Praise for
WORKING A BETTER WAY

"We think of HR as being about compliance, rules, and policies, but the heart of it is still human. Mr. Landrum understood the value of trust, and its connection to employee engagement, long before it was a 'thing.' *Working a Better Way* is not just a great story—it's a must-read for anyone growing a business. While many things about the world of work have changed, the importance of good relationships remains constant. People are still our greatest asset. Think of this book as a roadmap for building a company that attracts and keeps the right people— people who engage and do the right thing to help you build an unstoppable brand."

QUINT STUDER
Founder of the Studer Community Institute and author of
Wall Street Journal bestseller, The Busy Leader's Handbook

"*Working A Better Way* is a lesson filled chronicle of how this gentle but persistent entrepreneur founded and grew a successful, values-centered business based on the rock-solid principles of honesty, integrity, and fairness. Mr. Landrum's strategy for success was simple—'Trust and believe in yourself and your employees; find good people to help you; show them love and encouragement; and help them be all they can be.' "

ED RANELLI
Dean Emeritus and Professor, College of Business, University of West Florida

"It was a lot of fun to read about a former teacher who decided to do something entrepreneurial and was led to a vocation in HR services. It's a great case study for those interested in learning about people's experiences in business, the pursuit of new opportunities, and the 'why' behind the decisions that drive success."

JOHN HEER
Retired Health System CEO and three-time recipient of the
Malcolm Baldrige Award, the nation's Presidential Award for Quality

"This is the story of a boot straps start for someone with a willingness to forego current income in exchange for the future strength of his business. You have to respect someone with that dedication and bravery. It's just evidence of what Britt is as a man—what you see is what you get. It was as pleasurable to read the book as it is to be around him."

MORT O'SULLIVAN
CPA, LandrumHR Advisory Board member, founder and former
managing partner of O'Sullivan Creel (now Warren Averett)

"A fascinating story of how a guy started with an idea and built on it, who was willing to fail and experiment, smart enough to know when to walk away from bad ideas that seemed good at the time, persevered, and built a very successful company. It's a great American story."

AL STUBBLEFIELD
Former Baptist Health Care CEO and author of The Baptist Health Care Journey
to Excellence: Creating a Culture that WOWs!

WORKING A BETTER WAY©

WORKING A BETTER WAY©

A Fifty Year History of LandrumHR©

H. BRITT LANDRUM, JR.

Published by H. Britt Landrum, Jr.
Pensacola, Florida

Published by H. Britt Landrum, Jr., Pensacola, Florida
blandrum@landrumHR.com

Editor: Christine Broderick Emmanuel

Cover Design: 3SIXTY Marketing Studio - 3sixtymktg.com

Interior Design: 3SIXTY Marketing Studio - 3sixtymktg.com

Printed in the United States of America

Landrum, Jr., H. Britt

Working a Better Way: A Fifty Year History of LandrumHR

Library of Congress Control Number: 2020905835
ISBN: 978-1-7348244-1-4
First Edition
www.LandrumHR.com/WorkingaBetterWay

DEDICATION

This book is dedicated to the women and men, our employees, who built this company and made it what it is today. Some spent their entire careers with our company. Others worked for shorter periods of time, but all can be proud of what we have accomplished together. Their dedication, loyalty, and devotion to our mission of making LandrumHR a great place to work and to providing world class service to our clients has truly made our success possible. I can't thank them enough.

LandrumHR staff - 2015

ACKNOWLEDGMENTS

Years ago, I mentioned to a friend or two that I was thinking of writing a book about our company. Sometime after Ted Kirchharr came to work for us in 2003, he urged me to write the book, even going so far as recommending someone who could assist me or even write it for me.

On a trip to Freeport, Maine in 2006, my wife and I visited the famous L.L. Bean store. Leon Gorman, the retired president of the corporation and grandson of the founder, was out in front of the store signing his book, *L.L. Bean: The Making of an American Icon.* I bought one of his books and talked with him a little about the process of writing the history of his company. He told me it was one of the hardest jobs he had ever done, and he was glad it was finished. His wife was with him and echoed that sentiment.

Nevertheless, I read Leon Gorman's book and was inspired to go forward with my plan to write our history as well. I now understand how he and his wife felt.

The first person I want to acknowledge is my wife, Nell, who has put up with me now for over fifty-five years and has tolerated my spending many long hours writing my story. She thought when I retired that we would have time to do more things together. She also knows the importance of recording the history of our company and is fully supportive in every way.

Early in 2019, while attending a funeral for the wife of a friend, I ran into Marny Needle, whom I had known in connection with her work in fundraising for nonprofit organizations. She asked what I'd been doing in my retirement. I told her I was attempting to write a book and was looking for someone who might help me with that. Marny suggested that I speak with her friend, Christy Emmanuel, a recent retiree who was pursuing an interest in memoir and oral history writing.

So, I thank Marny for introducing me to Christy, and I thank Christy who has become my editor, producer, and chief encourager for more than twelve months. She has educated me about the technical requirements of writing and publishing a book. She has conducted numerous interviews, edited, and re-edited my work and helped me make decisions about final publication. I can't thank her enough for her dedication and invaluable assistance. Christy also put me in touch with her friend, Lorraine Lordi, who with 25 years of experience teaching writing at the college level, helped us by copyediting the manuscript.

I also want to recognize and thank CC Milford, founder and creative director of 3SIXTY Marketing Studio. CC designed the cover and interior of *Working a Better Way*. Her expertise proved highly beneficial as we charted new ground in self-publication, and she transformed the manuscript into a quality form made ready for print and electronic distribution.

Special thanks go to Peggy Fortunato, Denise McLeod, Susan Hunsucker, Ted Kirchharr, Andy Remke, Mike Perkins, Yvonne Nellums, and Britt Landrum III. Peggy, Denise, Susan, Ted, Andy, Mike, and Yvonne are all former employees of the company. Britt III is, of course, my son, and the president and chief executive officer of LandrumHR. All of these folks have a long history with me and with the company and agreed to be interviewed for the book. They have since answered emails from me asking for help in remembering people and events and confirming the accuracy of some of my statements.

I also want to acknowledge and thank Eric Nickelsen, Mort O'Sullivan, Dr. Ed Ranelli, Al Stubblefield, John Heer, Quint Studer, and James Hunter for reading and offering supportive comments on what I have written. Eric, a retired banking executive and now real estate developer, and Mort, the founder of O'Sullivan Creel (now Warren Averitt) accounting firm, are long-time members of our company advisory board. Ed is the former dean of the College of Business at the University of West Florida. Al is the former CEO of Baptist Health Care and the author of a book himself. John is the former president of Baptist Hospital and holds the distinction of guiding two hospitals under his leadership to win three Baldridge awards. Quint is now an accomplished author, speaker, and management expert, as is Jim Hunter who is the author of many books on servant leadership, one of which is referenced in my book.

Amie Remington, LandrumHR's general counsel, was kind enough to read the entire book before publication, and offer suggestions for improvement. Christy Arnold, the company's benefits compliance counsel, was likewise of assistance in advising me on the legal issues involved in publishing a book. Finally, I want to thank Rennee Edwards, Deborah Brousseau, and Tracy Herman of LandrumHR for their assistance in obtaining photographs and confirming employee information contained in the book.

H. Britt Landrum, Jr.

EDITOR'S NOTE

Working a Better Way reads as a compelling memoir and history of the human resources company H. Britt Landrum, Jr. founded fifty years ago beginning with a private employment business, and later, temporary staffing.

Inspired by an employee leasing article he read in *Inc. Magazine* in the early 1980s, Mr. Landrum then engaged and became one of the pioneers in establishing the Professional Employer Organization (PEO) industry we know today. With a dedicated team now 200 strong, Mr. Landrum has built a successful values-centered business that annually employs or provides services to some 20,000 people nationwide as a full-service HR outsourcer offering workforce solutions, human resources consulting, and job search assistance.

"I believe our company provides a real service to humanity, which truly is one of the greatest works of life."

H. Britt Landrum, Jr.

Derived from the Jaycee Creed: I believe that…service to humanity is the greatest work of life.

In the telling of LandrumHR's story through his journey as founder and CEO, and now chairman, Mr. Landrum reveals something of his integrity that set the course for his HR services company. Fundamentally, he understood that trust rests in people, and in order to build his business, he would be relying upon a vast network of people from whom and for whom trust opens doors. With trust, all things are possible, as illustrated time and again in the many anecdotes that color Mr. Landrum's memoir and his company's remarkable history.

It is fitting that H. Britt Landrum, Jr. pursued a path towards independent business ownership in the human resources field. Integrity is a fundamental value sought by employers in the people they hire as demonstrating sound moral and ethical principles at work. It likewise stands out as the quintessential mark that guided Mr. Landrum's actions and defined the HR services company he founded and has nurtured for fifty years.

Mr. Landrum led his team to success by developing relationships with, and earning the trust of peers, employees, clients, bankers, business partners, vendors, consultants, auditors, regulators, legislators–even competitors. True to form, he instilled *trust, integrity,* and *ethics* in his company's employees. With gratitude, Mr. Landrum invested in them as his most valuable asset, and the company has flourished all these years as a consequence.

Acknowledging the trust that Mr. Landrum placed in them, LandrumHR's employees were naturally inclined to do the right thing. In so doing, they made headway throughout the decades as they encountered emerging industry trends, business risks, competition, advancing technology, natural disaster, new business and acquisition opportunities, and developing regulations that demanded innovative ways to excel. With trust, the employees were handed the reins and were given autonomy to hire and train, create systems and procedures, make decisions and recommendations, and ultimately lead the company to its current prominence as one of the longest running and most successful mid-tier players in the HR services industry. Focused on the mission, the employees followed the Golden Rule instinctively, then watched doors open at every turn throughout a protracted period of growth and prosperity.

Mr. Landrum did not launch his human resources business until he was 32 years old. From modest beginnings, he talked to people, relied on people, and trusted people to help him get started and carry his company forward–fifty years forward.

Now looking in a rearview mirror, Mr. Landrum has every reason to stand proud. He is immensely grateful to the 700+ people who shouldered the weight of their responsibilities during his years at the helm and helped to build and to uphold the company's sterling reputation. He depended on them to do their best to deliver value. All of his employees and his family, as well, depended on him for their livelihoods. That is the weight that Mr. Landrum carried, seeing to it that they earned a respectable income in good times and in bad. Working a better way made that possible, as evidenced by the company's sustained financial stability and by the loyalty of Mr. Landrum's team members as employees, several having worked by his side for twenty, thirty, as many as forty-two years.

Working a Better Way is a feel-good story of a thriving family-owned business molded from Mr. Landrum's vision, his entrepreneurial spirit, his integrity, and his trusted relationships. In essence, this book recognizes the contributions of countless people whom Mr. Landrum credits for his company's enduring success.

Readers will learn about the fundamentals of human value creation, relationship-building, and beneficial business and HR management practices that have application for companies across all industries. Mr. Landrum's story is lightly sprinkled with a dose of practicality, self-effacing humor, with lessons learned, and with examples of human connection that underscore business vitality.

Mr. Landrum retired in 2017, placing the Pensacola, Florida-based business in the capable hands of his son, H. Britt Landrum, III as president and CEO. With his writing of *Working a Better Way*, Mr. Landrum leaves a legacy for his family and future generations of employees and employers that can help them to pave their way forward. In similar fashion, inspiration may well come to business owners, entrepreneurs, and organizational leaders everywhere.

Christine 'Christy' Broderick Emmanuel

PREFACE

As I wrote this book, telling the story of how LandrumHR came into being and how it has achieved the level of success it currently enjoys, my mind was filled with the images of so many people who have contributed greatly to that success. I am grateful to the many employees, both past and present, who have graced this company with their time and talent. A recent review of our records revealed that more than 700 employees have worked with us. Twenty-two of them stayed with the company for more than twenty years; five stayed more than thirty years; and two retired in 2018 with more than forty years of service to the company.

I have learned from them, leaned on them, and depended on them. Several of them were "pioneers" with me and built their departments using their own ingenuity with little or no real guidance from me. I am eternally grateful to them. All are part of our story. I cannot list them all, but there are some whose contributions were so significant that any telling of our story has to include them.

This book is both a memoir and a history. It's a story of my personal journey and how that journey impacted and included the journeys of the people who joined with me along the way. It is not intended to be a leadership manual or an instruction book on how others should run their companies. I will leave that to the management experts, some of whom inspired me and are referenced in my story. However, I would be pleased if there are some nuggets of information that inspire or instruct in some way.

The knowledge that I created a company that operates in almost every state in the country, continues to provide good jobs and good careers for our staff members, and has won awards for organizational excellence and for being a great place to work is a continuing source of pride for me. I am likewise proud to know that LandrumHR has become one of the most trusted sources for expert HR advice and good employees for so many employers.

CONTENTS

Note from the Author 3

Chapter 1   In the Beginning 7

Chapter 2   Managing Growth and Overcoming Challenges 29

Chapter 3   New Business Ventures 55

Chapter 4   Delivering HR Services Through the PEO 67

Chapter 5   Managing Risks 91

Chapter 6   A Focus on Leadership and Internal Controls 107

Chapter 7   Consolidating and Moving to Larger Quarters 133

Chapter 8   Making Advances with Information Technology 145

Chapter 9   Branching and Market Expansion 161

Chapter 10 Powerful Influences 183

Chapter 11 Corporate Culture 197

Chapter 12 Looking Forward 227

Afterward 241

Postscript 245

Reflections of Nine Leaders 247

Through the Years 258

Bibliography 267

Appendices 268

   Appendix A Acronyms 269

   Appendix B Business Evolution of LandrumHR 271

   Appendix C Companies and Ownership Interests Since 1970 274

   Appendix D Pensacola-based Office Locations Since 1970 275

   Appendix E People Referenced in *Working a Better Way* 276

   Appendix F Associations Referenced in *Working a Better Way* 287

About the Author 294

NOTE FROM THE AUTHOR

Readers should understand that this is primarily a history book and, as such, includes the names of many former employees. That information should be of most interest to those who recognize the names, or remember the people mentioned. There is also much written about our culture, business philosophy, challenges, and accomplishments which may appeal to a broader audience.

For the most part, the story is told chronologically as our history unfolded. However, I found it necessary to go back in time on occasion to give both the origin of the subject and its history up to the time of my retirement in 2017, or in some cases, to the present day.

Throughout this book, the reader will see various names for the Landrum operating entities, as well as the state and national organizations mentioned as they evolved. Insofar as the company is concerned, different names were used over time in an effort to differentiate one service from another or to create an awareness of expertise or focus in a given market. At the same time, the word "personnel" went out of use and "human resources" took its place. Some used the term "human capital," which we did not adopt. "Employee leasing" and "staff leasing" gave way to "professional employer organization (PEO)" and "human resources" became just "HR."

My first company was Landrum Personnel Associates, a private employment agency, also called a personnel placement firm. After a few years, we changed "Associates" to "Resources," and the full name became Landrum Personnel Resources.

The second company, Britt Landrum Temporaries, Inc., first did business as Landrum Temporary Services. Years later, as the jobs we filled were both "temporary" and "permanent," we started using the name, Landrum Staffing Services, shortened to Landrum Staffing. In

2019, that name became "Workforce Solutions," acknowledging that a significant part of the service we provide involves hiring and managing a portion of the workforce for a company.

The third company I created was American Staff Leasing Corporation, doing business as AmStaff. We used that name from 1983 until 2006 when an advertising and marketing firm convinced us to stop using any name that didn't include the name, "Landrum." AmStaff became Landrum Professional Employer Services, or Landrum Professional for short.

To complicate matters even more, around 2001 we created CU Personnel Solutions, an entity within AmStaff that focused on credit unions. We had quite a number of clients in that industry and used the name for several years before abandoning it in favor of Landrum Professional. Around that same time, we had a good number of doctors' offices and medical clinics as clients, and operated under the name Medical Personnel Solutions to reflect our expertise in that industry. It also became Landrum Professional.

Within a couple of years when we started doing a considerable amount of consulting in the human resources area, we created the name Landrum Consulting. All entities were listed as subsidiaries of Landrum Human Resource Companies, Inc.

There have been various other corporations and names created along the way, too many to list here. Our accounting staff stayed very busy keeping up with the numerous divisions and providing financial statements for each one.

During 2015, Landrum Human Resource Companies and its various subsidiary corporations and divisions started doing business as LandrumHR. It has taken a few years to get the website, building signs, stationary, business cards, and all other forms of digital and print media changed, but the transition is now complete with a new logo that distinguishes the "LandrumHR" brand.

There is one exception at this point, however, and that is the use of the name "hrQ," the consulting company we purchased in 2019. Prior to the acquisition, the "hrQ" name was well established with that company's many clients and HR professionals on assignment, so that name will continue to be used for the foreseeable future.

I hope these comments will help as you read *Working a Better Way*. Thanks for your interest in our journey.

CHAPTER 1

In the Beginning

Establishing a Private Employment Agency

MONDAY MORNING, AUGUST 3, 1970, after two or three years of dreaming, researching, and planning, I opened the doors of Landrum Personnel Associates (LPA), a private employment agency in Pensacola, Florida. I was excited, proud, and apprehensive. I had quit my job, borrowed money, rented and furnished an office, obtained a license, and hired an assistant.

The money to start the business came from my wife, Nell, who cashed in her teacher's retirement savings of $1,500, and an additional $1,500 that I borrowed from the Citizens & Peoples National Bank (C&P) with the help of my Army Reserve buddy, Eric Nickelsen, a new loan officer with the bank.

Just two short years before my opening day in August 1970, I'd never heard of a private employment agency. Neither had I ever taken a business course in college. (Twenty years after starting the business, I took my first accounting course along with my son, Britt III, in the summer term at Pensacola Junior College, now Pensacola State College.)

At age 30, with a social work degree, I was into my second year as a vocational rehabilitation counselor with the state of Florida and finishing up my master's degree in rehabilitation counseling at Florida State University (FSU). My job at "voc rehab" as we called it, was to counsel people who had some type of job-related disability and help them get medical treatment and/or vocational training that would prepare them for work. Sometimes, it meant helping them find a job.

I enjoyed my work and the friendship of my co-workers, but I realized that if I were going to achieve something in my life, I had to make a change. Those thoughts led me to the decision to start my own business. However, I had no idea at the time what type of business that would be.

Before my days as a voc rehab counselor, I had moved to Pensacola from Panama City where I grew up, to take a job as a probation and parole officer with the state of Florida. In Panama City, I had been a seventh-grade teacher of general subjects and taught math and algebra to ninth graders as well. I chose those jobs after graduating from FSU in 1959 when, to my considerable regret, my original plan of going to medical school and becoming a doctor, then joining my uncle, Dr. Louis G. Landrum, in his Lake City, Florida medical practice didn't work out.

In time, I realized that what I really wanted all along was to do something on my own and to determine my own destiny as my father, Henry Britton Landrum, did before me. He owned an automobile repair garage and a lawn mower sales and service business for many years. Later, he became a real estate broker. Doing his own thing made my father happy and provided a living for our family. I always admired my father's independent spirit and willingness to take a risk. I suspect he was inspired by his father, Britton Stamps Landrum, who owned and operated a gristmill and was a small-time homebuilder. Being in business for myself has given me that same sense of enjoyment and purpose, opened up opportunities to participate in business and community organizations, and enabled me to fulfill my goals and achieve far more than I could have imagined.

In the mid-60's, I joined the Pensacola Jaycees and became friends with a number of men my own age who in some way were doing their own thing–lawyers, small business owners, architects, engineers, insurance agents, and others. Also, during that time I was exposed to different "self-help" programs including "success motivation" tapes and books, all of which I devoured and took to heart. Those experiences combined to whet my appetite for doing my own thing and gave me the confidence to start planning for my future in business.

Breaking the news to my wife Nell that I was going to quit my job with a guaranteed salary and open my own business where our income was going to be very uncertain was stressful to say the least, made more so due to the fact that she had quit her job as a high school teacher and was very pregnant with our first child. To my great relief, she was very supportive and reassuring. She even offered to cash in her teacher's retirement to help out, which she later did.

After researching a few business possibilities, I learned that a former FSU fraternity brother, John Calhoun, owned a private employment agency business in Tallahassee. I drove over from Pensacola and spent the day visiting with him and the people who worked in his office. After speaking with them and learning about the business, I decided that was it. I had been helping people find jobs, so an employment agency seemed like a logical fit.

In my effort to learn all I could about the agency business, I investigated and gave some thought to buying a franchise. I even knew one of the franchisers, Guy Milner, who had a company called Southeastern Personnel Associates. (In the 'mid-50's' I had worked on Guy's team during a break from college one summer, selling Arcadian China.) After a visit with Guy at his offices in Atlanta and listening to his presentation, I was convinced that I wanted to do this on my own. I reasoned that being a franchisee might help me get started more quickly, but would take away my independence and a good bit of my money as well.

Still researching, I made contact with the head of the National Employment Association (NEA). He sent me several back issues of the organization's monthly publication that featured educational articles on the industry. Many of the articles contained advertisements for books and training films and tapes, which I purchased.

In January 1970, while still employed with the state of Florida, I attended a convention of employment agency owners sponsored by the Florida Employment Association (FEA). I was hungry for information and talked with as many folks as I could. Most were quite willing to share their experience and advice–especially since I wasn't going to be in their market area. Many of those people became close friends and proved to be very helpful in later years. I also learned from the experience and many others later on, that the most successful people in business are usually unselfish about their knowledge and are quite willing to help others just getting started. I tried to follow that example as I became more assured and knowledgeable in later years.

While still doing research, I created application and job order forms, chose a name, and created a logo for my new company. I had never heard of a business plan, so it didn't occur to me to create one. However, I did lots of daydreaming about what I would actually do once I opened my office–how I was going to operate, how I was going to earn a fee for finding someone a job, and how I was going to find someone FOR a job. Those visioning exercises helped me to think through all the details and gave me confidence in what I was about to do.

Renting an office was a huge step for me because it meant I was actually spending money, and there was no turning back. My Jaycee friends, John Schill, Jim Reeves, and Dick MacNeil had just refurbished an old building at 21 South Tarragona Street and were looking for tenants. I chose a small office suite of less than 500 square feet with three individual offices and a waiting room.

My next step was to sign up for a business telephone, which brought on my first experience with a Yellow Pages salesman. He called on me while I was still employed with the State. In all my years, I don't think I've encountered a more aggressive salesperson. He made me feel that there was no way I was going to succeed if I didn't go ahead right then and commit to purchasing the biggest and most expensive ad on the page. I resisted and bought a small ad but was exhausted and very anxious after he left.

Finally, still preparing for my opening day, I drove to Mobile, Alabama, to try and meet someone at Long's Personnel. Really, I was snooping just to see what another agency was doing and how it operated. The staff was friendly and offered to set up a meeting for me with Myrtle Long, the owner of that business. Myrtle and Tom Long had started their business forty years before and were very successful in Mobile. Tom had since passed away, and Myrtle ran the operation. She was very open and helpful, even offering to let me speak with her controller, Gonzalez Montiel, to learn more on the financial side. I met with Gon and was relieved that he was helpful and supportive. He even offered to be available if I needed advice in the future. Gon was the first person I called when I got the "jitters" the first week I opened for business. Basically, I had placed an ad in the newspaper looking for applicants, and no one applied. Gon assured me that things were going to be okay. I needed that!

First 'Help Wanted' ad before opening day – August 2, 1970

My small office at 21 South Tarragona was right across the parking lot from the *Pensacola News Journal*, which became significant because it was there that I made my first placement, a young lady looking for her first job after completing high school. Her parents were only too glad to pay the small fee I charged. I recall the pride I felt at having helped her find her first job and the good feeling I got when she paid my fee–the first for my new company.

Nobie Sparks was my first employee. Nobie had been my secretary at the Florida Division of Vocational Rehabilitation where I had worked for four years as a rehabilitation counselor. I was grateful to Nobie for making the move with me. I had not asked her to join me and was surprised when she volunteered. She had been a long-term state employee, and it took a lot of courage for her to leave that behind and take a chance with me. Her support gave me even more courage as I left the world of having a guaranteed income each month to the uncertainty of self-employment. Unfortunately, when Nobie committed to come with me, neither of us had a clear idea as to what her job would entail aside from the normal receptionist and typing duties. When I asked her to contact companies inquiring about job openings, she felt too uncomfortable making those cold calls. After about six weeks, she returned to her old job with the State, leaving me as the sole employee of my new company.

In addition to making curtains and helping decorate our new office, my wife Nell took on the role of accountant, a role she kept for the first seven or eight years of the business. As a business education teacher, she had taught bookkeeping in high school and understood much more about that subject than I did. She took me on as her student, gave me one of her accounting books to study, and helped me understand how to read a financial statement and a little about debits and credits. Nell's unwavering support, encouragement, and willingness to take a chance, starting with my announcement to her that I was planning to quit my job and open a business while she was very pregnant with our first child, Britt III, has always been of extreme importance to me and often made the difficult times a little less so.

Nell also kept me grounded, celebrated with me when good things happened, and encouraged me when things didn't go so well. She reminded me of the importance of family and of keeping things in proper perspective. Once, after weeks of staying late at the office and missing yet another dinner with my young sons, she telephoned me and asked what I was doing. I told her that I was working on something important, and I actually thought I was. She said, "Your children are growing up without you," and asked if that was what I wanted.

Nell and Britt Landrum - about 1980

Nell only had to say that once. I was reminded that while building the business was important, nothing was or is as important as family. From that point on, I did a better job balancing my time between the two. Nell has continued to be my biggest cheerleader, my most honest critic, counselor and supporter throughout our fifty-year history and in those ways has contributed greatly to our success.

Relationships have always been extremely important to me, and I believe have likewise contributed to our success. The friends I made in Jaycees later became my landlords, provided legal and accounting advice, and became my clients as well. People like John Schill, Dick MacNeil, Jim Reeves, Bert Brown, M.J. Menge, Bill Clark, Bob Crumpton, and others played an important role. As I mentioned, John, Dick, and Jim rented the office space to me. Bert owned Brown, Kirkland and Campbell, a CPA firm. He came to the office in our first week and showed Nell and me how to use the "One-Write System," a simplified check-writing bookkeeping system that we used for the first few years. Bert and his partner, Jerry Kirkland, did all of our accounting work for the first twenty years or so.

M.J. and Bill were lawyers and represented me at various times throughout the years. Bill filed the documents to incorporate Britt Landrum Temporaries, Inc. dba Landrum Temporary Services, and his firm has created many other Landrum corporations over the years. Bob Crumpton was an Army Reserve and Jaycee friend who left his job to buy a paint supply company. His example gave me encouragement to go out on my own as well.

A few years after starting Landrum Temporary Services, M.J. represented our company when we won the contract with the City of Pensacola to take over the workers at the Port of Pensacola. The former contractor, Manpower, didn't think the bidding was fair and filed suit. We won the suit and kept the contract for quite a few years.

While working in the vocational rehabilitation field in the late 60's, I met and got to know Pat Groner, the first president of Baptist Health Care. Pat was an innovator and was respected by hospital administrators all over the South. When I started focusing my recruiting efforts in the medical field, Pat gave me a letter of introduction to send to all of his fellow administrators. With that introduction, I was able to generate job orders and fill high-level, "fee paid" positions in several hospitals across the Southeast. As an added benefit, Pat placed me on retainer with Baptist for a couple of years to assist Jim Brown, his personnel manager, with recruiting. That $200 per month was a great help to me in those early days.

Relationships with my competitors were also important to me when I first opened my business, and I tried to get to know them. I was a bit naïve in expecting that they would all welcome my visit and want to know the new person who was working in their market. They were skeptical at first, but I knew we had issues in common (e.g., licensing regulations, legislation) that might give us a reason to work together. I was right and ultimately made some lasting friendships with one or two of the owners. Bob Bennett, a retired Air Force officer and the owner of Snelling and Snelling, became my closest industry friend. Even though we were competitors, his company later recruited and placed the manager of our new temporary help service–and I paid his fee.

Educating myself about the job placement business became my focus both before and after I opened my doors in 1970. The information I obtained from the NEA (later National Association of Personnel Consultants) encouraged me to join and attend their national and regional conferences. I also joined the FEA (later known as Florida Association of Personnel Consultants) and attended FEA conferences as well. Eventually, I was elected to the board of FEA, and after a couple of years or so on the board, I was elected president.

Hiring and managing people was a new experience for me. I knew I had to have people helping me to bring in income–I couldn't do it all myself. I had no training for hiring someone, so I turned to my friends and the articles I had read on the subject. My method of managing was to treat people the way I would want to be treated. That philosophy has stayed with me throughout my career and appears to be the essence of many management books I have read.

The first job placement counselor I hired was Joan Perryman. I had read in one of my magazine articles that having applicants perform some of the tasks they would be required to do on the job, an "in-basket" approach, was a good way to find out if they had the skills needed. I asked

Joan to come in after work so that I could test her. She was skeptical and asked me up front if this was *really* about the work. I caught on quickly and scheduled future sessions during working hours.

In the beginning, our agency had only telephones, a typewriter, and a copy machine that used smelly, chemically treated paper. Duplicates of anything copied on that machine would fade after a few weeks. We kept names and addresses on a Rolodex, a desktop device that had small, alphabetized cards on a wheel that you could easily roll to find the name you were looking for. A new device that I coveted was a speaker phone box that the phone company added to my phone. It enabled me to work hands-free while speaking to a client.

A couple of years after we opened, I was called on by a company rep who wanted to place a new piece of equipment in my office that could send a copy of a letter or other document over the telephone line. He called it a fax machine. The company was trying to get people accustomed to using these new devices, and it was offered to me free of charge. I just had to provide the space. The idea was to have people come in and charge them to send a fax to someone else. I was intrigued with this new gadget and had it installed. I don't think we ever had a paying customer, but we later used it ourselves when faxing began to catch on.

To attract applicants, I ran ads in the *Pensacola News Journal*. To create job orders, I called local employers who were listed in the Yellow Pages of the phone book and created coded lists of available applicants with brief summaries of their skills. I mailed those lists out and followed up with phone calls to the employers. My system worked pretty well and helped me build relationships and get job orders. It had its downside, though, especially when one or two employers I called told me that charging a fee to an applicant for getting them a job was illegal or ought to be. With time, I learned that employers and personnel managers with positive attitudes seemed to be more successful than those whose attitudes were negative. A few of those who had been rude to me later came to my office looking for help in finding a new job.

At first, I focused my attention on filling clerical (office and low-level administrative) and industrial (warehouse and factory) jobs for local companies, but basically, any job order I could get was acceptable. As I recall, the very first job order I received was for a truck driver. I didn't fill that one but later got a second job order from the same company for an accountant, which I did fill. From opening day in August until the end of 1970, my new company helped 25 people find jobs and helped 23 employers find an employee (one employer hired three people.) The fees I received in those first five months didn't amount to very much, but the fact that I had earned that money on my own gave me a really good feeling. Unfortunately, most of it had to be spent paying expenses, so there wasn't much left over for me.

During the early years of the employment agency, almost all fees were paid by the applicant. This was somewhat the custom and influenced by the recession in the early 70's when there were many more applicants than there were jobs available. Many applicants paid their fees when they started to work as they were asked to do. Others had to work awhile before they could afford it. Some just didn't pay at all. Working with an installment loan officer with the C&P Bank, I created a plan to finance the fees so the applicants could pay monthly. The only problem with that plan was that I had to co-sign all loans–a "full-recourse" loan, as they called it. That scheme was short-lived as I quickly learned that I was having to pay off too many of those loans.

I felt somewhat badly asking applicants to pay our fees. I remember sharing that feeling a few years later with someone whom I had placed on a job as a construction supervisor. His fee was $1,200, which was a lot in those days. He assured me that it was the best investment he'd ever made. He shared that he stayed with that company a few years, left, and started his own construction company, which had become quite successful. In any event, I learned that the best way to get fees paid and avoid collection problems, most of the time at least, was to look for job orders with companies willing to pay the fee.

Refining Our Business Model

Following the example of other placement agencies, I created areas of concentration or classifications of job orders and applicants, and hired a counselor for each one. One counselor specialized in filling office jobs, another engineering jobs, another data processing jobs, and another management and accounting jobs. After a year or so of working locally, my placement counselors and I began to broaden our search area to the Southeast, running ads in professional journals, and making phone calls to manufacturing companies and hospitals. We also coded resumes and mailed them out to prospective employers. This system actually worked and helped us develop good job orders where the company paid our fees. Plus, the fees were much higher.

However, sending out resumes to prospective employers had its risks. In our attempt to build volume, we sent out hundreds of resumes each week, being careful not to send a candidate's resume to his or her own employer. Unfortunately, on one occasion we made a mistake and did just that. We had already delivered the package of envelopes to the post office when I realized the error. Late in the afternoon, I raced to the post office on Jordan Street and begged the clerk to let me find that letter. Thankfully, the fellow I spoke with allowed me to make the search. I actually dug through what appeared to be thousands of letters in a large tub to find our bundled stack and pulled out the one that would have caused us and the candidate a lot of trouble. I'm sure that would not be allowed today with all the heightened security now in place.

The early years in the employment agency business at the Tarragona Street location were uncertain financially, but looking back, they were enjoyable and filled with learning experiences. Those working along with me in those days were my long-time secretary, Betty Bowles, and placement counselors Joan Perryman, Don Nelson, Eileen O'Brien, Grace Williams, and Frazer Banks. Our growth in numbers necessitated an increase in office space. Fortunately, Adcom, the advertising agency owned by Ray Howell, which was adjacent to our office, vacated the space, and we were able to expand to accommodate everyone.

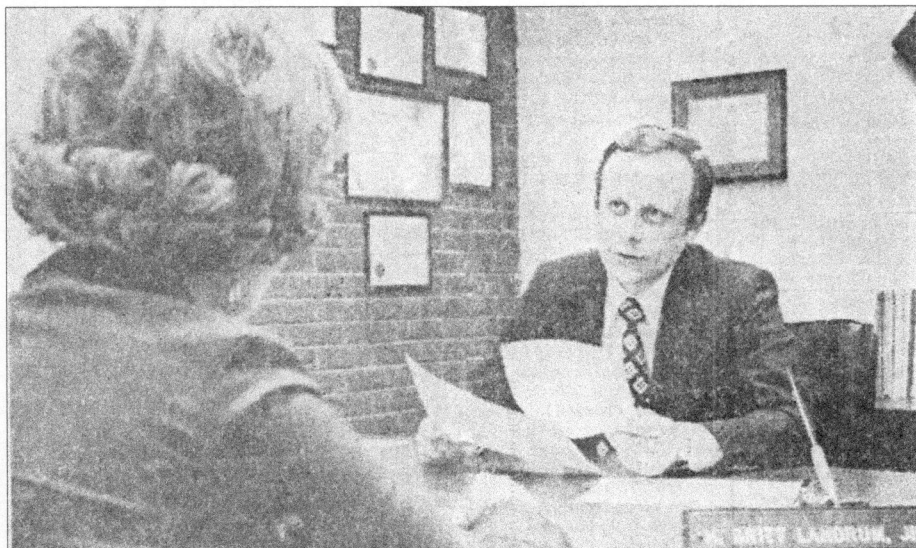

Pensacola News Journal article - 1975

LPA staff (L to R) Joan Perryman, unknown, Don Nelson,
Eileen O'Brien, Frazer Banks - 1973

LPA staff (L to R) Richard LaCour, Joe Dorsett, Linda Mock, Peggy Fortunato, Linda Haden, Don Nelson; Frazer Banks (back) – 1979

As a recruiter and placement counselor myself, I had many interesting experiences. I successfully placed engineers with area chemical and paper manufacturing companies, and physical therapists, medical technologists, nursing directors, other hospital department heads, at least one physician, and other specialists with hospitals throughout the South. These placements were challenging, but I enjoyed building relationships by telephone with personnel directors and recruiters around the Southeast and Southwest regions of the country.

One not-so-successful experience that stands out was my effort to recruit a director of surgical services for a hospital in Savannah, Georgia, an employer that had already hired several of my candidates in the past. I ran an ad for that position, and a candidate from Mobile saw it and called. He sent his resume, and we talked. He showed that he had more than sufficient qualifications for the job. It looked like a "slam dunk" to me as far as the placement was concerned. The HR director and I arranged an interview, and the candidate impressed everyone, even the doctors who observed as he assisted in surgery as part of his evaluation. On his way out of the hospital, one of the secretaries said she remembered him from a previous job in another state. Further investigation revealed that he was wanted by the Federal Bureau of Investigation (FBI) for attempted assault on an FBI agent, and I suspect for other things as well. A second and "final" interview was arranged, and when my candidate showed up, there were a dozen or so FBI agents stationed throughout the hospital waiting to arrest him. I didn't make the placement but thankfully kept the client for a few more years.

After placing employees on my own for a year or so, I learned of an organization that brought agencies together from all over the country to share job orders and applicants and split fees on successful placements. National Personnel Associates (NPA), headquartered in Grand Rapids, Michigan, was managed by its executive director, Chuck Marks, and had a membership of about 150 agencies in almost every state in the U.S. and one or two in Canada. My association with NPA in the early 70's and 80's was one of the most enjoyable experiences of my early career. I met many people there, established some life-long friendships, and traveled all over the US as well as Canada, England, and Bermuda to attend meetings. I eventually became a board member, officer, and ultimately served a two-year term as president of the organization.

It was through my membership in NPA that I became aware of the use of computers in facilitating the placement process. I've always enjoyed gadgets and was one of the first to purchase the first NPA computer, a small black box that would "talk" to other small black boxes via telephone lines and somehow identify candidates that matched your job order. The method was cumbersome and complicated and didn't catch on. Besides, technology was developing so fast that computers with better software became available soon after the black box was introduced. NPA soon installed such a system and set up a clearinghouse to serve the entire membership. From that point on, we used NPA's computer to route candidates, matching them to job orders and splitting fees with other members.

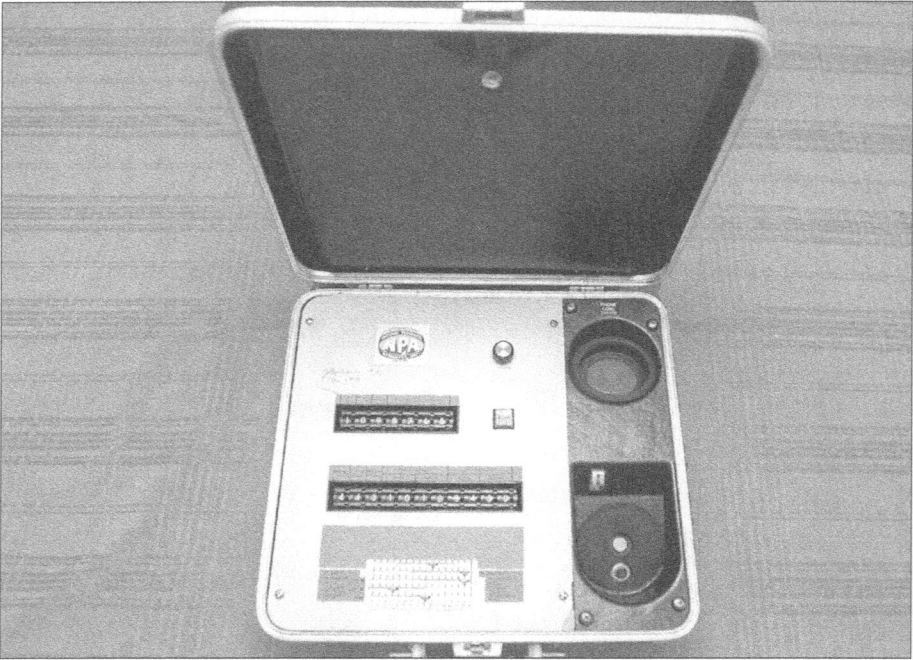

First LPA computer - early 1970's

Launching a Temporary Help Business

Over the decades, my employees have taught me many things. Grace Williams, a woman much older than I and near retirement age when she was hired, had an extensive career in the employment industry. She came to work as a job placement counselor for Landrum Personnel Associates in the early 70's and stayed for several years, riding the bus to and from work each day. I mentioned to Grace one day that I was intrigued by the temporary help business. She was a great encourager and brought me materials from a company she had worked for in Atlanta. With that information and after a good bit more research, I launched Landrum Temporary Services in December 1973.

My interest in the temporary service industry had a lot to do with looking for financial stability. Our placement service had too many ups and downs due to the contingency fee arrangement. No placement. No fee. This was the topic of many of our conversations during dinner with my family. My young son, Britt III, would often ask, "Did you make a placement today, Daddy?" Too often the answer was, "No." Even after making a placement, one could have a "fall off" which meant that you had to give the fee back or tear up the invoice if the person never reported for work. As often seemed to be the case, a good month was followed by a bad month.

At the end of my first full year in business, I remember telling a friend of mine that the company had sales of about $25,000. That seemed like a lot to me. It was more than I'd ever made. Unfortunately, there was very little left over after expenses were paid. My wife and I lived off an income of $500 per month for at least a couple of years. She was beginning to think that was the best we could do. I reasoned that the income stream from temporaries out on assignment week after week would be far more dependable and create the opportunity to build volume, which would give me a raise in pay. Thankfully, I was right.

The development and growth of the temporary service was exciting. I spent lots of time fussing over the details such as choosing a name, creating a logo, and developing forms. In January 1974, Frazer Banks, an experienced placement counselor with our personnel agency, recognized an opportunity for the new business. A government contractor came to us looking for four keypunch operators for a contract he had just won at the naval air station (NAS) in Pensacola. Frazer did the recruiting, and we were able to keep those four employees working for about six months. The steady income from that one job order convinced me that this was the direction our company needed to take in the future. We also needed space and someone to head it up.

The space issue was resolved when the area occupied by a small barbershop in our building at 21 South Tarragona Street opened up.

Before closing, the elderly barber who ran the shop had given my son, Britt III, his first haircut. When he moved out, we set up a two-person office in the expanded space, and Landrum Temporary Services officially opened for business.

My next step was to hire someone to manage our new company. As it turned out, I didn't fully appreciate all that had to be done, and the first person I hired didn't work out. After discussing this with my friend, Bob Bennett, owner of Snelling and Snelling, he told me he had just the right person for the job. An interview with Carolyn Davis was arranged, and shortly thereafter, she came to work as the new manager of our temporary help service.

Landrum Temporary Services began to thrive under Carolyn's leadership. She grew into her job and proved to be an energetic and resourceful manager. She helped structure the organization and focused on selling, recruiting, filling job orders, and getting employees paid. In June 1976, after moving to 1207 West Garden Street, we hired Denise McLeod, and she became the second employee in our budding temporary help business. As a recent college graduate with a degree in business focused on personnel management, Denise was enthusiastic and eager to help build the company. Operating out of two small offices in the rear of our building, Denise's initial task was to find and qualify employees to fill the job orders while Carolyn focused on sales.

In the beginning, we accepted all job orders. Nothing was too small or too risky for us as we were trying to build volume. We even took on the task of providing Santa's for the mall at Christmas. After finding out that there were no Santa suits available, Denise volunteered to make them. I don't know if she had any sewing experience, but she made some really fine Santa suits, which we used for a few seasons. Ultimately, we realized we weren't making any money off of Santa, so we stopped accepting those job orders.

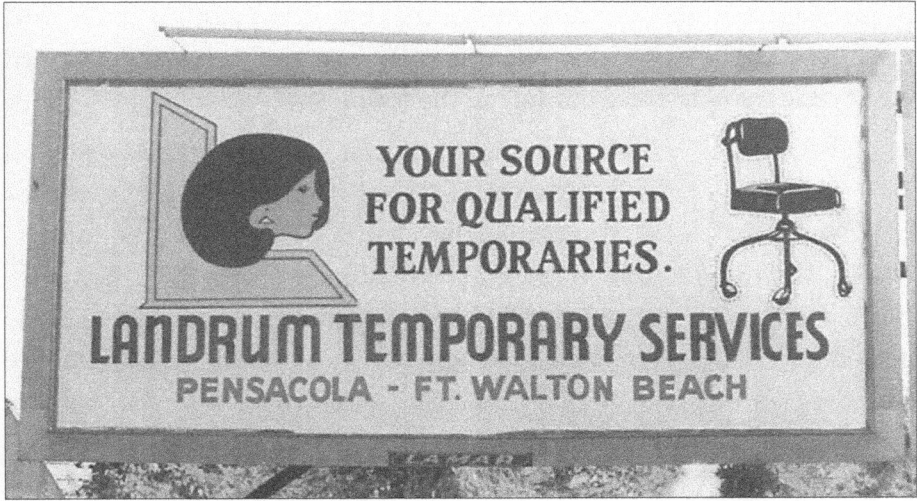

First billboard ad - 1977

My involvement in the temporary help business led me to join the National Association of Temporary Services (NATS), now American Staffing Association (ASA), where I met many others in the industry. I quickly learned that NATS was mostly controlled by the large franchisers such as Olsten, Manpower, and Kelly. There wasn't much for the little guy just starting out. Consequently, around 1976, about 15 of the independently owned firms decided to form our own organization so we could openly share ideas without fear of competition from each other. We chose the name, Independent Temporary Services Association, or "ITSA" for short. Wayne Josephson, the originator of the idea, served as our first executive director.

ITSA grew significantly over the next few years and became a great resource for our company and many others. I served on the board, became an officer, and in 1981 I was elected president. That same year, our company served as host of the national convention in Washington, D.C., with Carolyn and Denise serving as co-chairs of the convention. (It was at this meeting that I informed both Carolyn and Denise that I was promoting them to vice presidents of the company. Carolyn was named vice president of Landrum Temporary Services, and Denise was named vice president of the staffing side of the business.)

Now called TempNet, the organization has grown in size and significance and is a great source for training and sharing of ideas for independently owned companies. Because of the growth and success of our staffing service, in the late 90's some of our staff members, especially Denise McLeod and Sandra Smith, were often asked to make presentations at TempNet's annual conventions. Denise was by then vice president and general manager of Landrum Temporary Services and Sandra Smith was the manager of sales.

Expansion and Ownership of Our Building

Just as owning my own business was a goal to be achieved, so was owning the building in which my business was located. In 1975, after looking around for possible locations, I found and purchased a 1,500-square-foot building at 1207 West Garden Street that kept us near downtown. The building had been a retail store for years and needed extensive remodeling to make it ready for all of our staff. Because of my very limited resources at the time, I opted to do much of the work myself. I had been successful at building a den on my house (with the advice and oversight of an experienced carpenter), so I felt confident that I could remodel the office as well. To my surprise, Frazer Banks, Don Nelson, and Joe Dorsett, who had recently joined the company, willingly volunteered to help. Every Saturday and many weekday evenings for about six months, we worked to get the new offices ready and made the move in early 1976.

We added two key employees, Peggy Fortunato and Susan Hunsucker, to Landrum Personnel Associates after the move to West Garden. Peggy started as a temporary employee in April 1976 and became a regular employee one month later, serving as the office secretary and my assistant. Susan started with us in January 1980, assisting Peggy in supporting the placement counselors, answering phones, typing, and sending out resumes. Before being hired as a regular employee, Susan also worked for a time as a temporary employee. Both Peggy and Susan stayed with the company their entire careers and were promoted several times to more responsible positions before retiring from the company in 2018.

Landrum Personnel Associates seemed to do a little better after the move to the new office on West Garden Street. We added a few recruiting and placement counselors, including Billy Price. Billy was a former golf professional and member of my church, Holy Cross Episcopal. He joined the company in 1981 and focused mostly on engineering job placements. Over the years, he proved to be one of the most successful recruiters we ever had.

Office located at 1207 West Garden Street - 1975

LPA staff Christmas Dinner (clockwise) Carol Williams, Frazer Banks, Jean Broome, Britt Landrum, Jr., Peggy Fortunato, Margie Oakes, Billy Price, Michele Stinson, Darlene French - early 1980's

CHAPTER 2

Managing Growth and Overcoming Challenges

Gaining Control of Our Finances

IN 1979, THE FINANCIAL SIDE OF LANDRUM TEMPORARY SERVICES became more and more complicated as the number of employees and payroll volume grew. Peggy Fortunato, who by then had been on staff for three years, was responsible for paying the bills, invoicing and collecting from our clients, and keeping our books balanced. Our long-term CPA, Jerry Kirkland, helped us with payroll tax returns and payments and prepared quarterly and yearly financial statements for us. As the business grew, he recommended that we hire an accountant and suggested Margie Oakes, who maintained the books for one or two of his other clients. Margie maintained her office at home and agreed to work with us on a part-time basis. Over the years she was with us, Margie proved to be a dedicated, tireless worker who put in far more hours than her part-time status required. Much of that was necessitated by the startup and growth of AmStaff (the employee leasing company that I founded in 1983), which significantly increased her workload. Margie worked closely with Peggy and me for 14 years, resigning in 1993 to leave the area.

Margie Oakes (left) and Peggy Fortunato - mid-1980's

Before Margie left, our new accounting firm, Saltmarsh, Cleaveland and Gund, had advised that our company was large enough to need a full-time controller. In 1993, Peggy and I hired Leslie Gordon, a certified public accountant (CPA) who had not only worked in public accounting but had also served as controller for a successful local company. We were thrilled to have someone with Leslie's credentials and experience on staff.

Soon after coming on board, Leslie began to identify areas that needed the full attention of additional staff accountants. Mary Flynn was assigned the job of handling accounts receivable, and Rhonda Katona Freeman, whom Peggy had hired in 1989 to assist with accounts payable, continued in that role. Leslie took care of the general ledger, financial statements, daily tax liabilities, bank reconciliations, and state licensing, along with troubleshooting the daily postings, which were notoriously out of balance.

At the time, our accounting system didn't integrate with our payroll system, so everything had to be entered separately with the potential for input errors. A year or so after Leslie started, we began using the PayPlus accounting system, which was intended to integrate seamlessly with payroll with fewer errors. Leslie later recalled that I only gave her a month or so to create an entire chart of accounts and get the new system up and running by the first of the year.

(L to R) Andrea Johnson, Britt Landrum, Jr., Leslie Gordon – mid-2000's

The accounts payable role, which was originally filled by Rhonda, was next assumed by Lisa Nagem who was hired by Leslie in 1996. Lisa eventually transitioned to work full-time for Landrum Staffing Services, taking on the job of accounts payable and child support coordinator. The latter position was necessary as we had quite a few worksite employees who had been ordered by the court to pay child support. The law requires employers to deduct money from the employee's paycheck and forward the payments to the court (a form of "garnishment").

After a year or so, Lisa transitioned to payroll coordinator and eventually became our payroll and credit manager, serving in that capacity for about fifteen years. Lisa had a successful career and completed 23 years with the company before leaving in March 2019.

Learning to Manage New Accounts

Financing the payroll of our new temporary help service proved to be a challenge. I quickly realized that I was doling out money by the hour while getting paid very often by the month. At that time, we didn't have the extra funds available to pay the temporary workers without getting our fees paid rather quickly by our clients. Some were better payers than others. The city of Pensacola became a good client of ours at the time, but was not in a hurry to pay our invoices. I later learned that the city required several layers of approval before cutting a check, which usually took several weeks to accomplish.

I managed this problem at first by hurrying to deposit checks the first of each week after writing payroll checks on Fridays. My system worked fine until my friend Eric Nickelsen, by that time an officer with the C&P Bank, called me in and showed me a printout of my checks and deposits, which of course were not balanced. (The bank's practice was to hold checks for a few days before making the cash available.) He let me know that he had allowed this for a while, but we had to do something else as his superiors were aware of the situation and had mentioned it to him. Of course, those were the days when banking decisions were more local and personal relationships in banking meant more than they do today. Anyway, that was when I established my first line of credit and learned about pledging accounts receivable.

In the years following, I managed our financial ups and downs by borrowing money from the C&P Bank on a regular basis, always paying the loans back on time. I always made sure all of our vendors were paid promptly, and when I was short on funds, I borrowed the money. Establishing a reputation as a financially responsible company was as important to me then as it is now. That philosophy and practice has resulted in our company being courted over the years by many banks that have sought to earn our business.

Over the next few years, the sales volume of our temporary help business grew dramatically as we picked up some significant accounts. In 1976, Monsanto, a large chemical fiber manufacturer, selected our company as its exclusive provider for temporary help. In 1977, American Fidelity Life Insurance (AMFI), an insurance company and owner of three banks, four hotels, and a data processing company, selected our company to recruit and pay all of its employees, which totaled several hundred. My good friend, Henry Baggett, vice president of finance for AMFI, was responsible for encouraging his boss to give us a try. The insurance company and the data processing company became our clients initially. The other entities, except one hotel, were added later as we gained the confidence of AMFI's principals. In addition to those accounts, the popularity of our staffing company grew, and job orders from smaller companies also increased.

In the late 1970's and early 1980's, the temporary help staff, led by Denise McLeod, devoted a tremendous amount of effort to make sure AMFI's needs were fully met. We took care of all recruiting and the selection of employees, employee relations matters, some benefits management, and payroll. The account grew to become more than half of our volume of business, which made us vulnerable and became a cause for some concern to me.

AMFI and its properties were founded and principally owned by Charles P. "Chuck" Woodbury. I admired Mr. Woodbury for his accomplishments, and my relationship with him and with his board and key staff members was always positive. However, I was a little apprehensive a few years into our relationship with the company when Mr. Woodbury asked me to meet with him in his office. I was relieved when he showed me an article that he had recently read in *Inc. Magazine* describing something called employee leasing. He suggested that I look into it. I was intrigued by the article and realized immediately that the work we did for AMFI and its properties was pretty much what employee leasing was all about.

Sometime after we met, I was summoned to Mr. Woodbury's office for a second meeting except that this one included his board of directors. They offered to give our company the remaining property–one hotel, which had a hundred or so workers, and all we had to do was reduce our fee by 1%. That sounds so simple now, and any business like mine at the time would do most anything for that kind of an offer. Except we didn't. After several discussions with Carolyn Davis, the manager of our temporary service, she convinced me that if we took on those new employees and reduced our fee, we would essentially be netting the same amount of money for doing a lot more work. Against my better judgment, I gave in to her advice and turned down the offer.

About a week later, I was again summoned to meet with Mr. Woodbury and the AMFI board. They informed me that Manpower had offered to take over all of the accounts for a much lower fee, and they were letting me know that they would be leaving. I was upset with myself and unhappy, but I thanked them for the confidence they had placed in us and for their business. I asked them for time to adjust to the loss of their account. One of their board members spoke up and recommended that the move be made immediately. I was so thankful when Mr. Woodbury said, "Well, we're not going to drop you on your head. We'll give you six months to adjust." I quickly thanked him and offered to reduce our fees during those six months to the rate quoted by Manpower so there would be no financial loss to AMFI. This was a bitter pill to swallow, but it taught me a valuable lesson–there is always a competitor out there who will be glad to have your business at a cheaper rate.

(Ironically, AMFI came back to our company a few years later, after the state of Florida notified them that Manpower wasn't licensed as an employee leasing company and couldn't continue providing the service. By that time, we had made the decision to open an employee leasing company called AmStaff. Our license as an employee leasing company enabled us to take over the account once again.)

In December 1979, the city of Pensacola awarded our staffing service a contract to provide workers at the Port of Pensacola to unload bags of flour from boxcars to be placed in the port warehouses. The path to the award, however, wasn't without controversy, and the operation was an ongoing challenge.

The problem in the beginning was that Manpower had maintained that contract for many years, and the local franchise owner was very unhappy with the city for terminating its contract. He was so unhappy that he asked to appear before the city council and have the contract re-bid. We understood that some council members were sympathetic and considering that option. Of course, we saw that as being very unfair in that any company making another bid would have the benefit of our bid numbers from which to create its own bid.

At the council meeting, the franchise owner stated his case, saying that he was not given any notice and was given no opportunity to bid. I was asked to explain how I had learned of the bid offering. The truth was that we saw a notice in the *Pensacola News Journal* and submitted our bid as requested. I expressed my opinion as to why rebidding would be unfair. After some debate, the council agreed with me and voted to award the bid to Landrum. We were excited about this new area of business for our company, which would add one hundred or more laborers and more than a million dollars in annual revenue.

Our excitement didn't last long, however, when we received official notice from the franchise owner's attorney that we were being sued. They wanted to compel the city to open the bidding again. I immediately called my friend, M. J. Menge, with the law firm of Shell, Fleming, Davis and Menge, and asked him to represent us. The matter didn't drag on very long, and the court ruled in our favor.

From an operations standpoint, our job with the Port of Pensacola was to hire, pay, and supervise the workers. Following the pattern created by the previous contractor, prospective employees gathered around the warehouse platform. The supervisor would look over the group and point to the ones he wanted to hire that day. Sometimes, we needed only a few workers, and at other times we needed several. If they had not previously worked for us, those selected completed an application form before starting. It all seemed fairly simple and straightforward at first, but as we quickly learned, that was the worst method for hiring possible.

Two real problems presented themselves right away. First, the workers had to be paid by check each week and we didn't want them coming to the office. There were as many as 150 workers needing to be paid and our small office couldn't handle the traffic, nor did we have any extra parking spaces available. In addition, at the end of the day when payroll time came, the workers were hot and sweaty and covered with flour!

Our solution was to transform my 1980 Ford van into a "pay wagon," which we parked at the port near the workers. Denise McLeod and Carolyn Davis bravely handled that duty with one person issuing checks out of one side window and the other on the opposite side doing the same. Their system worked very well for a long time. Unfortunately, at one point, when both were leaving town to attend a convention, I was tasked with covering for them. All went well until, as instructed by Denise and Carolyn, I told one of the workers that he couldn't have his check because he hadn't filled out his paperwork correctly. That didn't go over well with him, of course, and after a few threatening remarks, I conceded and he got his check. After that incident, I decided to leave the issuance of payroll checks in the capable hands of Denise and Carolyn who told me that they had never been threatened and had always been treated with respect by the workers.

The second and even more serious problem was the frequency and severity of injuries at the port. The work was very strenuous (sacks of flour weighed 50 pounds or more each). The men were not screened properly, and many weren't in shape to handle such heavy work. All of the workers were rightfully reminded by law that if they got hurt on the job, their medical costs would be paid by the company's workers' compensation insurance, and they would receive a weekly paycheck from the insurance company as compensation for their lost time on the job. Whether the injuries were fake or real and whether or not their injuries occurred on our job, we couldn't always tell. However, our claims were enormous. After a few years, our workers' compensation claims experience rose to more than twice the book rate! We attempted to manage the problem with all manner of corporate maneuvering, which was all legal in those days. In the end, however, we decided that the risk was just too great, and there was no way to get around it.

I was already unhappy with the problems at the port and didn't think things could get much worse. I was wrong. Late one afternoon in 1983, I was sitting in my office when a man appeared at my door. He introduced himself as a representative of the Masters, Mates and Pilots Union. He presented a stack of about fifty cards signed by many of our workers at the port and said that his union wanted to represent them. I was pretty well in a state of shock by that time, but I managed to say that I would consult with my attorney and get back in touch with him.

My first call the next day was to Wayne Etheridge, personnel manager for the city. He recommended that I contact the city's labor attorney, Mike Miller, whose office was in Tampa. I called Mike immediately and learned from him that he could not represent both the city and our company. He recommended a firm in Jacksonville—Coffman, Coleman, Andrews and Grogan. The firm assigned a young attorney, Robert G. "Bob" Riegel, Jr., to represent us. Mike Miller and I became good friends a few years later when, as members of the Florida Employee Leasing Association, we worked closely to defeat state legislation that was detrimental to the employee leasing industry.

Bob Riegel proved himself to be a very capable representative for our company and worked very hard on our behalf. He spent many hours in our offices in Pensacola, interviewing staff, reviewing records, and educating us about the laws regarding unions, union organizing attempts, and the legal rights of employees to form a union. The matter took a great deal of staff time, finding and providing copies of documents, and testifying at depositions and in court. The case took about two years to resolve, but in the end, we won and the petition by the Masters, Mates and Pilots Union was dismissed by the National Labor Relations Board (NLRB) on October 2, 1985. Essentially, the NLRB ruled that the union had no jurisdiction since the matter involved the city of Pensacola, and that the petition should have been filed with the Florida Commission on Human Relations instead. The union had no appetite to continue the fight, so thankfully, the matter was closed.

We continued to provide workers to the port for a few more years but terminated the contract in January 1990. It was tough making the decision to walk away from so much business, but in the end, I decided that the injuries at the port just couldn't be prevented no matter how much we tried. Our workers' compensation factor (the experience modification or "mod rate" multiplier applied to the book rate) was so high at that time that it would take a few years to overcome. We had no choice but to cease providing workers to the port and terminated the contract. That was the first, but not the last time, we've had to give up clients who proved to be harmful to our business. Those decisions are always difficult and unfortunately made most often after the damage has already been done.

A pivotal year for the entire organization came in 1986, with the departure of Carolyn Davis as general manager of Landrum Temporary Services, the naming of Denise McLeod as her replacement, and the relocation of all staff members to a new building north of town. Shortly after making the move to the new offices, I invited Bob Liken, a fellow ITSA member, to come to Pensacola to perform a peer review of our temporary help company. Bob was the second-generation owner of a very successful temporary service in Pittsburgh, Pennsylvania. He was very complimentary of our staff and especially Denise, who by then was co-manager of the temporary services division with me. After my discussion with Bob and later with Denise, I decided it was time to promote her to general manager, giving her full charge of the temporary help company. As history has shown, it was one of the best decisions I could have made.

Because of the strong reputation our temporary help service staff had built with a few of the management staff at Monsanto, most notably the purchasing department, we were asked in 1989 to submit a bid to take over the staffing and management of all employees in the tire yarn area of the plant. This was uncharted territory for us in that it involved around-the-clock shift work inside a manufacturing plant, and we would be managing the employees, not just paying them and taking care of their HR needs. The contract required us to hire and supervise a site manager, four shift foremen, a safety manager, a trainer, and a human resources manager. We would be responsible for hiring, orienting, and training nearly 600 draw-twist operators who would be working three eight-hour shifts seven days a week.

At that point in time, Denise had been serving as general manager of our staffing division for about three years. After receiving the request for bid, she and I had a serious discussion as to whether or not we should even attempt to take on a project that large. We knew that it would require a tremendous amount of staff time and resources that could negatively impact our business with much smaller clients. Also, we remembered too well how the loss of AMFI and its hotel and bank operations had impacted our business. We didn't want to get into another situation where the percentage of income from one client was so high that it would cause us a financial setback if it went away. After much discussion, we decided that it was just too big an opportunity to pass up. We reasoned that we would survive when it ended, and we knew that it would eventually end.

The initial meeting of bidders included ten other companies, some of which had a wealth of experience in running similar operations in other manufacturing facilities. We were pretty sure that we were the smallest and least experienced company there. To help us with our proposal, we hired a consultant who was familiar with Monsanto and its bid requirements. That process took a few weeks, but when we submitted our bid and made a presentation to the bid committee, we were confident that we could do everything we were asked to do and would do the best job. To our surprise and delight, our bid was the one chosen.

The startup of that operation took several weeks with Denise and her team taking the lead. We chose AmStaff as the corporation to fulfill the contract because of the requirement to provide health insurance and other benefits that weren't at the time offered to employees of Landrum Staffing Services.

Under the terms of our contract, we had to do all things necessary to avoid being classified as co-employer of the employees–the opposite of what we were doing with all other AmStaff clients. Our management staff had to make the hiring decisions, conduct the training, make shift assignments as needed, and supervise the work of 600 employees or more. Denise and Yvonne Nellums, by then the HR manager for AmStaff, played key roles in the administration of the contract. Both spent countless hours at the plant in consultation with Monsanto leaders, conducting employee meetings, counseling individual employees, and working with our management staff and with Monsanto's managers.

We learned of the many nuances involved in running a 24/7 operation that required us to fully staff and manage workers in three eight-hour shifts. The rotating shifts took a toll on sleep patterns and families, which impacted recruiting, job satisfaction, and turnover. We partnered with the state employment office for skills-testing that had been certified specifically for Monsanto jobs and developed pre-employment physical exams relevant to the specific job requirements, as well as multiple-year medical testing and reporting that was required. We hired a training consultant, created comprehensive training notebooks, and conducted regular training sessions in our office building. The volume of paper files created for the thousands of employees hired over the duration of that contract was tremendous, consuming a good portion of the storage facility we rented for that purpose.

During the period of time we had the contract, Monsanto sold off some of its assets to Solutia, including the tire yarn operation in Pensacola. Solutia experienced some financial problems and eventually filed bankruptcy to shed some of its debt and get reorganized. Unfortunately, at the time of that filing, we were owed about $450,000. When that happened, we were somewhat in shock, and I wasn't sure if we'd ever see any of the money that was owed us. That was when I learned something about "factoring." After the bankruptcy became news, we began receiving letters from factoring companies that were willing to buy our accounts receivable from Solutia for a small percentage of what was owed to us. Andy Remke had come on board as our chief financial officer (CFO) by that time and worked with me in dealing with the offers. Andy was a good negotiator and managed to get the factoring company to accept more than the 35% it initially offered. I believe we eventually settled for about half of what we were owed. I learned a lot during that experience but hope I won't need that knowledge going forward.

In addition to learning about factoring and bankruptcy, our experiences over the fourteen-year period in which we kept this contract taught us quite a bit. The good part was the ability we had to place people in good paying jobs with decent benefits. The difficulty was keeping the plant fully staffed around-the-clock, which required us to force employees to come to work or extend them over to a second shift when another employee didn't show up. In addition, we had to discipline them if they refused to do so. We also had to get involved directly with the termination of worksite management staff on occasion when they didn't perform as expected. Having to personally meet a site manager early one morning and walk him out of the plant wasn't a happy experience for him or for me.

Overall, the managers and employees we placed at the plant worked hard and did a fine job for us, many times under difficult circumstances.

One of the more serious problems had to do with employee injuries. Safety is a huge issue in a manufacturing environment, and our staff worked hard to prevent "incidents" (events that could cause injuries) and injuries. The type of work done by our operators was tedious and tiring. In addition, they worked in a somewhat dangerous environment where unmanned machines were moving around the floor and long strands of string the size and strength of dental floss were being wound up on rapidly spinning spools. Preventing incidents and injuries was challenging. Harry Booros, our AmStaff safety and risk manager at the time, worked with Elaine Tracey, our site safety manager at the plant, to improve our safety program and to help our company receive ISO 9000 certification, which was granted in May 1999. That designation, awarded by the International Standardization Organization (ISO), is issued to companies that have demonstrated a commitment to quality and safety in their operations.

The number of injuries decreased as a result of our efforts, but the severity of the claims we experienced became too costly to ignore. Liberty Mutual Insurance Company, our workers' compensation carrier, let us know that our rates would be increasing as a result of the claims experience at the plant. We discussed these rate increases with the management staff at Solutia, but there was little interest on their part in paying a higher fee or in providing workers' compensation coverage themselves. Actually, they wanted to bid the contract out again to see if they could get a lower-cost contractor. In the end, we chose not to submit a bid and in 2003 gave up our contract.

Managing Timesheets and Payroll
for the Temporary Service

With an increase in sales volume, we experienced a corresponding increase in the number of payroll checks that had to be issued each week. In 1974, when we were just beginning, I used a "one-write" pegboard system to write the few employee paychecks that were issued each week. Small business computers weren't on the scene at that time, so everything was done using a tax schedule booklet, a calculator, and a pencil. (I also completed and filed all the federal and state tax returns each quarter.)

When Carolyn Davis came on board in 1975, she took on the job of issuing the checks for the temporary workers. When Denise McLeod started in 1976, she joined Carolyn in getting that job done. Peggy Fortunato, who also started that year, remembers typing the checks after the net amounts were given to her by Carolyn and Denise, who entered the amounts on the payroll stubs.

Denise recalls that she and Carolyn also manually figured all invoices and typed them each week. They had no means at that time of making sure we were paid correctly or on time, so they started a book of weekly invoice amounts, entering the date mailed and the date paid. The book was handwritten and helped them stay on top of accounts receivable and make collection calls when necessary. After about a year, we bought what Denise describes as a "super high tech" Olivetti calculator. The staff could then program the calculator to compute FICA (federal payroll withholding taxes), SUTA (state unemployment taxes), and FUTA (federal unemployment taxes), saving a lot of time. The calculator produced a tape for our records that contained all the calculations for each week's payroll.

By 1977, the number of temporary employees out on assignment had grown considerably. It was in that year that we purchased our first computer software system to help us handle the payroll job more efficiently. Caldwell Systems was developed and owned by Steve Caldwell, a friend I got to know through my association with NPA and ITSA (TempNet). Steve and his brother, Earl, also owned a placement agency and temporary help service, and were members of the two organizations. Our company was one of the first to purchase this new software.

First Landrum Staffing computer (using 8" floppy disks) - 1977

Nell and I also used that system to produce the internal staff payroll. As the number of staff members grew and payroll became a little more time consuming, I began to think more about letting someone else handle the job. Peggy was one to always ask, "Is there anything else I can do to help?" After watching me sitting at the computer for a while and struggling to get the staff payroll done once more, she said, "I'll be glad to help you with that."

That was all I needed to hear. From that time in 1978 until five months before she retired in 2018, Peggy was the person primarily responsible for the staff payroll. When she took on that role, we had about 15 members on staff. When she gave the job up in 2018, we had over 170. After she became corporate director of human resources in 2006, Peggy had lots of other important duties, but making sure staff members were paid accurately and on time was still a big part of her job.

In 1978, to accommodate the growth in payroll processing and the need for additional staff, the temporary help division moved from 1207 West Garden Street to an old house I purchased at 238 East Intendencia Street in the historic district downtown. The building needed significant remodeling to make it suitable for our staff. This time, I paid someone else to do the work!

After the move to the new office on East Intendencia, the volume of temporary workers grew dramatically as we took on more clients. It became necessary for us to hire a small staff just to enter employee information and print time sheets and payroll checks, all paper at that time.

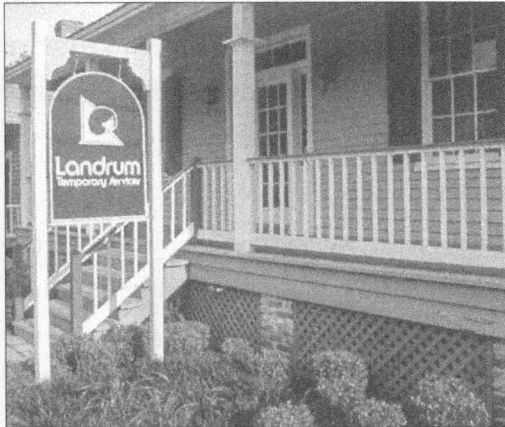

Landrum Temporary Services office at 238 East Intendencia Street - 1978

Our ability to manage both the reporting of hours worked and the processing of payroll for hundreds of temporary employees each week has improved dramatically over the years. For the first thirty years or so, we printed time sheets for each employee, which had to be completed, signed, verified by a client representative, and then delivered to our office by Monday evening each week. (The use of paper timesheets was eliminated several years ago. Now, the majority of our employees submit their hours worked each week through our online timekeeping software, Peoplenet. Our large clients utilize group timesheets and time clocks.)

In 1986, when we moved to 6708 Plantation Road, employees dropped their timesheet though a mail slot outside the front door. That practice continued when we moved across the street to 6723 Plantation Road in 1993. With the move, we created a mail slot in the front glass window and placed a container beneath it to receive the time sheets. We began to worry about someone reading personal information from another person's time sheet and decided to construct a special container that was more private. That led to what I suspect was the most expensive time sheet container on record. My friend, Larry Barrow, who was the architect for our building, having subsequently left to teach architecture at Mississippi State University, offered to have his students design and construct the container. I agreed, and I think we eventually paid around $2,000 for that device which replaced a cardboard box. In fairness, we had several requirements that added to the expense, but I suffered a little "sticker shock" upon delivery of the customized container.

Distributing checks to hundreds of employees each week was a time-consuming process. In the early days, some checks were mailed but most employees came to the office to pick them up personally, so there was lots of traffic in the parking lot on Tuesdays after the payroll was processed. As electronic banking came into the picture, more employees opted to have their checks deposited directly into their bank accounts. Those who didn't have a bank account were issued a "pay card" and their net pay was loaded onto the card each week. (Today, we don't print paychecks at all. All employees must either adopt direct deposit or use the pay card issued to them to receive their pay. Check stubs and other payroll records are available online to the employees on the LandrumHR website.)

Investing in Systems and Staff

Sometime after the move to East Intendencia Street, the need for an even more sophisticated computer payroll system became apparent, and we decided to make the investment. In 1983, we purchased a software system known as Spartin Systems, which was developed and owned by another industry friend, Murray Stinson. My investment in the computer system and staff to support payroll processing was significant, but it was necessary to handle the volume of work involved in managing the AMFI account. (After we lost the AMFI account, it took some time before volume picked back up sufficient to warrant that investment.)

Caldwell-Spartin computer system (DEC PDP 11) - 1986

I had known Steve Caldwell for a long time, and he expressed his unhappiness with me for not purchasing the next generation of software that his company had developed. I'm sure he accepted that my decision was made for business reasons, but it did put me in the awkward position of choosing one friend over the other. Thankfully, that situation resolved itself in 1984 when the two owners announced that they were merging their companies to form Caldwell-Spartin, Inc.

The software produced by Caldwell-Spartin was the most stable and sophisticated in the staffing industry at the time. It was well supported by a very capable staff. Murray continued to be very involved with the company and was always available to us. He visited our offices often over the years to perform upgrades or write a program or two that would enhance the operation in some way.

The system did all the things we expected, helping our staffing coordinators match job requirements with applicant skills so we could send out the "right" employee for an assignment, issue large numbers of paychecks and timesheets, print invoices for our customers, and produce volumes of related reports for accounts receivable, tax reporting, and record keeping. It also included a program to help our sales staff plan their sales calls and visits with our clients and prospects. We take all these things for granted now, but thirty-five years ago, this functionality was considered very advanced.

Caldwell-Spartin has since gone through a couple of mergers, most recently with a larger firm, Bond International Software. In 2016, we converted to the latest version of the software, known as AdaptSuite. On our twenty-fifth anniversary with Caldwell, we were invited to come to the company's headquarters in Atlanta, where we were given an award in recognition of being their longest tenured customer. At this point, that relationship has lasted more than 40 years.

Drug Screening

In 1992, Denise McLeod and I traveled to Mobile, Alabama to visit with Tom Damson, president and part-owner of Long's Human Resource Services. Tom is the son-in-law of the deceased founders of that firm, Tom and Myrtle Long. Tom and his wife Sarah had been industry friends for a number of years. Denise and I were interested in learning more about the in-house drug-testing program that they had successfully operated. We were impressed with what we learned and decided to implement a similar program at our office in Pensacola.

As a condition of employment with Landrum Temporary Services, applicants had to successfully pass a drug-screening process. We were proud to be the first staffing service in our market to announce a "drug-free workplace" policy for all of our employees. Our internal staff members were required to pass drug-screening as well. Knowing that employees assigned to our clients by Landrum had been tested and were drug-free gave the employers some peace of mind and a reason to use our service rather than a competitor's.

Initially, those tests were contracted out to local labs and the complete test was administered at the lab. Getting applicants to show up for the test and getting results back from the lab in a timely manner didn't work well, so we decided to bring the process in-house. Grace Whalen, a registered nurse, was hired in 1993 and became our first drug-free workplace coordinator. We contracted with a supplier to purchase the test kits and altered one of the restrooms so that applicants could properly provide the urine samples. We also hired a physician, Dr. Dan Mooney, to become our part-time medical review officer (MRO).

Our testing was primarily for marijuana and cocaine, but some testing included a few other illegal substances as well. We acknowledged that our lab was not certified, but our system was effective and legal. Just letting all applicants know that they must be drug-screened eliminated many of the offenders. Some tried to get by. Grace told stories about applicants borrowing someone else's urine for the test as well as other ways they tried to get around the test. Applicants who tested positive were told their test results were incomplete, and they were directed to show up at a certified lab within 24 hours. Some failed to show up. Positive tests were reviewed by our MRO. The benefit to our clients was the assurance that the employees they received through our company had been thoroughly tested and were clear of drugs at the time of hire.

The number of applicants tested each week was often one hundred or more. Grace handled the job by herself for quite a few years, but as the volume of tests increased, she hired a staff member to help her and became manager of the department. Grace was talented beyond her work, crafting Christmas ornaments and other items for auction at office fundraising events or writing lengthy, humorous poems that she shared with us at special company functions. Grace retired from our company in 2014 after completing 21 years and administering an estimated 100,000 drug tests.

Progressing from Temporary Help to Workforce Solutions

Getting the Landrum Staffing story out to prospective customers and building that business was the job of Sandra Kay Smith, one of the most accomplished and professional sales representatives I've ever met. In early 1997, we had lost our sales representative and had advertised our need for another. Sandra called and made an appointment to see Denise and me about the job. She described her extensive background in sales and management for a staffing service in Atlanta. She then told me that we needed her and that her salary requirements were higher than we advertised, which sounded pretty bold to me. At first, I told her, "No." Being a good salesperson, she countered by proposing that I hire her, and if after ninety days we didn't think she was worth the salary we were paying, then we could let her go. We hired her in 1997 and begged her to stay when she finally retired in 2016. She was everything she promised and more.

While Sandra's goal was convincing companies to let us help them fill their jobs, both temporary and permanent positions, it was the work of our staffing coordinators and the entire Landrum Staffing team to find just the right person to fill those jobs. And fill them we did, regularly paying a few hundred worksite employees every week, several thousand a year.

Landrum Staffing team - mid-1990's

The success of our staffing service operation over the years and the outstanding reputation it earned was due in no small measure to the dedication and skills of the staff members in that division of our company, and the systems put into place by their long-time leader, Denise McLeod, and her team. Six of those team members were with the company for more than twenty years. Two or three others are approaching the twenty-year mark. One has more than thirty years with the company. That longevity was and is important because it means that our loyal employees know their jobs very well. With years of service they get to know our repeat clients, which enables them to better match candidates with those employers and become a more valued partner.

Denise sings the praises of her team as she recalls the way they worked endless hours to tackle difficult recruiting assignments for companies that were undergoing a huge ramp-up in number of employees. In 2004, when Hurricane Ivan hit the Pensacola area, we recruited for Federal Emergency Management Agency (FEMA) contractors who needed more than 500 workers to help with the cleanup effort. We also recruited for AMFI, hiring several hundred workers to fill all positions when the company opened new hotels.

We did the same thing for Champion Paper when that company opened a large sawmill in the northern part of our county. After meeting with the management team and getting a clear understanding of the requirements, our team worked tirelessly over a two-day period to process over 1,200 candidates, initially hiring more than 400 workers that were needed to start the plant.

Landrum Staffing team - mid-2000's

The processes Denise and her team put into place included drug-screening, skills-testing, interviewing, criminal background checks, verification of education, employer-reference checking, and credit checks. The latter was done when the job to be filled involved handling money. The entire process was comprehensive and required a large staff and significant financial commitment, which in my view was much more than our competitors were willing to make. Those processes resulted in our being able to identify the very best candidates from the pool of applicants that came through our company. For that reason, I never hesitated to approve the hiring of another staff member when Denise made the request.

The protocols put in place gave our staffing coordinators assurance that the person they were sending out on assignment would represent us well and do the job they were hired to do. The standards Denise and her team adopted helped establish our reputation for quality, which translated to continued success in retaining customers and gaining new ones from those who were satisfied and recommended us to others.

Having a clear understanding of our clients' needs was and still is another key reason for our success. Our staffing coordinators regularly visit our clients to make sure they understand the jobs we are asked to fill and the culture of the company into which we are sending our employees. That important function continues today under the leadership of long-term staff member, Johanna Pohlmann, who serves as our client relations manager.

From a business perspective, our staffing service has always been profitable, with some years better than others, of course. Over the years, those profits helped us finance the startup of our PEO, buy property, and build and remodel office buildings. The financial gains also gave me peace of mind and afforded me the freedom to devote time to participating in industry organizations and community activities.

Just as important, and even more satisfying to me, is the reputation that we have earned in the communities we serve. In Pensacola, it is rare for me to run into someone who has never heard of our company. Most often, after hearing my name, they will ask, "Are you the owner of the staffing company?" They are surprised when they learn that the company was started locally and that I am its founder. That sounds egotistical as I write it, but I'd be lying if I said the recognition doesn't make me proud.

Over the years, I have run into former worksite employees at just about every place I visit–nurses and assistants at doctor's offices, secretaries at law firms, people in my church, and even one lady at Subway, who recognized me and made it a point to say, "I got my job through your company." She said that Denise McLeod placed her on a job twenty years earlier. She got to be the supervisor of her department, had a great career, and was now retiring. That story has been repeated many times over.

I get that same sense of satisfaction when a fellow Rotarian tells me an employee that we placed at their company was the best one ever hired. It also pleases me to know that our team is the primary source for employees at three of the largest manufacturing companies in the area. We have an onsite HR manager at one of the plants, and a site manager supervising several hundred workers at another. When one of the plants was hit hard by a tornado that came through Pensacola a few years ago, our team partnered with D & B Builders to quickly get the plant back up and running with very little downtime. Since then, we have been the "go to" company to supply construction, maintenance, and repair workers at their facilities, a relatively new area for us, but one that we are well equipped to handle.

The evolution in the services provided by our staffing services team over the years has caused us to change the way we refer to that service. In the beginning, we called ourselves a temporary help service, as that was indeed our main focus. When we started recruiting and placing people in permanent positions, we started referring to ourselves as a staffing company. Now, since the work that we do includes facilities staffing and management of the worksite employees as well, we refer to the division as "Workforce Solutions."

CHAPTER 3

New Business Ventures

False Starts

IN THE LATE 70's, I BECAME INTERESTED in two small business opportunities. The first was the establishment of a resume service in 1976. Since the beginning of Landrum Personnel Associates, I had been reviewing and improving hundreds of resumes for candidates looking for jobs. So, it seemed like a natural thing for me to do. My fee for preparing a resume was $25. The business was doomed from the start. It took too much time and didn't result in much money, so I quickly abandoned that idea.

The next business venture was the establishment of a medical transcription business I called, Medicom, which we started in January 1977. In my work as a placement consultant focused on the medical field, I became aware of the need for doctors to get their patient notes transcribed. That work had been going on for many years before I looked into it, but I felt the need was strong enough for me to get a share of the business.

The first step upon launching the business was to purchase a rather expensive remote call-in dictation machine made by Lanier Business Products. The machine had a row of cassette tapes that automatically advanced to the next tape when one was full and another was needed.

Physicians called the machine phone number at any time, day or night, and dictated their notes.

The second step was to hire a medical transcriptionist. My plan was to have the employee come into the office at night, sharing a placement counselor's office, to transcribe the notes left by physicians during the day–an efficient use of space, or so I thought. Unfortunately, finding an experienced medical transcriptionist proved to be more difficult than I expected. Even though she didn't have experience in the medical field, Peggy Fortunato, my assistant and an excellent typist and transcriptionist, volunteered to do the work for me. I took her up on her offer, and we developed a few physician customers as well as the Rehabilitation Institute of Northwest Florida.

Besides not being able to hire an experienced medical transcriptionist, there were other problems I didn't anticipate. Doctors typically paid by the word transcribed–at least that was the customary practice in that type of work. The doctors talked fast, many didn't speak clearly and distinctly, the medical terms were sometimes unfamiliar, and, of course, they didn't help by spelling them out. My transcriptionist simply could not type enough words in order to earn the kind of money she needed or that we needed in order to earn a profit. After doing this for an entire year, I calculated that I had earned a net profit of $50. I shut down the operation, donated the dictation machine to Baptist Hospital, and went back to focusing more attention on job placement and temporary help.

Testifying as a Vocational Expert

Another more interesting and much more successful venture involved my testifying in court as an expert witness on employment matters. In 1974, my good friend and attorney, Bill Clark, suggested that my background, experience, and knowledge of the job market might qualify me as an expert witness in employment matters. "Vocational Experts" as they are known, were often used by both plaintiff and defense attorneys to prove their cases in court. Shortly after that conversation, I started getting calls from lawyers involved in personal injury cases, workers' compensation claims, social security disability claims, and divorces. Sometimes I would be hired by the plaintiff's attorney, and on other occasions, I would be hired by the defense attorney.

Once, after testifying in a social security disability case, the Administrative Law Judge called me aside, complimented me on the quality of my testimony, and asked if I would consider working as a vocational expert under contract with the Social Security Administration (SSA). I was flattered and subsequently agreed. The judge invited me to attend a hearing at which another vocational expert would be testifying. After the hearing, I went over to meet the gentleman and compliment him for doing what I thought was a good job and to ask him a few questions, which the judge had suggested I do. He refused to shake my hand and walked away. I was a little shocked by that, but I later realized that he saw me as a competitor who would be a threat to his business. Thankfully, most competitors I've met over the years have been more cordial.

To prepare myself to give testimony and render an opinion about someone's employability, I developed a process involving testing and interviewing of the person involved and produced a written summary for the attorney. When I was hired by the SSA, I wasn't allowed to test and interview the claimant, but I could review the files and give my testimony based on the information provided to me.

Even though this work took me away from my normal business, I felt it was helping me build a strong reputation as an expert in the vocational and human resources area, which would be good for the company as well. I did this type of work on a part-time basis for over ten years, testifying in hundreds of cases. To assist in handling the cases and to free up some of my time, I hired my good friend, Cecil Lanier, whose vocational rehabilitation education and experience was similar to mine. Cecil assisted me with interviewing and testing the claimants. Our system worked pretty well for a year or so, and the fees earned were significant. Eventually the growth of my company demanded more of my time, however, and I decided it was best to stop doing that type of work.

A good many of the cases in which I was involved were disputes over claims for workers' compensation benefits by an employee who had been injured on the job. My evaluations and conversations with those claimants, discussions with their attorneys, and testimony in depositions and hearings before the state's Judges of Compensation Claims gave me a good bit of insight and knowledge regarding the laws and system for managing claims. That knowledge came in handy in later years as my company took on more responsibility for handling its own workers' compensation claims and creating programs designed to keep claim costs down.

Starting an Employee Leasing Company

Earlier I mentioned that in 1983, Chuck Woodbury made me aware of an article in *Inc. Magazine* about something called employee leasing. The idea intrigued me. Actually, the thought really excited me. I saw the possibility of having all of a company's employees on my payroll, not just a few as was the case with the temporary help service. Instead of having a few hundred thousand dollars in sales, we could have millions, and it meant closer and longer-term relationships with my clients.

The article was mostly about a California-based company, PayStaff, which had been in operation for a few years and boasted that it had over 200 clients and more than 1,000 employees. PayStaff had an array of benefits to offer the employees, which seemed to be part of the attraction, however, they also took over much of the administrative work of being an employer that reduced the burden on company owners.

Over the next few months, I read every magazine and newspaper article I could find on the subject of employee leasing. One of the articles I read was about a company in California, Contract Staffing of America. The article included a comment made by one of the company's clients, a small California manufacturing company. I made a phone call to the company officer quoted in the article who, thankfully, was quite willing to talk with me. I asked him why he chose to lease his employees, and he told me that he enjoyed not having to handle all the personnel-related issues on his own, which confirmed what I had read in the earlier article about PayStaff. Those words really started me thinking. I had always wanted to find a way to become more valuable to my clients, and employee leasing seemed to be the answer.

I also called Bill Morland, the owner of Contract Staffing of America. He was quite willing to share the details of his operation with me, but he seemed most interested in having me become a licensee of his company. He offered to teach me the business if I paid him a small percentage of all my sales. That part didn't interest me. I felt sure I could do it on my own.

One of the things I learned was that Contract Staffing of America, along with some other California leasing companies, had been successful in getting legislation passed by Congress that would enable a company that leased its employees to exclude those employees from the company pension plan as long as the employees were covered under a "Safe Harbor" pension plan, a plan that included certain minimum provisions established by the new law. The Tax Equity and Fiscal Responsibility Act (TEFRA) of 1982 created the "Safe Harbor" plan that seemed at first to be a strong reason leasing companies were gaining new clients. Of course, the leasing companies' assumption of some of the employer responsibilities appeared equally important.

In the course of my research, I learned that the new employee leasing industry was getting some national news coverage that wasn't very positive. In fact, it featured stories of how some employee leasing companies were providing self-funded health and workers' compensation insurance for their clients and the employees while defaulting on the payment of claims. Those same companies were collecting state and federal payroll taxes, but they were defaulting on remitting those payments to the government. Criminal charges were filed against some of the owners of those employee leasing companies, and a few went to jail. Some of the schemes appeared to be intentional fraud. Others appeared to be the result of well-intentioned people who didn't understand the business, were underfunded, or took on risks they weren't equipped to manage.

Regardless of the reasons for failure, the employee leasing industry gained a poor reputation at the start. State and federal legislators and regulators received complaints from constituents, and from the standpoint of the industry, unfavorable legislation and regulations were discussed. State unemployment and insurance regulators, as well as the National Council on Compensation Insurance (NCCI), considered new rules to curtail the industry.

In spite of all the negative publicity, I still believed that the industry had a future if owners obeyed the laws and provided a real service. It was at this point that I learned that several of my friends in ITSA were already discussing the possibility of opening employee leasing companies. The members included Richard Cruitt from Birmingham, Alabama, Wayne Josephson from Oklahoma City, Oklahoma, Bob Liken from Pittsburgh, Pennsylvania, and Lou Hipp from Stamford, Connecticut. In October and November 1983, I met with the group to learn more about their plans.

At the first meeting, the members were enthusiastic, and the talk was more about choosing a common name, pooling resources for accounting and benefits purposes, and the strategy of doing a "rollup" in order to create a publicly traded company. At the second meeting, Wayne Josephson and I were the only two who were still positive about getting started. The others were ready to back out fearing the unknown. There was much discussion regarding the risks involved in owning an employee leasing company and the impending legislation and regulations that could even shut down the new industry. In the end, only Wayne and I moved forward with our plans. Wayne opened and operated his company for a year or so before deciding it was not for him. I officially started my company in December 1983, by asking my friend and attorney, Bill

Clark, to create a new corporation with the name *American Staff Leasing Corporation* doing business as "AmStaff."

Starting this new company was exciting to me as I had a strong feeling that it was going to be successful and make us a more valued partner to the clients we served. Being a valued partner meant lower client turnover and ultimately, an increase in sales volume.

Remembering that the employee leasing companies I read about seemed to be focusing on physicians who wanted to take advantage of the Safe Harbor pension plan that Congress had approved, I had my attorney create such a plan for us and designed a marketing plan to approach them. My friend, Tom Fife, an insurance and investment executive, had been working with local physicians for many years and agreed to share his list of clients so I could approach them about AmStaff. As I remember, the list contained about 300 names.

My next step was to draft a letter that I could send to each physician, detailing the benefits to them of "leasing" their employees from AmStaff. I worked on it for a day or two trying to use just the right words that would persuade them to give me a call. For months my family had heard all about the new company and my optimism about its future. So, I thought it would be meaningful for them to participate with me in sending out the first letter. I can still picture the scene of my sons, Britt III, age 14, and Brian, age 8, and my wife, Nell, as we gathered around the dining room table at our home, folding letters and stuffing envelopes–a real family affair. The boys were a little less than enthusiastic that day, but both remember it quite well today and are proud of their participation.

I had high hopes that the letter to all those physicians was going to kick-start my new business. As it turned out, none of them were interested, at least not in the Safe Harbor pension plan. Actually, that was probably a good thing because the law creating the plan was amended by Congress a year or so later, taking away the benefit previously offered that I'd hoped would compel prospects to consider AmStaff.

I did get a call from one physician, a family doctor with two or three employees. He wasn't interested in the pension benefits but wanted someone to assist with the administrative side of his business–payroll, employee insurance, and benefits. I was only too happy to present him with a contract, and he became AmStaff's first client!

At that point I had created new employee applications and an orientation presentation. I envisioned sitting down with the employees to explain the new "co-employment" relationship to them while putting them at ease and making the transition from their employer to AmStaff as smooth as possible. The new client, however, had a different idea. As soon as he had signed the contract, he leaned out of his office door and literally shouted down the hall, "You're all fired!" He then laughed and was delighted to have me assume many of the responsibilities that he had shouldered up until then.

In August 1984, I received a phone call from Yvonne Nellums asking to make an appointment with me to discuss a business proposition. Yvonne had been the manager of a recruiting service in Mobile, Alabama that specialized in finding workers for offshore oil rigs. I learned from her that she and her friend, Kay Kendrick, had worked on a business plan to open a similar business in Pensacola, and after doing some research on me, they wanted me to own the business, allowing them to operate it for me. I liked their entrepreneurial spirit. But, after looking over their business plan, I told them I wasn't interested in their idea. I told them that I had created a new business that was going to be much larger than anything I'd ever done. I realized at the time that I needed help in selling and servicing the clients and worksite employees that we had gained, and discussed the idea of having them work with me in my new venture. After further interviews with Yvonne and Kay, I agreed to hire them both and they started to work in September 1984.

At that time, we had no office space available. Every office at the 1207 West Garden Street location was filled with a placement counselor for the employment agency or a member of our administrative staff. The only available space was in the break room, which was actually our small kitchen adjacent to the restrooms. So, the kitchen became our first AmStaff office, with the kitchen table serving as a desk. After a few weeks of being cramped in that spot, we rented a small construction trailer and parked it behind our building. Yvonne and Kay thought it was wonderful, dressed it up with curtains from Penny's Department Store, and turned it into a real office.

Yvonne Nellums entering first AmStaff office building - 1984

When Yvonne and Kay were hired, we only had three or four clients and not many worksite employees. Peggy Fortunato ran the small payroll each week, and I delivered the payroll checks and collected the payments from our clients. After Yvonne and Kay started, I turned that job over to them. They were also responsible for finding new clients, signing up new worksite employees, and handling any employee relations issues that came up. Yvonne particularly showed a great deal of skill in handling some of the more difficult problems. At the request of our clients, she would often have to counsel with employees and even take care of terminating their employment if things didn't work out. As we learned over time, many of our small business clients didn't want to deal with the difficult task of terminating an employee and were quite relieved to have us take care of that matter for them.

Not long after Yvonne and Kay started to work, I became acquainted with Jim Haggerty, who owned an employee leasing company in Sarasota, Florida, called Employers Management. Jim and I had previously met at a meeting of the Florida Employee Leasing Association. His company had been in operation for a few years longer than mine, and I was anxious to learn from him. Graciously, he invited me to bring my staff (Yvonne and Kay) to his office where he would show us his entire operation and allow us to spend time with his staff members as well.

Of course, we were curious to know how he got new clients. His advertisements were bold, showing a picture of a fire engine and the words, "Fire Your Employees and Hire Ours!" (This theme was popular in the early days, and we even used it ourselves on some of our advertising and brochures. Cooper Yates, our advertising consultant at the time, strongly advised against it, but I insisted, pointing out that others were successful in using that message. He was right, of course, and we abandoned that theme a short time later.)

We also visited with Jim's sales manager, Bill Mullis, who gave us a bit of the company's strategy in making new sales. (We didn't realize it at the time, but Bill Mullis and two or three other key members of Jim's staff were planning to leave his company and form their own. Not long after our visit, they started a company called Staff Leasing, and within just a few years that company became the largest employee leasing company in the country.) Jim ran into some trouble with state authorities a few years later and had to close his company, but I always appreciated his openness and willingness to share his experiences and those of his key staff members.

*Kay Kendrick, Yvonne Nellums, Peggy Fortunato
at Business Expo - about 1985*

Yvonne, Kay, and I continued to work to build AmStaff, primarily focusing on taking care of clients and worksite employees. On their first anniversary with the company, I sent Yvonne and Kay a memo of congratulations and mentioned that at that time in September 1985, we had 11 subscribers (prior name for clients) and 98 worksite employees. The business of employee leasing has grown significantly since that time, and members of the industry have now come to be known as Professional Employer Organizations ("PEOs").

CHAPTER 4

Delivering HR Services Through the PEO

A Full Complement of Services

SINCE ITS BEGINNING IN 1983, the primary focus of AmStaff (now LandrumHR) has been the provision of a full suite of services benefitting our client companies. We endeavor to help them control costs and to relieve them of some of the risks and many of the time-consuming responsibilities of being an employer. In short, what we do should cut down on the number of hassles most business owners experience as a result of having employees on the payroll.

Over the years, I've had a number of clients confirm that our services have made things easier for them and less complicated. Some have said that they don't see how their company could have done as well without partnering with us. I know that sounds like a commercial, but essentially, that's what we set out to do.

In broad terms, we deliver human resources services. The value we create for our clients comes from administrating payroll, health benefits, retirement plans, and workers' compensation plans. In addition, we help clients by assuming responsibility for safety, risk, claims and document management, employee relations, and training and leadership development. Each of those functions encompasses a broad spectrum of requirements and responsibilities made more complicated by the government. Keeping up with federal, state, and municipal laws and regulations and the changes that are made to them each year, is the job of our legal and human resources staff members. The challenge faced by employers without staff resources to stay informed and to remain compliant provides new business opportunities for us.

In the late 80's, I devoted my attention to perfecting AmStaff's offering to our PEO clients and our worksite or co-employees. After doing a fair amount of research, I produced our first employee handbook, which helped new clients' (worksite) employees better understand the arrangement entered into by their company. I also produced a sizeable client manual covering every aspect of the employee leasing arrangement and a fairly complete safety manual. I have no idea whether these manuals got used by our clients, but they were accurate, should have been helpful to them if they read them, and made us look more professional than our competition, or so I thought.

Employee orientation for new clients is extremely important. We had to get everyone to sign our application and agreement forms, which were legally compliant and designed to put our clients and AmStaff in the best defensive position in the event a claim for discrimination was filed against either of us. At the same time, the executed forms guaranteed all the employee rights required by law. Making sure our clients are in full compliance with all laws and regulations and that employees are treated fairly and in accordance with those laws is critical to our core mission. Unfortunately, those forms were not perceived as particularly employee friendly.

Yvonne Nellums and Kay Kendrick did the orientation sessions initially. Susan Hunsucker, who had returned to our company in 1984 after a two-year break, joined Yvonne and Kay in doing the orientations, getting the paperwork completed and forms signed, and explaining employee benefits.

We learned the hard way that things went much better if the client met with their employees first to explain the employee leasing arrangement. There were a few occasions when this was not done, and employees were understandably upset when they were given new application forms to complete. Some thought their company might have been sold or that by signing our application form, they were going to lose their accrued vacation or sick leave, which of course was not the case. To avoid this scenario, we designed a protocol that we urged new clients to adopt. It stressed the importance of an advance meeting with employees to explain why the company was entering into the arrangement with AmStaff.

Those orientation meetings were held at the client's worksite at a time convenient for them. In the early years, Yvonne recalls one occasion where she and Susan met with a group of employees for orientation at a concrete pipe manufacturing plant in Panama City. The meeting was held at 5:00 AM around a burning drum, which kept them warm in the freezing weather. Thankfully, Yvonne and Susan didn't have to work under such conditions very often, but it demonstrates their commitment to accommodate the needs of our clients, as well as their desire to assist our company in building its business.

In the early 90's, AmStaff grew in number of clients and worksite employees. Our focus was on improving infrastructure, adding benefits, and serving new and existing clients. We held staff meetings on a monthly basis to discuss various emerging issues of importance. A review of one of our old agendas reminded me that typical topics included legislative issues, new benefits offered, new clients coming on board, and time clocks–not unlike some of the issues we're discussing today. Staff members attending those meetings then included Harry Booros, Tom Downey, Peggy Fortunato, Susan Hunsucker, Darlene McClendon, Yvonne Nellums, Suzanne Walker, Betty Wright, and Lorita Bee.

As the only HR manager on staff at the time, Yvonne was responsible for handling all employee relations matters for all of our clients. In addition, she represented our company at unemployment compensation hearings in an effort to keep our unemployment tax rate under control. After some time, she let me know that the volume of claims and hearings had increased to the point where she couldn't properly prepare and attend them as frequently as she should. She also let me know that we were losing too many cases. On Yvonne's recommendation, I agreed to begin searching for someone to work full-time to handle those claims. I reasoned that the amount of savings that could be realized by reducing our claims experience would more than offset the cost of the new position.

In 1995, Yvonne reached out to a friend at the Florida Department of Labor who recommended Gayle Meacham, who was then working as an unemployment claims adjudicator for the State. As it turned out, Gayle had been the adjudicator who had most often ruled against our company in those unemployment hearings! After meeting with Gayle, I offered her the job as unemployment claims administrator, and she readily accepted. One of her first responsibilities as our new administrator was to file appeals in those cases we had lost and have them reheard. She did this, and to my amazement, got them overturned even in the cases where she had ruled against us as the adjudicator. The facts in those cases didn't change but knowing what to say and how to say it made a big difference.

Gayle remained with the company as unemployment claims administrator until her retirement in 2018, quietly answering thousands of claims and helping us win hundreds of judgments and appeals. Over her 23-year career with the company, I am confident that Gayle saved us millions of dollars in unemployment taxes.

In the period of time between 1984 and 1995, Yvonne gained a tremendous amount of experience, successfully passed her exams to become certified as a Professional in Human Resources (PHR) and was promoted to human resources manager for AmStaff. In 1995, Yvonne and I hired Carole Cox, an experienced human resources manager to join her in the department. As the company has expanded over the years to five locations, the number of HR managers has increased as well. As of this writing there are a total of nine HR managers and an HR relationship director in the department, with expert legal advice provided by our in-house employment attorney, Amie Remington.

Our HR managers are certified and considered experts in their field. They prepare or assist in preparing employee handbooks and policies on our clients' behalf. Among other services, they assist with writing job descriptions, conduct salary surveys, and advise on both employee recruiting and wage and hour matters. As warranted, they take great care to help clients determine whether or not an employee is classified correctly as hourly or exempt from overtime requirements. They are frequently called upon not only to advise clients and assist worksite employees with sensitive issues, but they often get directly involved in counseling, documenting any warning or discipline imposed, and terminations. Some of our HR managers are on site with larger clients several days each week. Others serve as the "off-site" HR manager for smaller clients and visit them less frequently. All of our clients have access to an HR manager for advice any time. After-hours and weekend phone calls are not unusual.

Yvonne reminds me that very often during those counseling sessions, the HR manager will learn that an employee is having a serious issue at home either because of an abusive spouse, a serious health concern, a problem with one or more of their children, or any one of a number of other issues. They bring their stress to the workplace, and it naturally has a negative impact on work performance. Often those employees are referred for counseling to our Employee Assistance Program (EAP), which is provided to them without cost. I have personally spoken with past employees who have let me know how much they appreciated that help when they needed it.

Our HR managers also conduct investigations into allegations of discrimination as required by law and work to resolve issues before they get out of hand. Most often, we are able to assist both parties in achieving some resolution to their dispute, avoiding the need or desire on the employee's part to file an official claim. One needs only to look at the cost of litigation in terms of time spent, legal fees, and sometimes damage to company reputation to realize the value of our service in those matters, and that doesn't include the monetary damages assessed against companies that lose their battles in court.

Preventing such problems is an important element of the service we provide. We have invested in obtaining the best legal advice in the area of employment law. Amie regularly consults with our HR managers to keep them current on changes in the laws and regulations and to assist with difficult cases. The forms we use, and the advice and counsel we offer to clients with regard to hiring, disciplining, and terminating employees are all designed to keep them in compliance with those laws and regulations.

A number of years ago, we began offering Employment Practices Liability Insurance (EPLI) coverage to our PEO clients. This important coverage is fairly expensive when purchased separately but relatively inexpensive when purchased through our group plan. For clients who chose to opt into our plan and who followed our advice, we offered to reimburse up to $10,000 of the cost of their legal defense if that became necessary. For clients who chose not to hire an attorney, we assisted them in responding to the employee, investigating the claim, and in writing a response to the charge. When clients had their own attorney, we were accustomed to doing most of the research, enabling them to limit their attorney's work to reviewing the final report. In both cases the cost savings to our clients was significant.

Over the years, our HR staff has learned that the best way to prevent problems and assist our new employer clients is to make sure they are in compliance at the outset. When that relationship begins, a human resources survey is conducted to determine if the company is compliant with wage and hour laws, if its employee handbooks are up-to-date, and if its hiring and supervision practices are in accord with Equal Employment Opportunity Commission (EEOC) laws and requirements.

We also recognize that our clients need access to training that will prepare their key employees for leadership roles or improve the skills of those already in those positions. In 2007, we started the Leadership Development Certification Series led by Yvonne. Training classes were taught by our human resources managers and, at that time, included such subjects as business ethics, selecting the best employees, conflict management, progressive discipline and termination, dealing with difficult people, harassment, and supervisory safety skills.

Several online classes were also made available to our clients. The Leadership Development Certification Series existed until 2014. Certification was earned if participants completed all classes in the series during the allotted two-year period. More than 160 participants completed the course work and earned a certificate of completion signed by me. Some of those certificates were, and I suspect, still are proudly displayed in the offices of those supervisors who successfully completed the program.

One of our most popular training programs is the Supervisory Boot Camp. That training, which incorporates the client's policies and practices, explores the basic employment laws and helps participants learn what compliance with those laws entails from a practical standpoint. The program is taught at our facility, and the classroom is usually filled to capacity.

The training programs that have been developed by our staff are offered to non-clients as well. Businesses, nonprofits, and governmental agencies contract regularly for this training through Landrum Consulting, a division of our company that officially launched in 2003, though it has been operating unofficially since the mid-90's. In 2010, our training program was certified by the Human Resources Certification Institute (HRCI) so that attending HR professionals could receive HRCI education credits.

In December 2019, after completing over 35 years with the company, Yvonne Nellums gave up her role as head of the PEO human resources department and retired. Those who reported to her knew her as a compassionate person and a fair and effective manager.

During her long career Yvonne successfully created and developed the outstanding human resources department that we have today. She grew into her role gradually as the PEO gained more clients and worksite employees over the years. She was called on to be our clients' HR manager, advising them on compliance matters, assisting them with the creation of employment policies and handbooks, and counseling their employees. In the early years before we had an employment attorney on staff, Yvonne was the person I consulted for all questions about wage and hour laws and other laws and regulations regarding discrimination in the workplace. The training programs she and her staff put into place have become the hallmark for our PEO. I am most grateful to Yvonne for her long years of service and contributions to the success of LandrumHR.

Big Company Benefits for Small Employers

Getting a group health plan for the PEO worksite employees when we started the business in 1983 was complicated. My industry friends in other parts of the state informed me that we had to have at least 50 employees before any insurance company would look at us. We had nowhere near that number. At first, we just added the new worksite employees onto our existing staff employee group health plan, which was very inexpensive by today's standards. Clyde Anderson's agency, Associated Insurance, assisted me with that initially.

As we grew and the need for a separate plan for the leased employees became evident, I came into contact with Ron Sedlacek, an insurance agent who became our friend and advisor for many years. Ron eventually helped us obtain a group health policy with Blue Cross of Florida. He was also instrumental in helping us manage that policy and others as the number of worksite employees grew from under one hundred to several thousand, and as the various insurance benefits offered to the employees increased.

Such benefits were (and still are) an important feature of the co-employment arrangement and helped us gain acceptance in the early years. Our initial offering in the late 80's included health, dental, life, and vision insurance, as well as a simplified retirement savings plan, tuition reimbursement, and adoption assistance. It also included an offer of membership in the Central Credit Union of Florida, notary public services, and confidential counseling sessions through the EAP program, which we provided at no cost to our clients or employees.

With time, benefits were added to include discounted prices on movie tickets and rental cars and to amusement parks such as Magic Kingdom, Busch Gardens, Circus World, and other entertainment venues. As we grew in number of clients and worksite employees, we created and offered a "cafeteria plan" and a 401K retirement plan. The cafeteria plan is a tax-qualified plan that allows employees to purchase disability and additional health insurance and to pay for other health-related services and products with pre-tax dollars up to an approved amount each year. The advantage to the employee is that no taxes are charged on the portion of an employee's paycheck that goes toward the payment of those insurance premiums or the cost of the approved services. Cafeteria plans and 401K plans are typically offered only by larger employers as they are expensive to set up and administer. Offering those plans through AmStaff brought additional value to our clients and a new slogan used by our sales team, "Big company benefits for small employers."

In 1986, AmStaff had about 300 worksite employees. Susan Hunsucker had already begun doing the administrative work associated with the management of all worksite employee documents and insurance plans. As stated earlier, she also participated in the orientation sessions for new worksite employees, explaining the benefits and getting enrollment forms completed. During that time, she enrolled in a program offered through the Wharton School of Business at the University of Pennsylvania in Philadelphia. After a few years of intensive study, Susan completed the program and passed all examinations to become a Certified Employee Benefits Specialist, a designation of expertise held by only a few in our part of the state.

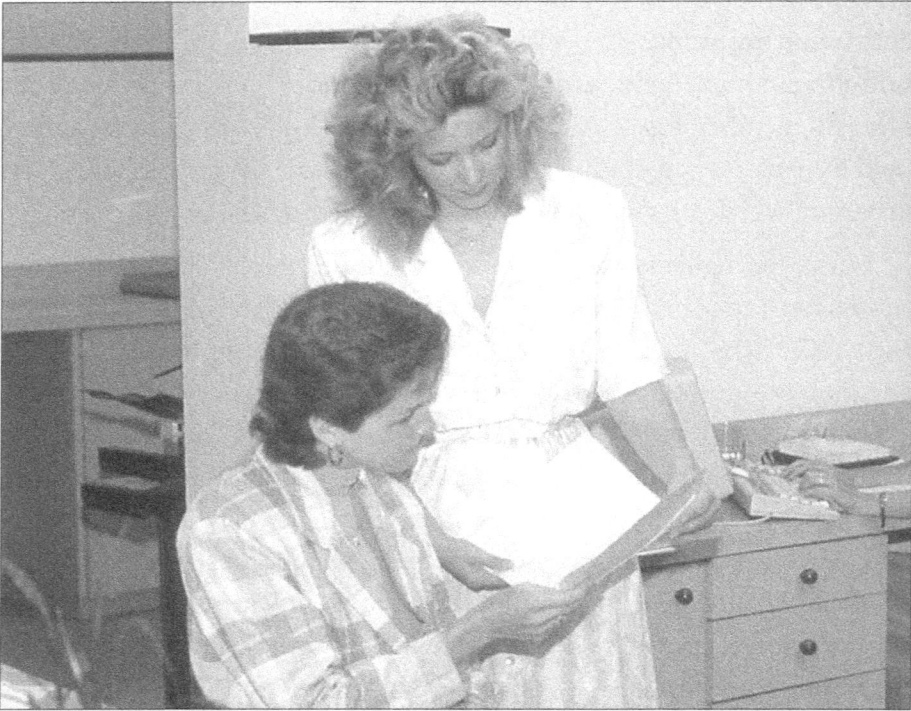

Susan Hunsucker (left) and Yvonne Nellums - 1986

In the early years, the matter of offering tax-qualified retirement or benefit plans to the worksite employees of an employee leasing company was not without controversy. With the passage of TEFRA in 1982, clients of an employee leasing company (PEO) could exclude their employees from their plan if the PEO covered them with a "safe harbor" pension plan, which had certain minimum contribution, vesting, and eligibility requirements.

Shortly after I started AmStaff in 1983, TEFRA was amended by Congress, essentially taking away the incentive for such a plan structure within the employee leasing relationship. Many had argued that employers were using the employee leasing arrangement as a scheme to avoid including their employees in their more favorable retirement plans. Internal Revenue Service (IRS) Section 414n was interpreted to curtail such discrimination from occurring. Over the years, amendments to 414n and rulings from IRS have provided some guidance regarding the relationship between clients of an employee leasing company, the employee, and the employee leasing company (PEO), and earlier controversies have gained further clarity.

Since our beginning, AmStaff (now LandrumHR) has taken the position that, for the purposes of plan discrimination testing, clients cannot exclude the worksite employees (our co-employees) from their 401K plans if the clients have one. Although a few clients still have their own plans that we co-sponsor, most adopt our 401k plan, which has been changed to a multiple employer plan.

Looking after the administration and investment of retirement funds for our clients and worksite employees is one of the most important functions we perform, and we take that responsibility very seriously. Not long after we developed the 401K plan, we chose Slavic401K as the firm we wanted to handle both administration of the plans and investment of the funds. The firm, owned by John Slavic, specializes in PEOs and has earned a stellar reputation in the industry. A few years ago, we contracted with another firm, Fiduciary Partners Retirement Group, to look over the shoulder of the Slavic organization to make sure they were properly administering the plan and making the best choices with regard to investments. We also established an Investments committee, which meets regularly with Fiduciary Partners to review the status and continued effectiveness of the plan and investments. To assure ourselves that we are receiving the best investment advice and management services at the lowest cost, Fiduciary Partners has periodically assisted us in reviewing bids from other firms. To date, none have offered better pricing or service.

In the late 80's and early 90's, health insurance carriers were reluctant to write policies at acceptable rates that could be offered to clients of employee leasing companies. As our growth continued in the 90's, we were fortunate to obtain a group health policy with American Life Assurance Corporation, a subsidiary of First National Life Insurance Company headquartered in Pensacola and owned by Pensacola residents, Martha and Skip Hunter. That policy worked well for us for a couple of years, but it was somewhat limited and unknown to prospects who were more interested in a policy with Blue Cross or another, better known carrier. We thought we had solved that problem when we were able to get a group policy with Liberty Life Assurance, a new venture for Liberty Mutual Insurance. Unfortunately, after a year or so, Liberty decided not to pursue that line of business, which forced us to look elsewhere.

In the mid-90's, we were able to obtain a fully-insured group plan with Blue Cross of Florida (now Florida Blue) with the assistance of Todd Torgersen and Ron Sedlacek. We were one of very few employee leasing companies afforded that opportunity, and we were told, the only PEO that had a fully-insured plan. The other plans were written so that the employee leasing company had to assume part of the risk for claims that exceeded a maximum threshold. At the time, Todd was a vice president with Florida Blue, and Ron was an independent agent. Ron continued to work closely with our company for many years before his retirement in 2016. After leaving Florida Blue, Todd formed an agency, Combined Insurance Services, Inc. (now doing business as Torgersen Causey) and continues to work with our company in managing all Florida Blue plans offered to the worksite employees. With thousands of employees on our health plan today, we remain with the same carrier for all covered employees in Florida. Now, however, we have to provide financial guarantees and absorb some of the risk if claims exceed a certain threshold.

Administration of these plans for the thousands of worksite employees and their families is a monumental task. Staff members in our benefits department have to make sure that every employee is properly notified about benefit choices and enrolled appropriately, that insurance cards are issued and received, and that payroll deductions and client billings are correct and properly entered into our computer system. The percentage of premiums paid by each client-employer and the cost of the policies offered under the various plans vary, which further complicates that process. Open enrollment each year is an especially busy time for the staff.

The proper administration of the requirements under the Consolidated Omnibus Budget Reconciliation Act (COBRA) and tracking of paid time off (PTO) are also the responsibility of our benefits staff. Both clients and employees want to have an accurate record of how much time they have used and how much time remains available to them. Tracking is somewhat complicated as the calculation of PTO can vary from one client to another. In the past, much of the effort was managed using Excel spreadsheets. Thankfully, most of that work is now automated.

In addition to administering all benefits, keeping up with the changes in employee benefit laws and regulations, amending plan documents, and filing Form 5500 tax returns, the benefits staff is frequently called upon to answer questions for employees and sometimes assist them with their claims. The benefits team is key to delivering the value that we promise to our clients and the worksite employees, and I'm proud to know they do it well.

At the time of Susan's retirement as the director of benefits in 2018, there were a total of ten staff members in the department. During her tenure, Susan is credited with creating the benefits department, hiring and training the fine staff of specialists who now run that department, and setting up systems and procedures to effectively and efficiently manage all the complicated insurance and tax-qualified benefit plans for several hundred small business clients and as many as 20,000 worksite employees each year.

Susan had a remarkable understanding of the complicated tax laws and regulations surrounding the treatment of "tax-qualified plans" such as cafeteria and 401K plans and was my source for information about testing for highly compensated employees, employee deferral rules and limits, and employer matching requirements. She obtained some expert help in that area with the hiring in 2015 of Christy Arnold, an attorney who serves as our benefits compliance counsel. I am truly appreciative of Susan's dedication to the company and her contribution to our success.

Susan Hunsucker and Britt Landrum, Jr. - 2000

Selling HR Services

In the beginning, I served as the only salesperson for AmStaff. In the mid-80's, there were only a few employee leasing companies nationwide, and AmStaff was the first one in northwest Florida. Hardly anyone had heard of the concept, so I spent much of my time educating prospects. To help market the company, I wrote articles for the local newspaper, and with the help of advisors, succeeded in getting an article placed in the *Florida Trend Magazine*. All of this helped to put our new company on the map and helped me sign up a few clients.

By 1986, my first AmStaff sales representatives, Yvonne Nellums and Kay Kendrick, who had been with the company since 1984, no longer had much time to focus on sales. Kay left the company in 1987, and Yvonne was busy with client and employee relations issues. I was doing all I could to assist, but to grow the company, I knew we needed help with sales and began looking for candidates. Unfortunately, the first few representatives we hired weren't successful and didn't last long. In all honesty, I didn't do a good job in identifying the best prospects or training them after they were hired.

In January 1988, Tom Downey, an experienced salesman who had sold a copy machine to me a couple of years earlier, came to see me about joining AmStaff. Tom had owned a part-interest in the copy machine company that he formerly represented, and I learned that he had since sold his interest. I was impressed with the way he had interacted with me on that sale and was pleased to offer him a job with AmStaff, which he readily accepted. It proved to be a good move for both of us.

Britt Landrum, Jr. and Tom Downey - 1988

For the next four years, Tom was our sole sales representative for AmStaff. His approach to the sales effort was professional, organized, and effective, and the company added many new clients and worksite employees. As our sales team grew to include other representatives, Tom continued to produce, and upon his retirement in 2011, he had accounted for thousands of new worksite employees and millions of dollars in new sales.

That same distinction belongs to three other long-term sales representatives, including Dave Keleher, who joined Tom in 1992 as the second representative in the sales department; Ted Holz, who joined the company in 2000; and Jerold Hall, who came on board in 2002. These three men added a significant number of clients over their careers, accounting for thousands of worksite employees and millions of dollars in new sales. Dave retired in 2018 after twenty-six years with the company. Ted Holz completed eighteen years before leaving in 2018. Jerold Hall was promoted to director of business development and served in that capacity until leaving the company in 2019 after 17 years.

In 1993, my oldest son, Britt III, returned to Pensacola and joined Tom and Dave to become the third person in our sales department, before the additions of Ted and Jerold. Britt III had graduated from college a year earlier and, while living in Atlanta, worked part-time for the company, doing client satisfaction surveys by telephone and investigating the opening of a branch office in Atlanta.

Our main goal for the Atlanta branch was to qualify as an approved vendor for Allstate Insurance, which at the time had made a corporate decision to require all of their licensed agents to use companies like ours to pay their agency employees. We had been very successful with Allstate in Florida and had 260 or so agencies signed up as clients, with all of their employees on our payroll. Unfortunately, the business didn't come as easily in Georgia, and we eventually abandoned the effort there.

Britt III was no stranger to the business, having grown up hearing all about it from me over the years. He had begun working for the company cleaning offices on weekends during high school, running computer back-up tapes during junior college, and delivering paychecks to worksite employees while home for summer breaks from Oglethorpe University in Atlanta. During the year or two he worked as an AmStaff sales rep, he added a number of new clients and worksite employees. One of his first clients has been with the company for more than 25 years.

Since 1993, quite a few men and women have joined our AmStaff sales department, many of whom stayed with us for several years and are credited for doing a fine job. In addition to Tom, Dave, Britt, Ted, and Jerold already mentioned, that list includes John Shattuck and Andrew Sowell. John joined the company in 1997 and was a very successful sales representative. He was promoted to manager of the department before his departure from the company in 2002. Andrew joined the company in 2011, continues to have an outstanding record in sales, and was recently named as senior business consultant in recognition of his additional role as sales trainer for the company. As I've learned over the years, selling the value created in the employee leasing arrangement can be challenging, and not everyone has the patience or skill set to be successful. In spite of the brief tenure of some of the sales staff, most were welcome additions and made a positive impact on the company by adding new clients.

During Tom Downey's tenure, I recall him wanting to meet with me to set goals for the year. He wanted to know what my long-term thinking was for the company. How large did we want to become? How many clients and worksite employees did we want to have? His questions certainly made me think about that subject much more. My answer to him then was still my answer when I retired in 2017. I have never aspired to be the largest. I have always wanted to be the best, and to have the most qualified people on staff who could deliver the best service and earn our company a reputation for excellence in all that we do. I certainly wanted to grow, but I felt that if our company's reputation was all about quality and we delivered a valuable service to our clients, then they would tell others and become our best source of referrals for new business. As a result, growth would come naturally. I'm not sure I satisfied Tom with my answer, but in those early years, many of our new clients did come to us by way of referral from existing clients who valued what we did for them and recommended us to their friends and associates.

Administering Payroll and Benefits

In December 1983, when AmStaff was established, we had ten years of experience in administering payroll and issuing paychecks for the temporary help service. As a result, we felt very confident in our ability to handle that function for the new company.

We initially used the Spartin Systems software designed for temporary help services to meet our payroll processing needs for the employee leasing business. That system was adequate for our purposes at the time since our service was limited to HR assistance, a few limited benefits, payroll administration, and coverage of the worksite employees under our workers' compensation policy.

In the beginning, I delivered the payroll and collected payments from our clients. Yvonne Nellums and Kay Kendrick took on that task after they started to work in the latter part of 1984. As they got busier and our client list got larger, staff members who lived close to the clients were called on to help. Mike Fortunato, Peggy's husband, assisted on occasion. After a few years, that led to a full-time job for him, and eventually for their son, Chris, who took over the payroll delivery job from his dad in 2007 after Mike passed away.

By the late 80's when our benefits program was expanded to include group health insurance, a 401K retirement plan, and a Section 125 "cafeteria plan," the Caldwell-Spartin system used by the temporary service was no longer adequate for AmStaff. While attending a meeting of the National Staff Leasing Association (NSLA), now known as the National Association of Professional Employer Organization (NAPEO), we learned of a new software program written especially for employee leasing companies. The PayPlus software system gave us much more flexibility for handling payroll deductions and billing and included modules that enabled us to do a better job managing employee benefits. We purchased that system in 1989.

Around that same time, with a few hundred worksite employees on the payroll, we began developing a payroll department for AmStaff. In 1986, we moved to a new location at 6708 Plantation Road and had space available for two payroll specialists. One of the earliest staff members to work in that area was Darlene McClendon who started with the company in 1990. Later that same year, she was joined in the department by Betty Riegler Wright. Betty had quite a bit of experience doing payroll when she came to work for us, so she became our first payroll manager.

The department grew to a half dozen or more payroll specialists when we moved the company to 6723 Plantation Road in 1993. The number of clients increased to a few hundred, and the number of worksite employees increased to a few thousand. In 2003, Betty chose to leave the company to join the staff of our payroll software vendor, PayPlus. Darlene transferred out of payroll after a couple of years. She is still with the company, now as a support specialist in the technical support and operations department.

Mary Griewisch followed Betty as the director of payroll and held the position for a couple of years before transferring to IT to assist with new client startups. Alice Malloy, a payroll specialist who started with the company in 1997, was then promoted to director of the department. In 2006, all staff members of the payroll department were moved to a newly purchased and remodeled building at 6715 Plantation Road, which is adjacent to and across the parking lot from the main office. We dubbed it the "Payroll Building."

As a part of our effort to become SAS 70 certified, which I address in more detail later, we invited Kevin Bowyer, a CPA with the O'Sullivan Creel accounting firm, to prepare us for an audit. In October 2007, we received a very lengthy and comprehensive risk assessment and preliminary audit plan, followed in January 2008 by a readiness report telling us in detail what we needed to do to get ready for the SAS 70 audit. One of the recommendations included in that report was to combine our payroll and benefits departments. At that time staff members performing those functions were located in separate buildings. They had access to all personal information on the worksite employees and were regularly accessing employee records to input personnel data into our system. To improve accuracy and security, it was recommended that we join the two departments and move them to the same location.

Britt III, by then vice president with responsibility for the two departments involved, recommended that we implement Kevin's recommendation. At his suggestion, we created the position of director of operations, combining the two departments under a single director. Susan Hunsucker was asked to accept that new role, while Alice Malloy was given the new title of payroll manager reporting to Susan. The new operations department was officially established in January 2010, and the building then became known as the "Operations Center" or "Ops" for short.

The operations department ran smoothly under Susan's leadership, but in 2013, we decided to break out payroll and benefits as standalone departments once again. Our concern was that our company was planning to set up our own insurance agency and begin offering benefits to the worksite employees through that agency, which was going to require a greater concentration of time in oversight. We also had plans to purchase the agency owned by Ron Sedlacek, who was retiring from the business. Susan had been identified as the logical choice to lead us through the transition and management of this critically important operation, which would require her full attention. She resumed her former role as director of benefits, and was well positioned to promote the purchase of life, disability, and health insurance through our new agency. As it happened, our plans to purchase Ron's business didn't materialize due to some unexpected technical issues, and we delayed the start of our new agency.

PEO Payroll Staff - 2007

Mindful of the recommendation from the 2008 readiness report that we consolidate payroll and benefits, we opted to separate managerial oversight of the two functions, but to keep the employees performing both payroll and benefits administration in the same building. After the separation of the payroll and benefits departments, Karena McCafferty, who joined the company in 2005 as a PEO payroll specialist, was promoted to director of payroll. Karena continues in that role today.

Timesheets and Payroll Processing

The reporting of hours by worksite employees is one of the many aspects of our operation that has benefitted from technology advances. Early on, AmStaff's smaller clients submitted payroll hours to us by fax or email. The transmittals were not secure and were often hard to read, resulting in input errors to our payroll system. Larger clients submitted lists, often handwritten, either by fax or by email. We then installed and maintained time clocks in the workplaces of the larger clients. The clocks we used had to be programmed to interface with our payroll system, and some of our staff members with the requisite skills took care of the installations. The clocks transmitted time-stamped data to our office over telephone lines, giving us what we needed to prepare payroll checks for the employees. Unfortunately, the system wasn't always reliable, and our staff had to make frequent trips to correct or replace the clocks.

For both small and large AmStaff clients, we installed several different time-keeping software systems over the years to address the need for improved security, functionality, and reliability. Today, all of our worksite employees use a timekeeping application on our website to securely log in and submit their hours, which are automatically uploaded into our payroll system for processing. Clients with a large number of our employees working for them use time clocks that export the data into our payroll system, greatly simplifying what used to be a labor-intensive process.

Delivering payroll checks to the PEO clients and worksite employees is likewise an important function of the payroll department. Delivering paper checks to the employees and paper-based reports and invoices to the clients, whether by our own driver, a courier service, or FedEx, is relatively expensive. Our first PEO clients were all located within a few miles of Pensacola, and personal delivery of payroll checks to their locations each pay period by existing staff was manageable. As we grew and obtained clients in surrounding cities, that system was no longer viable. At the time, overnight delivery services such as UPS and FedEx were used only for emergencies, and seemed a bit too expensive to use on a regular basis. We were hesitant then to add delivery charges to our client invoices even though we knew it was standard practice for other PEOs.

We have worked hard over the years to convert as many employees as possible to direct deposit. At the same time, we have encouraged clients to go completely paperless with all transactions handled via a secure portal on the Internet. Since we now have hundreds of clients and thousands of employees in almost every state and one foreign country, digital transactions and electronic banking are almost a necessity. According to Karena, over 95% of employees now have their checks deposited directly into their bank accounts, and more than 70% of our clients have elected to go paperless, receiving reports by way of the secure portal. We're still delivering a few checks and paystubs for the employees, but the number has been greatly reduced and is getting lower each year. The savings to the company and the benefits to the clients and employees with regard to security and efficiency are significant.

CHAPTER 5

Managing Risks

———————◆━◇━◆———————

A Focus on Safety and Claims Management

A KEY EMPLOYEE who played a significant role in the development of AmStaff's safety program was Harry Booros. Harry started with Landrum Personnel Associates in 1987 as a placement consultant. He struggled for a number of months trying to make placements, but after a while, we both realized that it wasn't the best job for him. As he was working out his notice to the company, Yvonne Nellums mentioned to me that Harry might have the background we needed to fill the job of safety manager for AmStaff, which we had been discussing. The need for that new job was becoming more evident as on-the-job injuries were increasing. After talking further with Harry, I learned that he had extensive background working as a supervisor in a manufacturing environment where he had overseen safety matters, so we offered him the job.

Harry stepped into the role with enthusiasm, overseeing safety and loss prevention, and ultimately created our safety and claims management department. The goal of the department was to prevent accidents and injuries and to control the cost of workers' compensation claims. This is a really big deal in the staffing and PEO industries. Workers' compensation claims can have a huge impact on the bottom line of companies, especially those that take on some of the financial risk as we have chosen to do. In the beginning, Harry spent much of his time visiting clients, performing safety audits, and working with clients to prevent injuries.

Britt Landrum, Jr. and Harry Booros - about 2000

In later years, as clients and worksite employees grew, we brought additional safety specialists on staff. We developed greater expertise and became more proactive in working with our clients, inspecting worksites, and observing work habits of the employees. We assisted our clients with understanding and complying with Occupational Safety and Health Administration (OSHA) regulations and reporting. We also developed supervisory training programs designed to prevent accidents. Each accident was carefully investigated and, even though we didn't have control over the worksite, we tried to get clients, as needed, to make improvements in operating equipment and procedures, and to provide personal protective devices.

Obtaining and maintaining a workers' compensation insurance policy has traditionally been a challenge for the temporary help industry. I found that out the hard way when we won the contract with the Port of Pensacola mentioned earlier. We had to provide hundreds of workers to unload boxcars full of heavy bags of flour. At that time, Clyde Anderson, owner of Associated Insurance, helped us obtain insurance through the Assigned Risk Pool and Liberty Mutual was the carrier. As a result of the frequency and severity of the injuries suffered by those warehouse workers, our mod rate (referred to earlier as experience factor multiplied by book rate) rose to well over 200%, which was the chief reason we terminated that contract.

The creation of AmStaff in 1983 presented new challenges in the workers' compensation area. Large insurance carriers weren't lining up to take on the uncertain liability presented to them by employee leasing companies that could, conceivably without their approval, sign up clients the carrier would not ordinarily insure. The only carriers available to AmStaff were in the Assigned Risk Pool that carried higher rates, or the self-insurance funds, which presented the risk of an assessment if funds weren't available to pay claims.

After a few years, we worked our way out of the Assigned Risk Pool. Since getting insurance from an admitted insurance carrier wasn't yet available to us, we obtained coverage through a self-insurance fund. These funds were created by various associations, mostly related to construction. For a time, we were insured by the Associated General Contractors Self-Insurers Fund and later by the Associated Industries of Florida Self-Insurers Fund. We went into it knowing that an assessment could be levied against us as participants in the event the fund didn't have enough money to pay its claims.

In fact, an assessment was levied on some friends of mine who obtained coverage for their employee leasing companies through a self-insurance fund created especially for our industry. The creator of that fund was a pioneer in the employee leasing industry in Florida and was thought to be knowledgeable in the insurance industry as well. Unfortunately, he ran into serious financial problems and the insurance fund failed. The participants were forced by law to pay their share of the claims accumulated by the fund, which was devastating to them.

The extremely high mod rate (2.13 as I recall) earned during our days at the Port of Pensacola was troubling to say the least. It was imperative that we take steps to get that number down to a more acceptable level. I devoted quite a bit of time to learning as much as I could about workers' compensation and how NCCI promulgated experience modification rates. Clyde helped me a lot with that. We paid experts to audit our records and found that some of the figures reported to NCCI had been overstated. The correction resulted in a more favorable downward adjustment to our experience modification factor.

Meanwhile, our base of worksite employees was growing, and the possibility of worker injuries was likewise increasing. Harry and I both spent much of our time educating ourselves and establishing procedures that would help us gain control over that situation. Using materials provided by Liberty Mutual Insurance Company and NCCI, Peggy Fortunato became an expert in the classification of employees and assignment of the proper workers' compensation insurance rates for each class.

After a time, we learned that a few of our new clients had misclassified the work done by their employees, which, in most cases, meant that they were paying lower rates than required. Making sure those codes were corrected was sensitive since our rates had to be increased to cover that change. The clients who had misclassified the work performed by their employees didn't like to receive news of the higher rate, of course, but our workers' compensation plan had to pass a rather stringent audit by the carrier each year. In addition, we didn't want any surprises in the form of additional premiums that we would have to pay.

We also resolved that, as much as possible, our staffing service would never knowingly accept another contract or temporary assignment where the likelihood of frequent or serious injury was present or where worker safety couldn't be reasonably assured. Through the years, we've tried to stay close to that commitment.

In 1996, to assist with the management of our claims, we hired Cindi (Opachick) Bigalow as a full-time claims manager. Cindi had worked as a claims adjuster for a large insurance carrier, and for a brief time, with a plaintiff attorney who specialized in workers' compensation claims. I thought at the time that her combination of experience would give her a unique perspective with regard to managing claims, and that has proven to be true. Cindi is still with the company and continues in her role as claims adjuster. Working with the adjusters with our major carriers, she has participated in resolving or settling millions of dollars of claims over the years.

Another key staff member in the Claims Management area was Lois Johnson. Lois started with the company in 1994. Her title was clerical assistant at the time, but she became a very active participant in the claims management process. Not only did she handle the necessary reporting requirements, but very importantly, she established a personal relationship and maintained contact with the claimants. She let them know that we were genuinely concerned about their injury and were going to do all we could to help them get the medical attention they needed so they could get back to work as quickly as possible.

We were and are still concerned about the full recovery of the injured worker, but we also know that claimants who don't feel cared for are more likely to seek help from an attorney, which increases our costs. A few years ago, Lois completed all requirements to become a licensed claims adjuster, enabling her to provide even more valuable assistance in the claims management area. Lois retired from the company in 2020, after completing over 25 years of service.

In the mid-90's, to keep medical costs low and thus lower our workers' compensation insurance mod rate, Harry, Cindi, and I devised a strategy to pay claims ourselves. In the early days, this was a rather common practice, often encouraged by insurance agents who sold the policies. The practice wasn't encouraged by carriers or the NCCI, but it wasn't prohibited either, so we proceeded to pay up to the first $2,500 of every claim including both medical treatment and indemnity (lost pay). We did this with the full knowledge of our insurance carrier and their claims adjusters. It often confused them, but we persisted and, because it lowered the total claims cost reported to NCCI, it seemed to work in our favor. Harry was successful in getting medical providers to charge us the lower rates that were approved under the workers' compensation regulations, saving us a significant amount of money on medical claims.

To keep indemnity costs low, we did all we could to get injured employees back to work as quickly as possible. This meant that, as soon as the employee was able, we had to work with our clients to encourage them to find limited or light work for the injured worker until he or she was able to resume full duty. We couldn't get the cooperation of all clients, so we came up with a plan to assign them to a light-duty job with local nonprofit agencies. We had to pay them anyway, and we felt it was important not to let them sit idle, but to remain active both mentally and physically. Most of the employees in the program reported that they enjoyed their assignments, the nonprofits appreciated the assistance, and we felt it did help the employees return to work sooner than they might have otherwise.

Unfortunately, the strategy of paying claims directly became more and more questionable, so we eventually stopped the practice. We also ceased the direct placement of the workers with nonprofit agencies because several of the injured employees preferred to continue doing that type of work rather than returning to the jobs in which we had placed them. We're still working closely with each claimant, doing all we can to get them back to work as soon as we can.

Another strategy we implemented was the hiring of nurse case managers to assist in the more difficult claims. Still in place, the case managers attend medical appointments to ensure the claimant sees the appropriate doctors, gets the diagnostic tests needed, attends physical therapy sessions, and takes medications as prescribed. The nurse case managers also assist with return-to-work planning, ergonomic job analyses, accommodations for restrictions, and more.

To get control over the cost of legal fees for representation in litigated claims, we managed to get our workers' compensation carrier to let us choose the attorneys we work with locally and negotiate with them on fees, resulting in improved outcomes and decreased litigation costs. Initially, we used a single attorney to handle all of our claims. The amount of the attorney's fees came to the attention of our in-house counsel, Amie Remington, who suggested that we might shop the work to other attorneys and compare fees. We took her advice and eventually chose to use more than one attorney, resulting in significant cost savings to the company.

The use of private investigators in cases where we suspect that a worker is not telling the truth about his or her injury or ability to return to work, has also proven to be effective over the years. More than once, the information gained by the investigators was persuasive in denying or settling a claim for benefits.

With years of experience, we developed the attitude that, in effect, we are just like an insurance carrier and need to do all the things a prudent carrier would do in every circumstance, which includes taking control over every aspect of a claim from prevention to settlement. That position has guided our approach and behavior in gaining expertise and in structuring our safety and claims management program, which in turn, has made us an attractive prospect for major insurance carriers.

In 1996, the leadership of the department passed from Harry Booros to Neil Thorsen, who remained with the company until the end of 2004. Harry served in the role of special projects manager until his retirement in 2005. Today, the safety side of the department is staffed by four highly qualified and experienced safety and loss prevention experts, including Mark Lundquist, a fifteen-year employee. The department is led by Jo-Anne Audette-Arruda who likewise has been with the company for fifteen years.

Entering the Captive and Self-Insurance Arena

In 2004, with the uncertainty of the workers' compensation market in mind, our executive team asked our visiting actuary, Tim Quinn, to give us his ideas on what else we could do to make sure that we always had coverage in place. Tim was an employee of Willis Towers Watson (formerly Towers Perrin), a global risk management consulting firm. He recommended that we look closely at forming a captive insurance company. We knew nothing about it at the time, but after weeks of researching and discussions with attorneys specializing in captives, we decided to proceed with it.

We established Accredited Insurance, Ltd., domiciled in Bermuda, in December 2004. The captive essentially issued an insurance policy to provide the first layer of insurance on all workers' compensation claims incurred by Landrum entities. Liberty Mutual agreed to insure all claims above that layer.

Ted Kirchharr, our VP of Risk Management, Andy Remke, VP and CFO, along with his wife, Pat, Ann McIntyre, our accounting specialist on captives, and Nell and I all traveled to Hamilton, Bermuda late in December. Ted, Andy, Nell, and I met first with the Bermuda Monetary Authority to sign the necessary papers and later attended the first meeting of our new captive insurance company. Liberty Mutual Bermuda, headed up by Peter Willetts, hosted our meeting and served as manager of the captive. Our Bermuda attorney also attended the meeting, wearing the traditional Bermuda attire—shirt, tie, jacket, dress shoes, knee-length socks, and Bermuda shorts. I bought the socks and had plans to dress the part when we came back home, but I just didn't have the courage to go through with it.

Owning the captive insurance company meant that we had to travel to Bermuda once a year for a meeting. It was fun at first, and we used the meetings as an opportunity for a few mini-vacations with friends. However, after about ten trips it lost its allure. Also, hotel room rates and food costs were exorbitant by most standards. Britt III traveled in my place once or twice. My final trip was just an overnight stay by myself.

When Britt III became president of the company in 2015, we moved the captive from Bermuda to Vermont, with Liberty Mutual still serving as manager. We did that because travel to Bermuda was getting more expensive, Vermont was easier to get to, and there was no penalty for bringing the company back to the U.S. A year or so after the move, the laws were changed, essentially taking away the tax incentives previously available under the captive arrangement and preventing our company from issuing any more policies to Landrum entities.

As a result of the changes in the law, we looked seriously at selling the captive and the "tail" (the accumulated incurred claims booked as reserves). We had a reasonably good offer, but after analyzing it further, we decided to keep the company and manage the claims, allowing them to settle as they will. The hope, of course, is that they will settle for less than we have them reserved, so that in the end, we'll realize a net gain. So far that has worked in our favor.

Creating the captive workers' compensation insurance company proved to be a great benefit to our PEO and staffing companies in that it enabled those operating entities to transfer all older claims to the captive, Accredited Insurance, Ltd. Landrum management could then concentrate on current safety issues, and not be concerned with older claims that had the potential to increase dramatically due to new or recurrent medical issues or litigation.

In setting up the Bermuda company, there was no attempt to circumvent the payment of all taxes due or to shelter income in any way. The captive paid taxes on all income as though it was a U.S. company. There were certain tax benefits available under the arrangement, and because of those benefits and our favorable claims experience, the company was able to accumulate a sizeable amount of cash, which made us more attractive to other insurance carriers. In a tight insurance market, that gave us some peace of mind.

In addition to owning the captive insurance company, in 2010 we decided to look carefully at starting our own insurance company in Florida. With several years of successful experience in structuring insurance plans, taking financial risks, and aggressively managing claims, we felt confident we could turn it into a successful venture. After discussing this with attorneys who specialized in that area of the law, we opted instead to form a licensed self-insurance company called "Florida Self-Insurers Guaranty Association, Inc." The plan, for Florida clients only, is structured so that our company will insure all claims below $500,000, and Liberty Mutual Insurance Company guarantees all claims above that amount.

This rather aggressive and comprehensive strategy of providing workers' compensation coverage to clients and all worksite employees isn't unique in the PEO industry, but we are one of just a few across the country that has taken this approach. The benefit to our clients is that the income earned from these endeavors has enabled us to offset the increased cost of providing all the other services to them, which has helped us keep our administrative fees relatively low.

Advocating for Industry Legislation

Early in my business career, I began to pay close attention to political matters, especially those that had some impact on our industry. My advocacy mostly consisted of writing letters to members of the state and federal House of Representatives and Senate, and placing occasional phone calls to business associates asking for campaign donations for candidates I was supporting.

In 1987, through a rather odd set of circumstances, I developed a relationship with Senator W. D. Childers, one of the most powerful men in the Florida Senate at the time. My relationship with Senator Childers didn't start out to be friendly. In 1987, the Florida Legislature had proposed placing a sales tax on all services, which would include temporary help and employee leasing services. The measure had strong support in the House and Senate, and there was general consensus that it would pass. Governor Bob Martinez had already signaled his intention to sign the bill into law.

Before the legislative session began, I attended a forum at Pensacola Junior College and addressed the local delegation, letting the members know that the new tax would be disastrous to the employee leasing industry. As it was written, the tax was to be applied to payroll and payroll taxes in addition to our fee. The additional amount would essentially price us out of business.

While I was speaking to the delegation, Senator Childers was walking around talking with the other legislators and paying no attention to me. The next morning, I received a call from a friend, Larry Lewis, who asked me for a contribution to Senator Childers' campaign. I shared my experience from the previous evening and told him there was no way I would help him. Well, actually I said, "Not no, but hell no!"

Within just a few hours of my conversation with Larry, I received a call from Senator Childers asking for an appointment with me. When we met, he apologized for not paying attention to me and said he would help me any way he could with the tax issue. I made a contribution to his campaign and raised additional funds from a few other employee leasing company owners around the State.

During the legislative session that followed, I joined two other members of the Florida Association of Employee Leasing Companies along with Mike Miller, our legal advisor, and traveled to Tallahassee to lobby members of the Legislature. We contacted as many senators and members of the House of Representatives as we could, explaining our problem and urging them to reconsider their vote on the sales tax. No one gave us any hope that this would be done. While we were there, the measure was taken up and both houses of the Legislature passed their bills, which applied the tax to all services including employee leasing companies. A conference committee of senators and House members was appointed to iron out any differences between the two bills. Senator Childers was on that committee. My colleagues and I were in attendance and were very disappointed when the conference committee completed its work and voted to accept the version of the bill that would apply the tax to employee leasing companies.

After the vote was taken, Senator Childers immediately came over to me and told me to stay in the room until he came back. At that point he left, and I now know that he went to see another powerful senator, Dempsey Barron. Both Senator Childers and Senator Barron had served as presidents of the Florida Senate and had tremendous influence in that body. After about thirty minutes, Senator Childers came back into the room looking very red in the face and told us the committee would reconvene. Within a matter of minutes, all the members of the conference committee came back into the room and reopened their meeting. There was a motion made to exempt employee leasing companies from the bill. That motion passed. The committee then adjourned and the members went back to their respective chambers where the amended measure was voted on and passed. As I was boarding the plane to come back to Pensacola, I heard that Governor Martinez had signed the bill into law.

I received lots of thanks from my industry friends for the part I played in getting our exemption, and many felt that it saved the employee leasing industry in Florida. At that moment, I was just grateful that Senator W. D. Childers was willing to use his influence on our behalf. (Ironically, the tax on services law was repealed in 1988, and the sales tax was raised by an additional 1% to offset the expected loss of revenue.)

In 1987, I made a presentation to the local association of used car dealers, telling them all about employee leasing and the benefits of becoming a client of my company, AmStaff. I thought things were going pretty well as there were several questions that indicated some of the dealers were interested. Then, one of the more astute business owners wanted to know what would happen if one of the leased employees was injured on the job. Of course, my answer was that the worker would be covered under our workers' compensation policy. He then asked whether or not the employee would be able to sue the dealership outside of workers' compensation since, technically, the worker was no longer its employee. I told him I didn't know the answer but would find out.

What I learned was that the workers' compensation law in Florida and most other states contains an "exclusivity provision" that basically prevents an injured employee in almost all circumstances from suing his or her employer to recover losses due to an on-the-job injury. The law was silent as far as temporary help workers and leased employees were concerned.

I needed to know more and had no idea how to do legal research. Fortunately, Sarah Entrekin, our good friend and Nell's maid of honor in our wedding, was visiting with us over the weekend. Sarah was a Mississippi attorney and at that time was serving as the county judge for Jones County, Mississippi. She agreed to help me with some research on the subject. Together, we went to the Pensacola Junior College library and researched the law and all the cases we could find involving customers of temporary help companies that had been sued by injured employees. There were no cases at that time that involved employee leasing companies. We found that in every case but one, the appellate courts had upheld decisions that applied the exclusivity provision to the customer of the temporary help service.

With that knowledge, in 1988 I began a campaign to get the Florida workers' compensation law (FS 440) changed. To do that, it was necessary to add a sentence to the existing law that basically said that the exclusivity provision would apply to employers who utilized the employees of a help supply company. With the help of Senator W. D. Childers and his staff along with Mike Miller from the Florida Association of Employee Leasing Companies, we were successful in getting that done, and in 1989, FS 440.11(2) became law. What that means is that clients of employee leasing companies and temporary help services in Florida no longer have to spend time and money trying to defend themselves and their company from employee lawsuits claiming damages outside the protection of the workers' compensation law. Finally, I had a good answer for my used car dealer!

Another important legislative event was the passage of the employee leasing licensing law, Chapter 468.520-468.535 in the Florida statutes. I was not directly involved in writing the licensing bill. That credit goes to Carlos Saladrigas, George Lehor, Bill Holt, and Mike Miller. Carlos, George and Bill were owners of employee leasing companies in central and south Florida. Mike, as previously mentioned, was the long-time legal advisor to our industry in Florida.

I strongly supported the bill and lobbied Senator Childers and our House of Representatives member, Buzz Ritchie, to get assurance of their vote in favor of its passage. I believed as others did, that in order to achieve a level of credibility with the business and banking community, as well as with state and federal regulators, we needed to become a regulated industry, and ideally, a self-regulated industry.

The bill provided minimum financial and operational requirements for all companies holding themselves out to be employee leasing companies, and I strongly supported that. I had seen too many articles in the newspaper about bad actors in our business who took advantage of employers, employees, insurance carriers, and state and federal taxing authorities, and I knew that something had to be done to prevent that from happening if we were ever going to be accepted as a legitimate industry. I also knew that CPAs and other business advisors would be more willing to recommend AmStaff to their clients if laws were in place to offer them protection.

The bill had the strong support of Senator Wilbur Boyd, an influential state senator who owned part-interest in an employee leasing company in south Florida. With his help and the lobbying efforts of many of us in the industry, the bill passed and became law in 1991. The new law created the Board of Employee Leasing Companies, which was granted the authority to issue licenses and discipline companies that did not follow the laws and regulations that were promulgated. I was proud to be appointed by the governor in 1992 to serve on the first board. I remained on the board until 1998, serving one term as chairman from 1995 to 1996.

CHAPTER 6

A Focus on Leadership and Internal Controls

———✦⟨✕⟩✦———

Executive Leadership

FROM THE BEGINNING, my philosophy and practice has always been to seek and listen to the advice of my most seasoned employees and act on those suggestions that seem most reasonable. I did that on an informal basis at first, with general discussions at lunch with a few employees or one-on-one conversations during the business day.

From 1987 to 1993, Peggy Fortunato, Denise McLeod, and Billy Price served as my first executive committee although there was no formal recognition as such. Each had been given the title of vice president of their respective division or area of responsibility. Peggy was responsible for administration and finance for the parent corporation, Denise was responsible for Landrum Temporary Services, and Billy was responsible for Landrum Personnel Resources. The four of us would meet on occasion to plan company functions and to discuss and offer some resolution to the issues we were facing at the time.

Clockwise from left, Peggy Fortunato, Billy Price,
Denise McLeod, Britt Landrum, Jr. - 1987

When Mike Perkins joined the company in 1997 as director of client services and general counsel and later as vice president and chief operating officer (COO) of Amstaff, the executive team was reconstituted to include Mike, Denise (then Vice President of Landrum Staffing Services), and me. In 2000 Andy Remke became part of the team when he joined the company as vice president and CFO for the parent organization, Landrum Human Resource Companies, Inc.

Shortly after Ted Kirchharr joined the company in 2003 as director of strategic initiatives, the executive team took a more formal approach, calling ourselves the Senior Leadership Team (SLT). In addition to Ted, Denise, Mike, Andy, and me, the SLT included Britt III, vice president and chief technical officer (CTO). Bill Cleary joined us as vice president and director of client services in 2006, the same year Mike left the company. Johnathan Taylor, who had been hired as Andy's replacement, started attending meetings in 2006 and became a member of the team shortly thereafter. Andy retired in 2014. Ted left the company in 2016, and Mandy Sacco, Denise's replacement as head of Landrum Staffing, joined us in 2017.

Senior Leadership Team (L to R) Andy Remke, Denise McLeod, Britt Landrum, Jr., Britt Landrum III, Ted Kirchharr, Bill Cleary – 2010

Senior Leadership Team (L to R) Ted Kirchharr, Britt Landrum III, Johnathan Taylor, Britt Landrum, Jr., Denise McLeod, Andy Remke, Bill Cleary - 2013

Although the makeup of the SLT changed quite a bit over the years, the executive team remained steadfast in its commitment to the success of the organization. We discussed the issues before us at length, often to excess as some boards have a tendency to do. We listened to the opinions of each member and, as much as possible, we used the collective wisdom of the group in making decisions of importance to the company.

In 2007 we engaged the services of Sperduto & Associates, Inc., a group of PhD psychologists specializing in executive and team coaching. The SLT met with them as a team and individually each month on a continual basis through 2016. As a group, we studied Patrick Lencioni's book, The Five Dysfunctions of a Team, and we got to know and understand each other better. The exercises we did improved how we interacted and shared our thoughts and opinions with each other, and in the end, made us a better team.

The second level of leadership, our department heads, are considered our key leadership team. For years, we have met with them regularly at brief "stand-up" meetings to keep them informed. This practice of holding brief meetings where everyone remains standing was borrowed from both Baptist Health Care and Ritz Carlton Hotels. The expectation is that the meeting will be brief but meaningful. The department heads in attendance have an opportunity to ask questions, get clarification, and offer suggestions. Information shared is then made available via email to all employees following the meeting.

Early on, the stand-up meetings included a "thought for the day," many of which I brought forward. I intended for these messages to inspire the leadership team along with their staff as the meeting information was shared throughout our organization. Following are some thoughts I addressed in meetings with the supervisors in 2012, which Peggy recently pulled from her archives.

EXCELLENCE

In the dictionary, "excellence" is defined as the quality of being outstanding or superior. It is the opposite of mediocrity.

Our company's stated goal is to be the best HR services company in America. To achieve that goal, we have to commit ourselves individually and corporately to being the best that we can be.

We have to know what excellence looks like in payroll processing, documents management, IT, sales, staffing, greeting customers by phone or in person, supervising employees, and every other function that is performed both inside and outside of this company. We must never be satisfied with just doing our jobs. We must always measure what we do by the gold standard of "excellence."

HONESTY

Honesty, integrity, and fairness are three values found in our 'Best People' foundation (one of "Five Foundations" adopted by the company at that time).

> *Thomas Jefferson – "Honesty is the first chapter in the Book of Wisdom."*

> *William Shakespeare – "No legacy is so rich as honesty."*

> *Britt Landrum, Jr. – "Trust is born out of relationships that are honest."*

PASSION

This word is contained in one of our company's core values, as in "passion for progress and improvement." The word passion implies many things, but in connection with our company and our work, I mean for it to imply "enthusiasm."

Having passion for progress and improvement means that we are never satisfied with the way we are doing things today. We're always looking for a better way. Our company's chief goal is to provide the very highest quality HR services to our clients.

If we are to achieve that goal, we will have to continuously look for ways to improve the quality and the means and methods we use to deliver our services. As Bill Cleary commented recently, "Every decision we make and every action we take should be guided by the question, 'Is this the highest quality we can offer our client?'" Be passionate about improving quality.

HARMONY

"Harmony is such a significant word. In music, it involves different notes that, when played together, create a richness of sound that didn't exist before and that couldn't exist if only one note was played." (Brianna Keen–my great niece and Britt III's cousin.)

*In work, harmony involves different people striving together to achieve the same goal, the same purpose. I believe the management experts call that "alignment." We can call it, "**working a better way.**"*

In music, the notes played are different. In work, the people are also all different. Different skills. Different personalities. But, when working to achieve the same goals and for the same purpose, we can do far more together than we can do alone.

This business has achieved the level of success it has because of all the many people who work here now and who have worked here in the past, all striving for the same purpose, all working in harmony with one another. Let's always keep it that way.

PERSISTENCE

*"The power to hold on in spite of everything, the power to endure–
this is the winner's quality. Persistence is the ability to face defeat
again and again without giving up, to push on in the face of great
difficulty, knowing that victory can be yours. Persistence means
taking pains to overcome every obstacle and to do what's necessary
to reach your goals." (Author Unknown)*

*Napoleon Hill writes, "The majority of men meet with failure
because of their lack of persistence in creating new plans to take
the place of those which fail."*

*There are many wise sayings about persistence. Calvin Coolidge's
saying is certainly among the most notable: "Nothing in the
world can take the place of persistence. Talent will not; nothing is
more common than unsuccessful men with talent. Genius will not;
unrewarded genius is almost a proverb. Education will not; the
world is full of educated derelicts. Persistence and determination
alone are omnipotent."*

*I chose this word as our theme for the week in tribute to the
members of our fine sales staff who go out day after day in search
of a prospect who will say, "Yes–I am interested in your services."*

*Please remember each one of them and all the "no's" they have
to encounter before getting to that "yes." And when things don't
quite go right in your day, always remember–persistence is the
winner!*

RESPONSIBILITY

One of the core values of our company is responsible behavior.

*To me, being responsible means taking ownership and being
accountable for our actions. It means that people (employees,
supervisors, customers, applicants) have trusted you to perform*

your job to the best of your ability; they trust that you genuinely care about them and are looking out for their best interest.

Think about it. Our clients trust us with their money and their information, some of which is quite confidential and important to their success, including important legal employment matters that involve deadlines and accuracy. They trust each one of us to behave responsibly and to always do the right thing in the right way.

If we will each commit to doing the right thing the right way all the time, we will continue to build trust and further our reputation as one of the most responsible HR companies in America.

PURPOSE

Most, if not all of you, have heard the story about the man who came upon a construction site and saw three men working. He approached the first worker and asked him what he was doing. The worker, who appeared bored, answered, "I'm mixing mortar." Still curious, the man approached a second worker and asked what he was doing. That man also showed little enthusiasm for his job. His reply was about the same, "I'm laying brick." He then approached the third worker who was likewise laying brick, but he appeared happy and went about his job with enthusiasm. When the man asked him the same question as he did the others, this worker's reply was, "I'm helping build a cathedral."

The moral of the story is this: Knowing and understanding the purpose of our work makes it more enjoyable and meaningful.

So, what's our purpose here? Getting job orders? Issuing payroll checks? Processing forms? No, I believe what we're doing here is providing real services to humanity, which truly is one of the greatest works of life.

A few weeks ago, I told most of you the story about a young woman who approached me at Baptist Hospital and told me that she got her job through our company. Two years earlier, she had graduated from college and could not find a job. After giving up the effort on her own, she came to Landrum for help. She was very complimentary about all the friendly people she met and how they helped her. We got her a job at Baptist Hospital where she has done well and received a couple of promotions. Needless to say, she is very happy and tells everyone how much we helped her.

About a month ago, I received a call from a man who asked me to help his son find a job. The man reminded me that thirty years earlier I had helped him get a job at a Pensacola manufacturing plant. He stayed there his entire career and rose to the position of plant manager.

Over the years, I've heard lots of stories like that and I'm sure many of you have, too. I've also had employers tell me that we found just the right employees for their companies and that they rely on us to do that for them. I've had PEO clients tell me how we have taken so much of the burden of being an employer off their shoulders and how we've helped them get better benefits for their employees.

When you find yourself a little less than enthusiastic about your particular task, just remember that you're really helping another person, maybe a father or mother trying to make enough money to provide for a family. Remember that you're helping a young person get started in a career, or helping a business to find and hire the right people.

And you're giving the small businessman or businesswoman peace of mind by making the complicated, time-consuming task of being an employer so much easier.

We may not be building a cathedral, but what we are doing is extremely important to the people whose lives we touch.

So, remember our purpose!

RESPECT

"Respect for the dignity and worth of every individual" is one of our company's core values. What that means to me, and I'm sure to all of us, is that we should treat everyone the way we ourselves want to be treated. Follow the "Golden Rule."

In his book, The Servant: A Simple Story About the True Essence of Leadership, *James C. Hunter talks about respect and how people want to be treated. His words apply to all of us who have authority over another person (and believe me, that means every one of us). We want that person to be patient with us, to give us attention, to give us appreciation, to give us encouragement, to be authentic with us, to treat us with respect, to meet our needs when they arise, to forgive us when we screw up, to be honest with us, to give us feedback, to hold us accountable, and ultimately, to be committed to us. I suspect we all want to be treated like that.*

Let's remember to respect the dignity and worth of those whom we serve and those with whom we work.

RELATIONSHIPS

Humanity is all about relationships. Family is all about relationships. Business is all about relationships. Building and maintaining healthy relationships in every aspect of our lives is the most important thing that we can do.

The key to healthy relationships is love. Not "love" as in how we feel about one another but love as in how we treat one another. In every situation, always be guided by the Golden Rule—treating one another the way we would want to be treated.

ATTITUDE

Much has been written and much has been said about the word "attitude." We can have a positive attitude or a negative attitude. We can see the glass half-full or half-empty. We can hold a grudge against someone, or we can forgive that person. We can feel sorry for ourselves for the things that have happened to us or for what we don't have. Or we can give thanks for what we have and accept ourselves for who we are and strive to be the best that we can be.

When we interact with someone–a family member, friend, co-worker, subordinate, or boss, our attitude can determine the outcome of that interaction. It's not what you say, but it's the attitude that you convey when you're saying it that determines how it is received. Attitude is one of the few things in life over which we have absolute control. No one can take that choice from us. We have the power to choose our attitude.

I have known rich people who are miserable, and poor people who were content with their lives. It's all about attitude. Take charge of your attitude and you take charge of your life. For me, I believe that an attitude of gratitude is the key to happiness. I find that being truly thankful for what I have keeps me from spending useless time worrying about what I don't have.

VISION

The theme for this week is "vision." I have chosen this word because I am trying right now to write a vision statement for the company, so it's definitely on my mind.

A few years before I started this company, I had a vision of what it would look like–what I would be doing and how that would feel. I had read several books on "imaging" and the part it plays in determining future success. So, I spent time trying to put myself visually in my office and doing the work of finding jobs for people and people for jobs. I got pretty specific in my imaging and ultimately made a plan to carry out that vision.

That's really what I'm trying to do now—only we're 42 years older and much more complicated. Still, I have a vision of what I'd like to see this company look and feel like in the next few years, and I'm just trying now to articulate that in a way that will make sense and inspire all of us.

What is your vision for your job, your department? What do you hope to accomplish in the next eight years? Do you have a vision for the company that you would like to share with me? If you do, please let me know. Clear vision helps us see where we are going in business and in life. Give some thought this week to your vision.

DISCIPLINE

The word "discipline" has more than one meaning as you know. When used as a verb, it generally refers to some type of punishment for wrongdoing. As a noun the word refers to being diligent about a task or "stick-to-it-iveness," so to speak. That's the meaning that I'm referring to today.

The word "discipline" has a companion word – "consequences." When we determine to take some action and stick to it, we can expect those actions to have consequences. Those consequences can be good as in brushing your teeth regularly results in having healthier teeth, or exercising regularly results in better health. Or consequences can be bad as in smoking for years results in bad health.

All of us have seen consequences of not being disciplined about various aspects of our lives.

I remember driving my two sons to school many years ago and talking to them about the importance of discipline in their lives. At the time, I was mostly referring to exercising, but I wanted them to extend that to all areas of their lives. They may have rolled their eyes a little at that time, but I made sure they got my message.

In business, we see the need for discipline as well. Our business development managers have to be disciplined about making phone calls or visiting prospects even when they don't feel like it. The consequence of not making those contacts can be disastrous.

Our payroll coordinators, staffing coordinators, reference checkers, HR managers, computer programmers, finance specialists, and in fact all of us have to be disciplined about the tasks that we know we must do to realize successful consequences. Not doing those tasks can and will be disastrous for applicants, for clients, and ultimately for our company.

So, be disciplined about the tasks you have before you. Think long term, and always keep the consequences in mind.

Improving Financial Controls

Leslie Gordon, who came on board in 1993 as our first controller, hired accounting staff and organized the department so that we could gain better control as our accounting needs became greater and more complex. Producing financial statements, accurately accounting for and making timely payments of tax liabilities, keeping track of worksite employee wage garnishments, and producing thousands of W-2's each year were just a few of the many important tasks to be managed by the accounting staff and Leslie, who by the year 2000, had become director of finance and accounting.

In 2000, our auditing firm, Saltmarsh, Cleaveland and Gund, recommended that we hire a CFO for the company, preferably someone with experience in a large company. The first name that came to my mind, after hearing their recommendation, was Andy Remke. Andy had recently taken early retirement from Baptist Health Care (BHC) after serving as that organization's CFO for a number of years. As a long-term member of the BHC board, I got to know Andy and had the opportunity to listen to his reports to the board. He was well versed in the complex financial issues of the Baptist organization.

After discussing the possibility of his working for our company, Andy expressed interest and suggested that he might first serve as a consultant. His idea was to perform a review of the department to get a clear understanding as to how it was organized and what improvements might be needed. I was impressed with his report and offered him the job.

One of the first steps Andy took after joining the company in August 2000 was to create a new position for a financial analyst. When the opening was announced internally, Melanie Rhodes applied and got the job. Melanie was already working for the company, having been hired earlier that year as an assistant in the HR department. Andy and I both were pleasantly surprised to learn that we had someone already on staff with just the right credentials for the job. I have to confess that when Andy first discussed the idea of hiring a financial analyst with me, I couldn't see the importance or need for the position. After seeing the reports that Melanie and Andy produced, I became a believer.

Andy recognized the importance of making financial information, in various forms, readily available to top management so they would be better informed as company decisions were made. He introduced charts that showed trends and projections in every relevant area of the operation. He pushed the accounting staff to provide financial statements on a timely basis.

During Andy's tenure as CFO, the company had a large deductible workers' compensation policy with Liberty Mutual Insurance. Liberty Mutual required that we post a rather large letter of credit, guaranteed by our bank. It also required that we deposit a significant amount of money up front in order to fund the reimbursement of claims that were under the million-dollar cap for which we were obligated. Setting the amounts tied to each obligation was subject to some negotiation each year. Before Andy took over those negotiations, I had mostly accepted the amounts put forth by Liberty and by the banks that guaranteed the letters of credit. Andy saw this as a challenge and each year was able to win significant reductions in those deposits. He was likewise successful in getting fee reductions from our banks, which saved our company a lot of money over the years.

Andy's experience as a senior level executive with BHC meant that he was very familiar with the tools and strategies used by Baptist in its planning and operations. As a result, we began a structured investment program with Highland Associates, of Birmingham, Alabama. We also began the relationship mentioned earlier with Sperduto & Associates, of Atlanta, Georgia. Both firms had provided services for BHC and proved to be very helpful to our company over the years.

Early in 2005, Andy expressed to me that we didn't have anyone on staff at the time who was qualified to take his place when he was ready to retire. This prompted the discussion of finding and hiring someone he could groom to take his place when that time came. Coincidentally, I had just heard from Johnathan Taylor, a friend from Rotary who was the CFO for Killinger Marine in Pensacola. Johnathan had just assisted the owner, Gene Killinger, with the sale of his business to Marine Max, a publicly traded boat sales and service company. That meant that he would need to find other employment for himself. I arranged an interview with Johnathan and Andy, and we both agreed that he was perfect for our job.

Johnathan started to work with our company in 2005 as controller, reporting to Andy. They worked closely together until 2009 when Johnathan became CFO and Andy began reporting to him as our corporate treasurer. In Andy's new role, he assisted in looking for acquisition opportunities for the PEO, an area of responsibility that he had enjoyed while serving as CFO.

Switching roles like that is certainly a little unusual, but both Andy and Johnathan made it work with very few issues or concerns. Prior to making the change, both had worked closely with Gary Sperduto of

Sperduto & Associates, who helped them anticipate problems and work through them in advance of the change.

During his fifteen-year career, and especially since assuming the role of CFO, Johnathan has demonstrated his commitment and tremendous worth to the company. He has played an essential role with Britt III in performing due diligence on companies that we were considering purchasing. He has assisted me in decisions regarding the evaluation and purchase of property, and has prepared and presented meaningful financial data to our SLT and to our advisory board. He has also prepared information for meetings of our family board (comprised of family members who are officers and directors of the various Landrum corporations) and for our former estate attorney, Bob Hart. In addition, he has hired and oversees the performance of the accounting staff, at least four of whom are CPAs like himself.

After becoming CFO, Johnathan was my chief confidant. He could always be relied upon to provide sound technical advice with regard to any finance or accounting-related issue. I cannot say enough good things about the value he continues to bring to the company. It gives me great comfort to know that he is now providing that same level of support to Britt III in his role as chief executive officer (CEO).

SAS 70 Audit

Rigorous financial reporting requirements are placed on our PEO by both the State of Florida and the Employer Services Assurance Corporation (ESAC). In the mid-2000's, our SLT made the decision to subject Landrum Human Resource Companies, Inc., the parent corporation, to an audit of our internal controls, known in the accounting industry as a Statement of Auditing Standards 70 (SAS 70 was later changed to SSAE 16—Statement on Standards for Attestation Engagements). Andy Remke, our CFO at that time, reminded us that auditors for some of our clients, primarily the credit unions, wanted to know what controls we had in place and were asking for an audit report from us. For that reason, and because we felt it was the prudent and responsible thing to do, we proceeded with the SAS 70 Audit. As mentioned earlier, we engaged Kevin Bowyer with the O'Sullivan Creel CPA firm, to consult with us and conduct the audit. Kevin was a CPA with an additional specialty in the analysis of business internal controls.

Our CFO Johnathan Taylor recalls that even before we received the SAS 70 audit plan, we decided to move forward to truly improve the controls we had in place. We spent considerable time in the organization examining and changing some of our processes. One particular concern was the unlimited access to the payroll check processing and packaging area. This is the physical area of the company where worksite employee checks were printed and packaged for delivery to our clients. I never felt that we were at risk of having checks stolen or lost, but with unlimited access, the possibility was always there. To remedy that exposure, we instituted a process to require badge verification for access to the area.

Another weakness we identified had to do with the process of making changes to worksite employee records in the PayPlus payroll system. Such entries had been made by payroll and benefit staff members as they received information from employees or clients. To strengthen control over the information, we decided to reassign the task of making employee record changes to our documents management team managed by Andrea Johnson. That department, created in 2006, was tasked with processing and ensuring the accuracy and completeness of the thousands of employee records entered into our computer system each year. The department was located in a secure area of our building that required badge access. At the same time, as discussed earlier, in an effort to improve communication between payroll and benefits staff members and enhance the efficiency of sharing information on clients and worksite employees, the decision was made to consolidate the two departments into a single operations department.

One of our biggest concerns had to do with the limitations of our PayPlus software system, which, at one time, had no effective ability to track changes that were made to the payroll data. Those limitations required that we put extra controls in place to make up for some of the software weaknesses.

Client communications was another important area that the report addressed. At that time, clients sent emails to us containing employee names, salary information, social security numbers, and other sensitive data. We also produced reports containing that same information and regularly sent them as email attachments. To prevent identity theft, it was recommended that we develop a more secure way to transmit and receive data from our clients. The result was the creation of a portal for each client, which utilizes data encryption technology so that both incoming and outgoing transmissions are secure. The system is less user-friendly in that it requires a few more steps to gain access, but the increased security and peace of mind warranted the change.

The extra steps we took to shore up our processes as a company seemed like "overkill" to some, but our SLT and I believed that the protections put into place were in the best long-term interest of our clients and the company. In addition, the audit of our internal controls was another strong statement about our commitment to those who put their trust in us.

Hiring an Employment Attorney

To ensure that our HR managers give correct advice and take proper action on all HR matters, we obtain legal advice from qualified employment attorneys. In the beginning and through most of the 80's, we called on Bob Riegel, the Jacksonville attorney who helped us defeat the unionization attempt at the Port of Pensacola.

In the late 80's, I met Mike Perkins, who was introduced earlier in this chapter. Mike was an employment attorney with the Clark, Partington, Hart law firm in Pensacola. When we met, he was serving on the board of directors of the 90 & 9 Boys Ranch, a home in Escambia County that housed more than twenty boys who were either abandoned by their parents or removed from their homes by the court. I joined that board and worked with Mike for a few years trying to make improvements to the home and take better care of the boys. Mike and I each served one or two terms as chairman of the board. I got to know Mike very well during that time and began to turn over all of our employment law questions and problems to him.

I learned very quickly that Mike was a terrific attorney. He gave us good advice and seemed genuinely interested in our company and its challenges. He also had a real flair for marketing and client development. Mike was trying to build his law practice at that time, and we were, as always, trying to find more clients for AmStaff.

In early 1994, Mike suggested that his law firm jointly sponsor an Employment Issues seminar with AmStaff and that we hold it in Destin (for non-natives, that's about 60 miles east of Pensacola). This was a comprehensive seminar complete with big notebooks full of information on all the important topics relevant to employment law. I saw this as a great opportunity for AmStaff in that associating ourselves with a well-known and respected law firm would add to our credibility in the eyes of the business community.

Mike agreed to be the key presenter at the seminar. My role was to be limited to making introductions. Two days before the seminar, Mike announced to me that he had a slight problem. His wife, Kim, was nine months pregnant, and the baby was due on the day of the seminar. Of course, he told me not to worry, that he would have it covered if he couldn't make it. You can imagine how comforting that was to me– actually not at all. Thank goodness and thanks to Kim, little Alex Perkins wasn't born until after the seminar, within a few days as I recall.

To help Mike get up-to-speed with regard to the employee leasing (now PEO) business, I invited him to attend one or two national conventions with me. NSLA (now NAPEO) was beginning a legal advisory committee, and I thought it would be helpful for Mike to participate on our behalf. It wasn't long after attending those meetings that Mike hinted that if I ever thought about hiring an in-house attorney, he would be interested in the job. I really didn't think we had enough work to keep an attorney busy on a full-time basis, but his interest caused me to think more about my need to have someone assist me in the overall management of the company.

Initially I was concerned about my ability to pay Mike what he expected. We were already spending a fair amount of money each year on legal fees, conferring with him about various employment issues that our clients and HR managers confronted. I reasoned that having him as our employee would do away with those expenses. After many discussions and some negotiating on salary requirements, Mike and I agreed on terms, and he accepted the job. In January 1997, he came to work as our director of client services and general counsel. He was later appointed as vice president, COO, and general counsel.

When Mike joined the company, Landrum Human Resource Companies (all operating entities) had a staff of 49; AmStaff had over four thousand worksite employees, and annual wage revenue for AmStaff alone was just under $73 million. When he left the company in 2006, we had 120 staff members, just under 11,000 worksite employees, and our wage revenue from those employees was approaching $300 million per year. It was a phenomenal period of growth.

That growth was due in no small measure to Mike's efforts. In addition to being a tremendous resource for legal advice to our HR managers, he was passionate about taking care of clients and inspired the staff to do the same. During his time with the company, we sponsored a number of seminars and client gatherings where he would give legal updates and speak about employment issues important to the business community.

At one of those events, to educate our clients about the laws on sexual harassment and discrimination, we put on a mock trial. The scenario we presented had me in the role of the owner of a company whose top sales representative was accused of sexually harassing a female staff member of the company. I had refused to fire the mock representative, arguing that he was my best sales rep. The female staff member sued, and I was placed on the witness stand to defend my actions in allowing that behavior to continue. Casey Rogers, before she became the Honorable Casey Rogers, District Judge of the United States District Court of the Northern District of Florida, played the role of attorney for the female employee. Her questions put me on the spot, and I thought were particularly unfair–but realistic. When I jokingly asked her about her merciless line of questioning afterwards, she said I deserved it. The mock trial was fun to do, very well received by our clients, and an excellent teaching tool. It certainly got my attention.

In addition to his other duties, Mike Perkins led our sales team for a period of time and helped bring in a significant number of new clients. He also relieved me of many of the operational issues in the company, which allowed me to become more engaged with industry and community organizations.

(L to R) Mike Perkins, Congressman Joe Scarborough,
Britt Landrum, Jr. at staff briefing - about 1999

During Mike's tenure with the company, we established referral relationships with Fisher Brown Insurance Company, AmSouth Bank, and the Florida League of Credit Unions. Fisher Brown's sales agents and the agency itself were offered a commission for referring prospects that became clients of AmStaff. We were successful over a few years and signed up several new clients with an estimated annual payroll near $20 million.

In the late 90's, AmStaff had a close relationship with AmSouth Bank (now Regions Bank). AmSouth was the primary bank for AmStaff and processed thousands of checks on a weekly basis. AmSouth's President, Bill Watson, invited me to serve on the bank's advisory board. I proudly accepted the opportunity and served for quite a few years before having to give it up when I accepted a board position with the Jacksonville Branch of the Federal Reserve Bank of Atlanta.

Mike and I made presentations to officers of AmSouth Bank in Pensacola, Mobile, and Panama City, explaining the benefits of AmStaff's services and encouraging them to refer their small business customers to us. AmSouth offered to set up new accounts to all new AmStaff employees at no charge to them, so for a while, we included the bank's material in every employee packet. Since all of our payroll checks were drawn on that bank, it seemed better for the employees to have an account there. Promoting AmSouth to our new worksite employees was a little sensitive, however. We had two or three other banks as clients at the same time, and they weren't very happy about what they perceived as our preferential arrangement with AmSouth.

In spite of the effort, I can't recall a single new client who came as a direct result of our relationship with AmSouth. Still, our association with the bank and its endorsement of our company enhanced our credibility in the greater business community.

Our relationship with the Florida League of Credit Unions worked out much better. The League existed to provide various services to credit unions around Florida and was looking to expand in the area of HR services. The league itself became our client, and we created a division within AmStaff known as CU Personnel Solutions. Over the years, more than twenty credit unions have become clients of AmStaff. Some have since merged with larger credit unions and are no longer our clients, but the vast majority are still with us today.

The growth of our company during Mike's tenure created the need for more talent within the company. He was a past president of the SubWest Rotary Club in Pensacola, and over time, encouraged me to hire three men whom he knew well, and who had also served as presidents of that club. Jerold Hall came to work as a sales representative in October 2002, was later promoted, and contributed significantly to our continued growth as director of business development until he left the company in 2019. Ted Kirchharr, an expert in organizational development and strategic planning, came to work in October 2003 as director of strategic initiatives. He was later promoted to vice president over several departments in the company, served on our SLT, and contributed significantly to our success before leaving in 2016.

Bill Cleary, the last of the three former SubWest Rotary Club presidents recommended by Mike, came to work for us in July 2006 as director of client services. As an officer of AmSouth Bank, Bill had worked with our company for a number of years as customer service representative for the bank. We were impressed with his skills in that area and eager to have him join our team. During his time with the company, he was promoted to vice president, managed several key departments including sales and risk management, and served as a valuable member of our SLT. He resigned from the company in 2018 and resumed his career in banking.

Mike left the company at the end of 2006, after accepting a call to become a houseparent of eight boys at the Big Oak Ranch in Gadsden, Alabama. We hated to see him leave, but respected the sacrifice that he and his wife, Kim, were making in order to enrich the lives of those boys.

A year before he left the company, Mike introduced me and the other members of our SLT to Amie Remington, an employment attorney whom he greatly respected and recommended we hire. At that point in time, his role as COO was taking almost all of his time, and there was a need for more legal representation for the HR team in the company. After interviewing and getting to know more about Amie's background and experience, it was clear that she would be a tremendous asset to our company, so we offered her the job as general counsel. She accepted the position and started to work on a half-time basis in September 2005.

(L to R) Britt Landrum, Jr., Amie Remington, Britt Landrum III - about 2014

Amie has certainly lived up to all expectations, not only in providing much needed legal advice and representation for our HR managers, but also to the company in writing employment contracts, keeping the legal requirements in staff employee handbooks up-to-date, negotiating contracts for services with larger clients and their attorneys, advising me on various legal matters, and more. She is an outstanding presenter and has given numerous seminars for clients and to the business community at large. She has also appeared in many webinars providing legal updates on employment laws and regulations. After the Affordable Care Act became law, Amie appeared on one or more webinars explaining the complexities of that law and its impact on businesses and employees. She represents our company on the NAPEO Legal Advisory Council and has served on the board of directors of the Florida Association of PEOs as well.

In November 2015, attorney Christy Arnold joined our legal department with a specialty in tax and benefit law. Christy initially assumed the role of compliance benefits attorney primarily for the PEO, making sure that all of our tax-qualified benefit plans are kept current with changes in laws, regulations, and court rulings. Her role has since expanded to include corporate-level work related to reviewing and negotiating contracts with prospective clients, as well as business acquisitions.

CHAPTER 7

Consolidating and
Moving to Larger Quarters

————— ✦◗◇◖✦ —————

Relocating and Combining Operations

AROUND 1985, AFTER FIFTEEN YEARS IN BUSINESS, our overall growth as a company caused me to begin looking for larger quarters. I was also interested in consolidating the businesses in a single location to improve communication, gain better control, and save money by pooling resources.

After much research I settled on a new office park being developed in the northern part of town. The park consisted of four buildings fronting on Plantation Road near University Mall and Interstate 10. The lot I chose was located at 6708 Plantation Road on the corner of Plantation and Creighton Roads. This choice would prove to complicate our lives a few years later when we learned that the Florida Department of Transportation was planning to widen Creighton Road and possibly take some or all of our property.

Office located at 6708 Plantation Road - 1986

Construction of the new building took many months, but we finally made the move in the latter part of 1986. The building had several amenities we previously did not enjoy, including a conference room, large kitchen, lots of storage space, more bathrooms, and room to expand.

One other important feature–the new building was declared SMOKE FREE! I had checked with my attorney to make sure I could issue that rule to our employees, and after getting his blessing, I made the announcement before the move. In those days, smoking in an office building was common. Several of our staff members were smokers, and a couple of them did not take the news very well. One decided to quit her job before making the move. I offered to pay for smoking cessation classes for all the employees who wanted to attend. One took me up on the offer and has been a non-smoker ever since.

All three divisions of the company, Landrum Temporary Services, Landrum Personnel Resources (changed from Associates), and AmStaff, were assigned respective areas for their staff members, and the common reception/waiting area supported all of us. For the first time, we also had a specific area for the administrative and accounting staff as well as a computer room and workroom for mailing equipment used by the staffing service to mail checks and invoices, and by the personnel service for sending resumes. We were proud of our new building and held a ribbon-cutting ceremony to announce our new location. Howard Rein,

Mayor Pro Tempore for the city of Pensacola, came to cut the ribbon. He said many good things about our company and mentioned that he was proud to represent the city, but that our building was actually located outside city boundaries in Escambia County, a fact that I had overlooked.

Ribbon cutting for 6708 Plantation Road offices – 1986

Pensacola Chamber official making presentation to Britt and Nell Landrum - 1986

Joni Kee Humphreys was our first full-time receptionist and telephone operator at the new office, joining the company in 1986. After a couple of years, a sales position opened up in the temporary help service, and Joni was picked for the job. She remained in sales for a number of years, but her skills in computer graphic design eventually led to her being utilized in that capacity, creating brochures and flyers, designing letterhead and business cards, and publishing newsletters for all Landrum entities. As our first director of marketing and communications, Joni developed skills in the social media area and created the company blog and posts on Facebook and Twitter. In addition to her work in those areas, Joni served as our community relations representative, scheduling company fundraisers and heading up our very successful annual United Way campaigns. She completed thirty-one years with the company before leaving in 2018.

Landrum Temporary Services staff (L to R) Lori Esser, Valerie Cole, Luz Pitre, Dee Langan, Joni Humphreys, Dianne Milling, Denise McLeod - 1986

Luz Pitre succeeded Joni in June 1989 as the receptionist and telephone operator for the company. Luz was known for her ability to recognize the voices and remember the names of our clients, which made them feel welcome. She remained in that position for 19 years before leaving the company in 2008.

The growth of the business brought with it an increase in the number of calls and the need for more telephone operators. Wanting to retain the personal feel that welcomed those who called our offices, we resisted moving to a more automated answering system. At one point, we had as many as four people answering calls in addition to the receptionists who manned the front desk–all part of our "First Impression Team." (In 2018, given the expense of maintaining all those telephone operators, the availability of sophisticated telephone systems, and the public acceptance of automated attendants answering the telephone, we decided to catch up with the times. Just one person is now assigned to answer the phones when a caller asks to speak with an operator.)

In 1984, Peggy Fortunato was promoted to manage administration and finance, a role that also included responsibility for data management and office administration, primarily for Landrum Personnel Associates. After moving to the new building in 1986, the staff size increased along with our sales volume and new clients for both AmStaff and Landrum Staffing Services. With that growth came additional responsibilities, and Peggy's title was changed to vice president of administration, finance, and systems.

Peggy excelled in her use of the computer as she set up and maintained our accounting software and the new PayPlus system we acquired. In 1989, when that new system was installed, Peggy took the lead in learning it so she could teach our payroll coordinators how to use it. During the course of learning, she spoke with and got to know several other users of the system around the country. Eventually, she was chosen to head up the vendor's newly formed PayPlus users' group.

In Peggy's new role as head of administration, finance, and systems for our small company, she hired and supervised the clerical staff, ran computer programs to produce accounting information, and became our "go to" person for just about anything that involved ordering supplies, installation of new equipment, or building repairs. We both worked on the installation of our new telephone system, literally determining the polarity of the wiring in the walls, installing telephone jacks, and making terminals for the cables. We also made minor repairs to the large company computer used by the temporary help service and by Peggy for payroll and accounting. Those repairs, of course, were made with some advice from the technician who couldn't always get to our office when repairs were needed. I'm sure our current IT staff would be horrified to see Peggy and me pulling out a large circuit board from the back of our computer to swap it for a spare one that we thought would work better. But we did it, and occasionally it worked.

One of the employees hired by Peggy in 1989 was Rhonda Katona Freeman. Rhonda had worked for our company at the Garden Street location a few years earlier just after graduating from high school. At that time, she served as an office assistant, leaving the job after about a year. When she was re-hired in 1989, she worked as an accounting assistant, helping Peggy with accounts payable. She later transferred to work for Billy Price as an assistant in the Landrum Personnel division. Shortly after starting her new job, Rhonda saw the need for an automated system to track resumes and job orders, and she began working on a computer-based solution. After successfully creating that program, she continued studying on her own and became an expert in computer hardware and software.

Over the next eighteen years, Rhonda progressed from computer technician to software developer. As a technician, she reported to Britt III who by then had been promoted to manage IT. She installed new computers and printers, loaded software, and generally served as our computer "fixer." At her ten-year anniversary we played the song, "Help Me, Rhonda" as that was the message most often sent to her by a staff member with a computer issue.

We purchased the PayPlus software program during Rhonda's tenure to assist in keeping track of worksite employees and handling the payroll for AmStaff. As mentioned previously, Peggy was our first expert user of the system. Working with Peggy, Rhonda not only learned how to use the new software, but over the years, she learned how to program the system and make changes as needed. She eventually became one of the top experts among PayPlus users in the nation and consulted often with the vendor's system developers. She left the company in 2018 to work full-time for PayPlus, which was a real success story for her.

In 1987, Billy Price, who had been with the company for six years, was placed in charge of Landrum Personnel Resources and given the title of vice president. Billy had done an outstanding job as a placement consultant specializing in placing engineering candidates with regional manufacturing facilities. Under his leadership, the volume of placement income increased, primarily due to his own production.

Even with the increase in sales volume, the placement side of the business continued to be uncertain. In an attempt to improve, we hired a number of new consultants as more experienced ones left. We paid them a small base salary and a percentage of the placement fees collected. In spite of all we did to help, they just couldn't earn a consistent income for themselves or the company and left to find better jobs.

As my investment of time and money in Landrum Temporary Services and AmStaff grew over the next few years, my interest in Landrum Personnel Resources declined. The income from the employment agency side of the business was just too uncertain compared to the other two divisions. Meanwhile, Billy Price developed the urge to go out on his own. After some conversations with him about this, in 1995 I decided to cease all activity under Landrum Personnel Resources and let Billy have all the information he needed from the company to start his own operation, including his files, office furniture, and the computer retrieval system he was using at the time.

A Forced Move

As mentioned earlier, the 1986 move to consolidate offices at 6708 Plantation Road proved to be complicated. One morning in 1989, I was meeting with a friend in the conference room of our building, and he casually mentioned that an engineer friend of his was working on a drawing of the widening and extension of Creighton Road (our building was on the corner of Creighton and Plantation Roads). This same road was scheduled to pass right through our building! We had only been in our new building about three years, and I thought he was kidding. Just to be sure, I decided to check it out. Sure enough, the Florida Department of Transportation plans showed most of our building situated in the path of the new extension of Creighton Road. My staff and I were all shocked and disappointed at this news and a little aggravated that we weren't told sooner. Reality set in, however, and I began to look for alternative space.

We liked our location near University Mall, which was relatively new at the time, and we liked being near Interstate 10, which was good for our staff and easy for our staffing service applicants to find. Fortunately, right across the street from our building were two vacant lots, adjacent to each other. After some investigation, I chose to make an offer on the larger site, and it was accepted. (Years later I bought and had to pay a higher price for the adjacent lot for additional parking and regretted not buying it earlier when I had the chance.)

After acquiring the property, I engaged the services of an architect, Larry Barrow, a friend from Holy Cross Episcopal Church, who had also been the architect on the building we were then occupying. On Larry's recommendation, we chose D & B Builders as the contractor for the new building. David Denham, the owner of the construction company, became a good friend and has done several construction projects for our company and for me over the years.

During the planning of the new building, we learned that the Creighton Road plans were changed somewhat, and that the new road would only take away our parking lot and not the entire building. This was good news and bad at the same time. This meant we could stay in the building longer, but the State might not pay for the building as it was only taking the parking lot. Of course, without space for parking the building would be unusable for us, so we had to file suit against the State.

Groundbreaking ceremony at 6723 Plantation Road – 1992

Bill Clark, my attorney friend for many years, informed me that the State actually expected me to sue them, and it would even pay his fee in the matter. This was strange but good news as well. Eventually, the State agreed to buy the building and let us pay rent until we were ready to move to the new location.

We completed construction and moved to our new building at 6723 Plantation Road in 1993. We had held a groundbreaking ceremony at the beginning of construction, and shortly after making the move, we held an open house, preceded by a blessing of the building by The Rev. Michael Schulenberg, rector of my parish, Holy Cross Episcopal Church. It was a great event attended by our staff, many clients, vendors, and friends.

Open House celebration at 6723 Plantation Road headquarters - 1993

6723 Plantation Road Office - 2020

After moving to the new building, our staff increased from about 25 in 1993 to over 170 in 2017 when I retired. (With the acquisition of hrQ in 2019 the number of staff members is now over 200.) In 1995, just two years after completion of the first building, we built a sizeable addition and bought the adjacent property for parking. Two years after that, we added another large section and subsequently bought the small office building on the corner of Creighton and Plantation Roads, which was adjacent to our parking lot. The need for more parking and possible expansion led us to purchase seven of the eight small properties in the Stonegate Office Park located adjacent to and just north of our building. In 2016, in anticipation of building a new office complex that would be large enough for all our future needs, we purchased the 3.5 acre-site across the street from our main office building. At this point, the future of that site is uncertain.

I'm sure if I had enough money at the time and the foresight to know that we would grow as rapidly as we did, I would have done more to plan and would have constructed a building with office space large enough to accommodate everyone at the outset. But I didn't. By delaying, I'm also sure I paid more money in the long run for construction and for the land we needed for extra parking. Nevertheless, I have no regrets. We have borrowed very little money over the years, and we were virtually debt-free when I retired.

CHAPTER 8

Making Advances with Information Technology

———✦⟨⟩✦———

Keeping Pace with the Introduction of New Technology

DURING THE 70's AND UNTIL THE LATE 80's, all of our memos and letters were typed by secretaries. If I wanted something to be read by all staff members, I asked my secretary to type it, make copies, and distribute it to everyone. If I wanted to send a letter to someone, I dictated it, my secretary typed it, and she sent it out for me. Lengthy reports were entered into a dictation machine, which were later transcribed by my secretary. Any math work I did or needed done by others was figured on a calculator.

By the late 80's and into the early 90's, we began using spreadsheet programs like Excel and Digicalc, and word processing programs like WordPerfect and Word. Office calendars on computers also became popular. I resisted at first, but my assistant, Meg Harris, insisted that I give up my paper calendar, which I had kept for thirty years or more, and start using the program on my computer. That was hard for me to do, but

I soon gave in to it. The demand for these new tools spread quickly, and more employees were given computers to increase their productivity. Staff members, myself included, began to write their own letters and memos. Secretaries became administrative assistants and took on other, more responsible duties.

Those new computers were expensive and not always reliable. Peggy Fortunato was responsible for buying the new equipment and keeping it in working order, and contracted with a computer technician to provide that service. At some point, the technician began building computers and selling them to us at a reduced price. Each computer he sold us was loaded with the Microsoft operating system and Microsoft Office Suite to include Excel and Word. WordPerfect was also popular at the time, and some of us continued to use it.

As we adapted to new ways of managing internal communications, we began to recognize the need for process automation. In the mid-70's, we were producing a large volume of letters and resumes sent to prospective customers. That led to the purchase of a word processor from Digital Systems, a company based in Pensacola and owned by Wally Yost and Sandy Sansing (before Sandy entered the automobile business). Shortly thereafter, we invested in new computer and accounting software from Caldwell Systems to produce a growing volume of payroll checks for temporary employees, to create invoices for our customers, and to track information for our internal needs.

The accelerating AmStaff business volume in the late 80's and early 90's required an upgrade of those systems to computers that were faster and with capacity to handle the information load. They featured a disk-to-reel tape "back-up" system that was time-consuming to operate but more efficient than the floppy disk system we were using before.

The computer, keyboard, and display terminals (known then as CRT's...an acronym for cathode-ray tube) used by our temporary help service's payroll operators were made by Digital Equipment Corporation (DEC) and maintained by its technicians. As the operating system became more complicated, we became dependent on local contractors to maintain it and install updates.

Initially, AmStaff's payroll was produced using the DEC computer and software designed for the temporary service. We quickly acknowledged the limitations of that system given the amount of data required to manage human resources, benefits, and workers' compensation. We solved that problem in 1989 with the purchase of PayPlus, a new software system designed especially for employee leasing companies.

PayPlus Software, a California-based company, was owned by Dr. T. Joe Willy who was a pioneer in the employee leasing industry. We were one of the earliest customers of his new company. Barclay Bourdeau, the program designer, came to our office to install the new system. Peggy and I were excited to be getting what we hoped would significantly improve our operation. As we watched Barclay unpack an older portable DEC computer with a cracked keyboard, we lost a little confidence. He actually had to prop something under one end of the keyboard to hold it together!

In spite of that questionable beginning, the system worked reasonably well and solved most of our issues. Peggy took the lead in learning the new system and initially doing the payroll. Sometime later, "T. Joe," as we called him, came to the office to participate in a companywide planning session, and while he was with us, he installed some updates and did more extensive training on the system.

Bringing Information Technology Systems In-house

In the mid-90's, my oldest son, Britt III, was in the sales department and used the computer a good bit to write sales proposals and create spreadsheets. He talked with me about the frequent problems we were having with individual computers. It was his opinion that the computers we were buying from our contractor were assembled using cheap and unreliable parts. He told me that he was sure he could do a much better job taking care of the company's computers than our contractor, and he wanted a chance to take it on.

I knew Britt was light on experience, but I recognized his passion to make some improvements. I also knew he was very knowledgeable about computers, having watched him work with equipment and software while growing up, and I had confidence that he could learn what he didn't know. So, I said, "Yes." Looking back, it was the best decision I could have made.

One of the first things Britt III did was to stop buying second-rate computers, which in itself reduced downtime and improved performance. He also discovered that none of the computers using Microsoft products were properly licensed. All were copies of the former contractor's original. He recommended that we promptly obtain licenses for all the computers and "get legal." I agreed with his recommendation, and we mailed a check to Microsoft for almost $100,000.

To better qualify himself for the job, Britt III set out to become an expert in Microsoft products and systems. Over a period of many months, he studied intently and successfully passed written examinations, earning certifications in at least a half-dozen areas critical to the operation of the systems department, including recognition as a Microsoft-certified systems engineer and certified customer relationship management (CRM) consultant. As a result, he brought exciting new tools to the company that facilitated our work and improved our productivity.

The Intranet was one of the first technologies Britt III introduced to the company in his new role managing information technology (IT). This was a huge advancement to our internal communications. I'd never heard of an Intranet before he presented the idea, but it was an instant success in terms of sharing information around the company. In choosing a name for it, Britt III suggested that we create a contest for the staff members. We asked them to submit a name or names, offering a cash prize for the one chosen. Yvonne Nellums submitted the name, "LINK," an acronym for Landrum Information "NetworK." We accepted her suggestion and the name caught on quickly. To make sure it was used, everyone's computer was set to open to the LINK screen when they booted up in the morning. This went a long way toward keeping us all on the same page within the company and reduced the need for memos that had to be typed and distributed.

Email and the Internet were also added about this same time, around 1997. I confess that I was a little slow in understanding how this new communication system worked, and who was going to be able to use it. I wasn't the only one. I recall discussions about local Internet service providers (ISPs) and upload and download speeds and bandwidth, which practically no one outside of the "geek world" knew much about. As expected, however, this new method of communication caught on very quickly with fellow staff members and outside of the office with everyone who had access. Now we can't imagine doing business without it.

Another bold step Britt III took in his first year as head of the new IT department, was to require that all employees use only Microsoft Office software, notably Word and Excel. That meant those who were using other spreadsheet programs like Digicalc, or word processing programs like WordPerfect (myself included), had to give them up. There were good reasons for that decision as history has shown.

As mentioned earlier, Rhonda Freeman was the first computer technician hired by Britt III to assist in the IT department. Rhonda handled troubleshooting, installed new equipment, and downloaded software. Early on, she also worked with Peggy in writing PayPlus reports and ultimately learned to write programs and troubleshoot in that system.

The Caldwell-Spartin payroll software system for Landrum Staffing Services was maintained by the vendor and was very stable from the outset. AmStaff's payroll system, PayPlus, however, was relatively unstable at that time, and we were responsible for hardware and software maintenance and upgrades with some help from PayPlus systems personnel. The system ran on a UNIX platform. As the expert on PayPlus at the time, Peggy hired an outside contractor to maintain the UNIX software operating system while Britt III was responsible for maintaining the hardware. This created some confusion as to who was responsible when things didn't go well.

Britt III was not an expert on the UNIX operating system, and our dependence on an outside contractor who was in great demand left us vulnerable. I recall one incident when the system crashed. It was after hours, and no one was available to help get it back up and running. We were down to a final backup tape that could restore the system to normal with current data. Britt III was out of town, but I got him on the telephone. He talked me through the restore process, and we prayed that the backup would work. Thankfully it did, but we both knew from the experience that we had to do something to prevent that from happening again. One employee leasing company I knew was forced to shut down because it couldn't recover its data from a computer crash. It was time for us to make a change.

In order to gain more control over our situation, Britt III recommended that we change operating systems for PayPlus from UNIX to Windows so he could maintain it. The systems engineers for PayPlus didn't have a lot of experience with the Windows operating system and were reluctant at first but eventually consented.

Britt III recalls being pretty much on his own in setting up the new operating system for PayPlus. Initially, there was a problem with it being extremely slow, which was a real concern for our folks attempting to look up information, enter payroll data, and produce checks. Britt III determined that the problem was a lack of server memory and network bandwidth, which was resolved by beefing up our network infrastructure. With those problems fixed, the move to Windows proved to be a viable alternative to UNIX, and other PayPlus users followed our lead.

As CTO for the company, Britt III was responsible for all computer hardware and software systems purchased and placed in operation.

He hired and supervised the technical staff and did much of the work himself. As with most companies around the turn of the century and still today, we were totally dependent on our computer systems for the success of our company. And with virtually every company, we had to deal with something called, "Y2K."

Sometime in 1998, Mike Adkins, audit manager with the accounting firm of Saltmarsh, Cleaveland and Gund, met with our leadership team to talk about "Y2K" (referring to the year 2000) and the potential impact that it was going to have on computer systems all across the country, including ours. Today, this is referred to as the "Y2K Apocalypse." Many people expected the Y2K computer "bug" would cause worldwide problems, including the disruption of electricity due to power plants going down, and the same for water services, transportation, food distribution, and other services. Some people expected a complete breakdown of society.

When Mike made that presentation to us, Y2K was not a familiar term, at least not to me. I honestly hadn't given any thought as to how it might impact our company, so Mike's warning was timely. The problem, as I understood it, was that computer programs had been written in the 20th century to allow space for only two digits for the particular year in which the information was stored. The year 1999 was just 99 and so on. Experts were not sure how some systems would react when the digits became "00." PayPlus software was written just that way, i.e., two spaces instead of four to specify the year. Thankfully, PayPlus provided us an upgrade to work around the issue.

Britt III identified and upgraded all of our non-compliant hardware and software in preparation for Y2K. As a consequence, when the clock rolled to January 1, 2000, the feared "Apocalypse" was a non-event for us. Nothing weird happened. We continued with business as usual, and the lights never went out.

It worried us both that Britt III was the only person in the company who had the technical skills necessary to keep all systems running smoothly. Our vulnerability was resolved in January 2003 with the hiring of Jason Heuer, an experienced and highly skilled systems engineer. Now in his 16th year with the company, Jason has proven his value many times over and has been an integral part of the growth and success of the IT department and our company.

Managing a Growing Volume of Data and Documents

The story of how our company's technology has evolved over the years probably mirrors that of others in many ways. However, the changes we faced have been real for me and nothing short of dramatic. For several years, Britt III and Jason Heuer worked together to build a complete data center with racks of computer processors, data storage systems, advanced power supply systems, special fire protection systems, and more things that I didn't understand and don't remember. I do recall that Britt III was coming to me very often explaining our need, first for one piece of equipment and then another, all very expensive.

The fear of equipment failure or damage from fire or hurricanes was also an issue. Redundancy was built into every system. We packed so much equipment into our small computer room that it was hard to keep it cool, which meant we had to purchase a larger, single purpose air conditioner and modify the building to accommodate it. When we became dependent on the Internet for time-keeping systems, payroll submissions by our clients, and a host of other requirements, we set up redundant ISPs and even signed up with a satellite ISP, which required us to purchase and install a satellite antenna.

Backing up computer files was another big issue that saw many changes over the years. After moving from the large reel tapes that we used with our DEC PDP 11 system, we progressed to cassette tapes which someone took home with them every night as a safeguard. After a few years of utilizing that system, we arranged with a service in Atlanta to download our information to its computers on a nightly basis via the Internet.

We gave all employees access to the system, which necessitated personal computers (PCs) at every desk, all linked to our central processing center in the building. Printers were placed all over the building as well. Microsoft Office software was loaded on every PC and properly licensed. Staff members working for the PEO had access to the computer hosting the PayPlus software on their computers. Those working for Landrum Staffing had access to the computer hosting the Caldwell-Spartin software on theirs. Keeping all the equipment and software running and updated was highly demanding, requiring the addition of more staff as we grew. New computers and displays were always stacked up in the IT department, waiting to be installed so old ones could be given away, recycled, or trashed.

Much of the demand for computer software was driven by the enormous amount of paper associated with having thousands of employees on the payroll. Large printers were regularly spitting out reports on the often-used green and white striped paper that we felt needed to be saved for long periods of time–at least seven years as we were told. Application forms, medical records, drug testing results, I-9 forms, counseling forms, and attendance records also had to be maintained. Federal laws require us to keep I-9 forms in one file and medical records in another, necessitating three separate folders for every employee.

We addressed records management in earnest by creating a file room with several four-drawer filing cabinets and a full-time records clerk. The clerk was constantly creating new files, retrieving information from the files that staff members requested, and filing paperwork of some kind in the existing files.

Moving to a larger room, we graduated from that system to an even larger filing system with rolling shelves and vertical files that resembled the medical records department in a hospital. We were proud of the efficiency of our "new" system but soon outgrew it. To create more room, we regularly moved older files to boxes, then on to one of two rental storage units outside of the office. We were literally drowning in paper.

The digital storage and retrieval of documents for small businesses was still in the early stages of development in the 80's and 90's. Britt III was very interested in exploring systems that might offer some relief to our situation. Over time, he hired two or three consultants to help us work out a solution, yet none seemed to have the answer for us. In 2005, after evaluating several available options, we purchased a documents management software system called PaperWise. Jason, by then our director of IT, worked diligently with each department head to document workflows and other necessary procedures for programming into the system.

The process of integrating PaperWise began with scanning or digitizing all files that were stored in our office file room, along with automating the "onboarding paperwork," i.e., essentially all forms signed by or created for new employees. In 2006, about nine months after the PaperWise purchase, we finally put the new software into production. Between 2006 and 2008, Jason and his staff customized and streamlined the software to automate countless tasks that had involved manual paper processing. It took some time for people to get comfortable with not having a piece of paper in their hands, but they soon realized that the new system made information storage, sharing, and retrieval much faster and more reliable, and made us far more efficient as a company.

When we began using PaperWise, we stored records in two rented warehouses and in the dedicated areas of our two buildings. Today, we use only a small space onsite solely for our most current documents. However, getting rid of paper hasn't been as easy as we'd hoped.

AmStaff's contract with Monsanto, which ended many years ago, required that we hold onto, or have access to, some of the forms indefinitely. That involves thousands of files and lots of paper. Also, decisions made by the U.S. Supreme Court placing the burden of proof on the employer with regard to employee claims of discrimination make it difficult to decide what must be kept and what we can destroy. Thankfully, Amie Remington, our in-house counsel for employment matters, has helped us make those decisions. With time, all those paper files should be a thing of the past.

In 2014, the decision was made to phase out our computer operations center and move production to Atlanta, Georgia as part of a data center colocation arrangement with Flexential Corporation. For a few years prior to that decision, we had been using Flexential's data center (then known as Peak 10) as a failover site just in case our system was to have a problem locally. We now own very little hardware or infrastructure. Today, almost all of it is provided by our vendor, which offers "Infrastructure as a Service" at their secure site in Atlanta.

PCs with Microsoft Office software on them that used to be on every staff member's desk, have been replaced by what our tech-savvy folks call "thin client machines," a term that is new to me. It is essentially a computer display connected to a small black box (my description, not theirs) that communicates with our software at Flexential in Atlanta via the Internet. This new system took a little getting used to, but it has proven to be much more secure, efficient, and reliable. It is also easier to maintain and far less labor-intensive for our IT staff to manage.

Creating Operational Efficiency with Advances in IT

ClientSpace and Employee on Board software played an integral part in improving the operational efficiency of our company. ClientSpace is a product of NetWise Technology. It is a CRM system written especially for the PEO industry, which integrates workflow, makes information available to staff members, clients, and worksite employees, tracks the underwriting of prospects in the sales pipeline, and prompts staff in every department to take action as warranted.

Employee on Board was written and installed on our system by a former member of our IT staff, Paul Randall. Before it was introduced, only paper applications were used, and the data had to be manually entered into our computer system. The new software enabled PEO worksite employees to enter their own application information and complete and sign the various required forms via the Internet. That information was then reviewed or audited by our documents management staff to confirm that the application was complete. Employee on Board reduced errors and saved us a lot of time and money.

In 2016, after many discussions about the need for a better software system for the PEO, our SLT authorized Ted Kirchharr to begin a process of evaluating alternative human resource information and payroll systems. Ted was vice president over the IT department at the time. The decision to pursue alternatives was not made lightly. PayPlus was our legacy system, which we had used for more than twenty-five years. We had built our processes and procedures around it. We were (and still are) part-owners of that company and had a vested interest in wanting it to be successful. Nevertheless, we needed functionality that was not yet available nor scheduled by PayPlus as a planned upgrade. Also, we were maintaining spreadsheets and running calculations using Excel, which had not been automated as part of their system. We reasoned that a new system with that capability would save our staff hours of work and save the company considerable money.

Ted put together a team of nine people from all major departments in the company and tasked them with coming up with criteria for evaluating prospective software companies. After weeks of discussion and visits by the contenders, the committee selected Prism Software as the new provider. The expectation was that the new system would help our company become more efficient, offer more self-service options, and provide our clients with more and better access to their information. Some, but not all of those expectations have been realized.

In a recent conversation with LandrumHR's payroll director, Karena McCafferty, I learned that the conversion from PayPlus to the new payroll software, Prism, had gone well and enabled her to get more work done with fewer employees. Because of some of the enhancements available on the new system and the reduction in the number of manual calculations required of the staff, payroll entry takes less time, and the specialists can take on more clients and worksite employees than before. As a result, the department now operates with seven fewer staff members. The volume of work continues to rise with the team issuing well over thirty thousand vouchers (paper and electronic checks) each month.

Our part-ownership in PayPlus came about in December 2001 when nine users of the system, including AmStaff, joined forces to purchase the company from Zurich Insurance Company, which by then had purchased it from Dr. T. Joe Willey, the originator of the software. The new owners elected George Gersema with Employers Resource of Boise, Idaho, John Heaton with Pay Plus Benefits (different from PayPlus) of Kennewick, Washington, and me to serve as the management committee for the company. George was elected chairman, John as vice chairman, and I was elected secretary/treasurer.

We hired a new president, consolidated key staff to a single location, and set a goal to develop a more modern payroll and accounting software system for our group of about 100 users. We had high hopes that since the company was now run by people who understood the PEO business and who had a vested interest in making the company successful, the system would improve as our needs evolved.

Over a period of ten years or so, it did get a lot better, and we began developing new software. Still, we were not able to keep pace with some of the newer companies that were able to start from scratch to develop proprietary software using modern architecture frameworks. We did not have that luxury since we were attempting to develop new functionality while accommodating a myriad of users, solving their immediate problems, and keeping our system current. Just as important, it would have taken a lot more money than we had available to invest in development of a competitive new product.

As vice president and CTO for our company, Britt III attended many of the PayPlus board meetings with me over the years. Around 2007, I stopped attending the meetings and turned the responsibility over to him. He was eventually elected to the board and served until 2016 when we stopped using the PayPlus system.

Leslie Gordon, Britt Landrum Jr., Peggy Fortunato, Britt Landrum III - early 2000's

The advancement of technology over the years brought with it the need to continuously upgrade software and hardware just to keep current with the changes and to take advantage of the latest innovations. The initial thought was that more automation would result in more efficiency and lower costs. It has certainly brought about more efficiency, as described in the comments above about timekeeping and payroll, but it has been increasingly more costly. The size of our IT staff has continued to grow each year as we have tried to automate many of our processes and give clients and employees ready access to their information while making the systems more secure.

Jason Heuer, Britt Landrum, Jr. - about 2013

In the last three years, the IT department has been reorganized and expanded. New positions have been created. New staff members with greater expertise have joined the department. Jason's title is now lead enterprise architect, and the IT department has expanded to include other related functions within the company. The once small department comprised of Britt III and Jason has grown to reflect the changing needs and significant advancements in technology that have occurred in the last few years. It is now one of the largest operating units in the company.

CHAPTER 9

Branching and Market Expansion

————◆◇◆————

Establishing Branch Offices for the
Temporary Help Service

AFTER LOSING AMERICAN FIDELITY and its properties as our client, which as mentioned became a significant share of our business a decade or so after its beginning, Carolyn Davis, Denise McLeod, and I came up with the idea of opening branch offices for the temporary help service. We looked first at Panama City, my hometown. I still had family there and often traveled to visit them. After making some inquiries, we learned that a small temporary service, Professional Personnel Services, Inc., was looking to sell its business. After further investigation, we decided to purchase the company, and opened our first branch in June 1983.

Panama City branch office - 1983

Fort Walton Beach branch office - 1985

Carolyn devoted a good bit of her time getting the new branch established. Finding and training the right employee to manage the office was more of a problem than we anticipated, however, and the business suffered because of it. Not to be deterred, we stuck with the plan and in 1985, opened an office in Fort Walton Beach, renting space in a strip mall located on Mary Esther Cutoff. The office was actually in Mary Esther, Florida, a small community near Fort Walton Beach. Again, we hired a manager and one or two employees to run the operation. Carolyn spent a fair amount of time with the staff doing training and going on sales calls. We were a bit more successful there, and after a year or so in operation, were able to build a small volume of business.

It was during this period that Carolyn and I developed significant differences of opinion as to the way the operations should be run, and in January 1986, she left the company, later to go into business for herself. With that new development, I was feeling a little overwhelmed with all that we had going on and, after some long discussions with Denise, decided to get out of the branch operations as quickly as we could. A short time later, Denise and I traveled to Panama City and officially closed the office there.

By that time, the Fort Walton Beach branch was doing a little better and we decided to continue the operation and attempt to find a buyer. I contacted Larry Cowan, a friend from church and former client who was then working as a business broker. Larry was successful in finding a buyer for us, and in 1988, we sold the operation and devoted our attention to building the business in Pensacola instead.

We learned a few lessons from the experience of operating those branch offices. The first lesson was that we simply weren't ready. Finding the right staff to operate those offices was difficult. Managing the staff from Pensacola was complicated and took much more time than anticipated. Closing one branch and selling the other seemed like a defeat at first, but after devoting time, attention, and resources to the Pensacola operation, we soon grew that volume of business with far less investment.

We were much more effective in building a stable and capable staff locally. In January 1988, Valerie Cole, a long-time Manpower staff member, joined our company. Valerie had been in charge of industrial staffing in her previous job and brought significant strength to us in that area. Now in her 32nd year with the company, Valerie continues to be a valuable employee in our Workforce Solutions Division (the new name for Landrum Staffing), working closely with our long-term client, General Electric (GE), to staff and employ several hundred production workers in their Pensacola plant.

Anniversary celebration for Valerie Cole
with Britt Landrum, Jr. - 1993

(In 2019, thanks to the exceptional work done by the entire Workforce Solutions team including Valerie, our other staffing coordinators, our GE site manager, Chris Fountain, and the company's other supervisory staff at GE, LandrumHR was presented with a North American Supplier of Excellence Award from GE Renewable Energy, recognizing our fulfillment and support of the GE Renewable Energy facility in Pensacola.)

After ridding ourselves of the branch operations, we devoted more attention to sales and advertising in the local Pensacola market. We began buying space on a few billboards and bus benches to get our name out in the marketplace, using the Dodson, Craddock and Born agency to assist us in those days. We also tried radio advertising. I recall one ad in particular that seemed to be effective. It featured the voice of a pregnant secretary being taken to the hospital by ambulance telling her boss not to worry, that she had called Landrum Temporary Services to send over a replacement for her while she was away. A siren could be heard in the background. I got the idea for that ad from Susan Hunsucker, our own staff member who worked until she was quite ready to deliver her baby. I asked her every day how she was doing, wondering if she would make it through the day. It was a fun ad, and we got lots of feedback from listeners of WCOA, a popular local AM station at the time.

In 2011 we made the decision to once again establish branch offices in Fort Walton Beach and Panama City. The office in Fort Walton Beach was established primarily for the staffing service, but also functions as a servicing center for PEO applicants. When we began discussing the establishment of the offices, we acknowledged that it had been more than twenty-five years since we opened our first branch and we felt we had a far better understanding of what the venture needed to be successful. We had staff available to travel and train, we had sophisticated telephone and computer systems—even closed-circuit television cameras that could facilitate video conferencing and monitor activity in the remote offices. Denise McLeod and Britt III were responsible for getting the Fort Walton Beach office up and running, and the venture has proven to be a success.

Welcome and Open House celebration at
Fort Walton Beach office - 2011

The Panama City office was opened in 2012, primarily to serve clients and co-employees of the PEO. In 2018 we were making plans to move to a larger office and begin offering staffing services to clients in the Panama City area. Unfortunately, Mother Nature had other ideas. Hurricane Michael, which landed hard in that section of the Panhandle of Florida in October 2018, destroyed our office as well as many others and placed many people out of work. After that event we decided to close the Panama City office and revisit the plan at a later date.

Stepping into Business Acquisitions

For quite a few years, I had watched as other PEOs grew faster than our company. There were lots of reasons–larger markets, larger sales staff, lower pricing, and taking on construction and other high-risk clients, which we most often rejected. But some were growing by acquisition, that is, buying other PEOs. Most of the PEOs we followed were owned, either fully or jointly, by venture capital firms. Their owners had taken on investors in order to provide the funding for their purchases, which was something we had vowed not to do.

In his role as CFO, Andy Remke encouraged me to consider making some acquisitions as a means to grow our business. At that point in our history, around 2004, we had already acquired one or two small companies. As mentioned earlier, in 1983 we purchased a very small staffing service in Panama City, Florida, and opened an office there. It didn't take off, in part because we really weren't ready to operate a branch office. Moreover, the seller did not have a strong base of customers nor widespread name recognition. We had paid little for the business, and since running the branch was costing us more than we were making, we opted to close the operation.

The second purchase, made in 1999, was for Evergreen Systems. This was a local staffing service that provided quite a few technical employees to the Monsanto chemical plant in Pensacola. The owner was an engineer who had been an employee of Monsanto and seemed to have an "in" with the managers who placed the job orders with Evergreen. Significantly, most of the employees were former Monsanto employees who had retired and were brought back in as consultants on the payroll of the staffing company.

Evergreen had two key employees running the operation, Angela Thornton-Jones and Dawn Danforth. After acquiring the company's assets, we relocated all the files and the two employees to our offices. They continue to work for our company today, and I have often told them that they were the best part of the whole deal. As I recall, the purchase price for Evergreen was reasonable, with a payout that depended on sustaining the same volume of sales. After two or three years, we were able to generate enough income to recoup the money we paid for the business and earned a reasonable return on our investment. Monsanto eventually became Solutia and now Ascend, and we continue to provide the plant a number of technical staff members.

Around the time we purchased Evergreen Systems, we looked seriously at a small PEO in Birmingham, Alabama, that was owned by an acquaintance. After evaluating the financial aspects, we made an offer of nearly one million dollars, contingent on sales continuing at the same level or better. Our offer wasn't accepted, but the experience of evaluating, pricing and negotiating such deals was helpful to us in looking at other opportunities.

We also approached PEOs in our northwest Florida market, both directly and through a CPA friend, and tried to interest the owners in selling. We reasoned that buying a PEO in our market would give us the highest return on our investment since we could cut out duplicated costs and improve profits. Unfortunately, our plan didn't work out at the time. Of those we contacted, two were not ready to talk, and another had significant problems that we felt would be too expensive to resolve. During that time also, Joe Baldi, the owner of Staff Payroll, a Pensacola company, approached us about buying his company. After providing us with all the information we needed to evaluate his company and make him an offer, he changed his mind, saying that the timing wasn't right for him to sell.

Our acquisition strategy for the PEO in the mid 2000's was somewhat influenced by the natural disaster that wreaked havoc in our community on September 16, 2004. Hurricane Ivan struck Pensacola and other northwest Florida cities, inflicting catastrophic damage to structures along the western Gulf Coast. The damage to our building was relatively minor, and our backup generator provided electricity, which enabled us to continue operations with only a little downtime.

We faced significant challenges as several of our staff members suffered severe home damage and were unable to come to work. We did lots of things to help them during that time, including establishing a temporary day care center in our building for their young children and bringing in meals for them during lunchtime. We also issued emergency bonus checks to help with expenses for them. We were able to open the office and restore operations fairly quickly. This was and still is an essential requirement for us since clients located in unaffected parts of the state expect us to provide services for them without interruption.

Many of our clients suffered severe damage to their businesses and had to lay off some or all of their employees for quite a number of weeks. Since our income was derived from a percentage of the payroll of those employees, the earnings for Landrum Professional, our PEO, took a hit. Thankfully, our sales representative for Landrum Staffing had anticipated such an event and had established relationships with other firms that had contracts with federal disaster relief agencies. Our staffing income rose during that time as we placed around 500 workers with companies involved in the cleanup and reconstruction of buildings across the western Gulf Coast. The additional income from the staffing side of our business offset the loss of earnings from the PEO, so overall the company did not suffer a loss.

That experience made us keenly aware of the need to diversify the PEO geographically. We simply could not afford to continue putting "all of our eggs" in the Northwest Florida "basket!" Building our PEO business in other states became an important goal for the company. It was during this time that we began to work more closely with Wanda Silva, a PEO broker whom we had met previously at meetings of our national organization, NAPEO.

Wanda spoke regularly with our CFO, Andy Remke, discussing PEO clients who had listed their businesses with her. Those prospects were mostly located in North Carolina, South Carolina, Georgia, and Florida. We looked carefully at several, but nothing seemed to work out. With each opportunity, we got more proficient at evaluating the companies we were trying to purchase. We were also surprised to learn how some of the companies operated, ignoring some of the rules that we felt important to follow.

We didn't rely solely on Wanda to provide us with prospects. We also obtained a list of all the PEOs in states where we wanted to have a presence and sent letters expressing our interest in buying them out. It was not unusual for PEO owners to receive such a letter from a broker or venture capital firm. For many years, I received at least two or three such letters each week, which I quickly discarded. (Well, for a while I saved them, thinking that if I ever decided to sell, I would have someone to contact.) I thought that receiving a letter from a fellow PEO owner might get more attention than contact by a broker. We did generate interest from one or two prospects, but nothing resulted from that effort.

Our first sizeable acquisition, made in January 2012, was not a PEO itself but a portion of their "book of business." The PEO, located in south Florida, had made a decision to get rid of all small clients and focus on larger ones in their niche market. They were secretive and didn't want their name used in any announcements that we might make. As I recall, they had fewer than one hundred small companies as clients, with roughly two to ten employees each–around 800 worksite employees. At the time, even though we didn't market our services to very small businesses, we were open to taking them on if they didn't pose an undue risk for an excessive rate of employee injuries, poor credit, and legal non-compliance. We also compared their pricing model to ours to make sure we could turn a profit. When the prospective small client pool was presented to us in aggregate, the deal seemed attractive.

From a financial perspective, the acquisition was a success. We paid a reasonable multiple of earnings before interest, taxes and amortization ("EBITA") for the business, we didn't have to borrow money, and we recovered our purchase price in just a few years.

In December 2012, we purchased the assets of two PEOs, Employer Administrative Services (EASI) in Asheville, North Carolina, and Synergetic in Columbia, South Carolina. EASI was a small PEO with roughly 200 worksite employees. The firm was owned by a husband and wife who were both eager to sell. The business had been operating for several years out of a small, rented office space in a dated "store front" office complex. Both owners worked in the business with one additional employee. They had accumulated several loyal clients over the years, provided a lot of personal service to them, and were profitable, due in part to very low overhead.

Synergetic, with just under 1,000 worksite employees, was owned and managed by a single shareholder. Significant income came from the owner's HR consulting practice. Located in Columbia, South Carolina, the fourteen-year old company had loyal clients and several long-term employees who were integral to the success of the business. The company also owned a life and health insurance agency, Tangent Insurance, which was principally operated by the owner's wife. Synergetic, we determined, was profitable with the income generated from the insurance agency and consulting practice.

With both EASI and Synergetic, we purchased the assets of the businesses and kept the employees on staff to facilitate the transition. Keeping the clients on board after the sale is of utmost importance to both buyer and seller, as the purchase price always includes an "earn out" provision, which means that if sales decrease, so does the purchase price. The transition can be challenging as some clients and their employees are resistant to change, so keeping staff in place tends to reduce the anxiety level for both parties and increase the likelihood that the transition will go smoothly.

As in all of our asset purchases, getting the newly acquired companies' clients to sign our contracts is the first hurdle. The owner of the acquired company is usually quite willing to assist since the purchase price is based on all the clients staying onboard. The next task is to get all incoming worksite employees, often several hundred, to sign new applications, I'9's, W-4's, and a few other forms. They also have to select and enroll in our benefit plans. Getting all that information accurately entered into our computer system in time for the first payroll, often within just a few days' time, is a monumental task. To their credit, our staff members worked tirelessly, many times on nights and weekends, and they have always come through.

In making these two purchases, we were establishing our first remote branches for the PEO. The EASI office was deemed to be inadequate because of its location and appearance, so within just a few months we rented new space in a more modern office park in a newer business section of Asheville, and we upgraded the furnishings and technology. We purchased Synergetic's office as a part of our deal with the company's owner. The building had been recently renovated and was located in a modern office park in a busy commercial area of Columbia.

The Synergetic purchase proved to be more difficult than expected. The owner and his wife had built a fine company, and both agreed to stay on for two more years to assure a smooth transition of the clients and worksite employees to Landrum as the new owner. The long-term staff members also agreed to stay and become Landrum employees. To keep things as normal as possible for the clients and the staff in Columbia, we decided to make the former owner the president of our new South Carolina location. Our thinking was that he could run the office for us and make the transition easier for us as well. Unfortunately, our management styles proved to be quite different, and this arrangement didn't work very well. Eventually, we decided to bring in someone from the outside, and we hired John Slavich, who had a strong background in human resources, to manage the office.

During the two-year term of his contract, the former owner focused primarily on providing consulting services to the select group of clients with whom he had worked before selling his company. When his two-year term expired in 2014, we honored his relationship and obligation to those clients by allowing him to keep them. We accepted that this would amount to a reduction in sales for our company but felt it would foster a more cooperative and supportive relationship going forward, which was beneficial to the staff, the clients, the seller of Synergetic, and me.

The blending of our two cultures and resolving of differences with the former owner were only some of the challenges we encountered in acquiring Synergetic. There was also the issue of timing. When we acquired the company, the Synergetic staff was in the process of converting their payroll and all human resource information from PayPlus, which they had used for many years, to a new software platform called Darwin. We were approaching 2012 year-end, and the conversion was far from completion. We knew this could have a disastrous impact on the company if W-2's and other tax reports couldn't be produced in a timely manner. Some clients and employees had been entered into the new system, but many, including clients with more complex setup requirements, had not.

After considerable effort and much discussion with staff members from both locations, all agreed that there was not sufficient time before year-end to get everything properly set up in the new system. Thankfully, our PayPlus expert, Rhonda Freeman, was able to transfer all records back to PayPlus in order to close out the year in an orderly manner.

At the time we made this acquisition, our company, which had been using the PayPlus system for many years, was taking a serious look at other software systems that might be better for us. The Darwin system purchased by Synergetic was one that we had decided to evaluate. So, in the beginning of 2013, we chose to continue using Darwin for former Synergetic clients and worksite employees, requiring our staff to make an all-out effort to set up parameters and to input and test the data before the first payroll was due in 2013. Jessica Beal, the leader of that project in Pensacola, recalls that the effort was monumental and involved several of our departments and staff members, sometimes working late evenings and early mornings to get the job done. We operated that way for the first six months, maintaining and comparing both payroll systems, but in the end, we decided that our best course was to convert all Darwin users to PayPlus.

Prior to making the purchase of Synergetic and its insurance agency, Tangent, our company had already made the decision to enter the insurance agency business. We had created our agency, Garden Street Insurance, in anticipation of buying the assets of Sedlacek Insurance Service, which was a tenant in one of the office buildings adjacent to and owned by our company. The agency owner, Ron Sedlacek, was a long-term friend and agent for our company's health, life, and disability insurance policies. He was not in good health at the time and had plans to sell his business. Our plan to purchase the agency was put on hold while we made sure we had covered all aspects of licensing and regulation. We eventually abandoned the idea in favor of an arrangement with another long-term agent and friend, Todd Torgersen. Our subsequent purchase of Tangent gave us much clearer insight as to how the PEO and the insurance agency could work together for the benefit of all concerned.

Synergetic did not have a group health plan to offer its clients and worksite employees, but through its insurance agency, licensed agency employees were able to assist them in finding and purchasing separate group policies that would be written in the name of the client. All the while, Synergetic administered the plans and collected and paid the premiums on the clients' behalf. That model seemed to work well, and, after the acquisition, we incorporated Garden Street Insurance in South Carolina in 2013, and all clients of Tangent became clients of our new agency.

Inevitably, unexpected issues have to be dealt with in any acquisition. We didn't anticipate how much time and attention the Synergetic acquisition was going to require, but the result proved to be worth the effort. We have some very dedicated and capable staff members there, and the business gives us a presence in a very important market in South Carolina.

In 2013, another acquisition opportunity came up unexpectedly. The attorney for Staff Payroll of Pensacola, which we had once considered, approached me to see if we were still interested in purchasing the company. The owner, Joe Baldi, had passed away and his wife, Irene, wanted to sell the company.

Joe Baldi had been a friend. His company used the PayPlus software system, as we did, and he occasionally needed our help. His small company did not have an IT department, and we were most willing to help out when we could. We also referred business to one another. We referred small employers who didn't seem to be a good fit for our company to Staff Payroll. Joe referred larger clients that wanted group health insurance and retirement plans to us. The arrangement worked well for both companies for a number of years.

After meeting with Irene and her attorney and having an opportunity to review Staff Payroll's financial data and the list of clients and their employees' workers' compensation classifications, we agreed to make the purchase. Again, only purchasing the assets, we moved the company's records to our office, and two of their staff members came to work for us, assisting in the transfer of all clients and employees to our company. Steve Durko, Joe and Irene's son-in-law and a minority owner of Staff Payroll, joined us as a customer service representative and proved to be a great employee. Unfortunately, within six months of starting with us, Steve suffered a heart attack and passed away. He did such a good job during those months that we created an award in his honor, the "Steve Durko Customer Service Award."

In January 2017, we purchased The Employee Management Team, a Sarasota, Florida PEO owned by a long-time industry friend, Rick Ratner. Many years earlier, Rick and Ed Bongart owned an insurance agency and helped me obtain workers' compensation with Liberty Mutual Insurance. Rick and Ed also owned Modern Employers, Inc., a Sarasota PEO, which they sold in 1999. Rick started the new business, The Employee Management Team, about ten years later.

Before he and his partner sold Modern Employers, Rick and I often attended state and national industry meetings and occasionally enjoyed taking our morning exercise runs together. In 2016, I again met up with him at the annual meeting of NAPEO. While there, Rick approached me to see if my company was interested in purchasing The Employee Management Team. At that point, his new company was about seven years old and had grown to over 400 worksite employees. Rick shared that he was looking to get out of the management side of the business.

To facilitate the negotiation of the purchase, we both agreed to bring in Wanda Silva, the PEO broker who had helped us with every previous purchase except Staff Payroll. After some negotiation and signing a letter of intent, Britt III and Johnathan Taylor performed the due diligence, examining financial records, and traveling to Sarasota and the surrounding area to meet with all clients of The Employee Management Team as well as a key staff member, Melissa Redmon. The deal was closed at the end of the year, and we began operations on January 1, 2017. Melissa agreed to become an employee of LandrumHR and continues today as our client services specialist, working at the Sarasota office location.

I realize that all of our acquisitions through 2018 were for small PEOs and don't compare to the multimillion-dollar stock deals made by larger PEOs and their venture capital owners. My comfort level has always been in buying businesses that were smaller than ours. Going "small" enabled us to assimilate the staff members and clients of the acquired company into our business without a major disruption to our operation or culture. I wanted to control the acquired company, not be controlled by it, as often plays out with larger acquisitions.

Our CFOs, first Andy Remke and later Johnathan Taylor, tracked the acquisitions we made on a quarterly basis, pointing out to me that we were making a much higher return on our investment in purchasing those businesses than we were earning with the money we invested in the stock market. Over the years, the rate of return on our investment (ROI) in the purchase of other PEOs has ranged from a low of 15% to a high of 148%. Considering that the annual earnings on our managed investment of savings was yielding around 5% on average, acquiring companies produced a much higher return on our investment of funds.

With regard to funding the acquisitions, I personally did not want to go into debt even though at least one of our advisors had recommended against using our own money. In discussing this matter with Jonathan Taylor, our CFO since 2011, he reminded me that until 2019, we had made all purchases from cash flow without requiring the use of any of our invested funds.

Those invested funds have built up over the years to a respectable amount as we have left most of the annual earnings in the company. That financial strength has given us the ability to look at acquisitions without fear of taking a major hit if things don't go well.

Having a strong balance sheet has also made us attractive to banks and insurance providers, both of which require considerable collateral when establishing lines of credit or writing risk-sharing insurance policies. Our healthy cash reserves have also provided a cushion to handle unsecured accounts receivable from larger clients of the staffing service, which often delay payment of invoices by as much as two to three months. In essence, we are lending money by the hour and getting paid by the month, and sometimes much longer–a rather unattractive aspect of owning a staffing company. Accounts receivable, especially due from some government entities and large manufacturing companies, often run into the millions.

Buying another PEO is more than just making an investment in order to get a higher return on our money. It's also about getting into new markets, gaining new clients, obtaining qualified staff, and having the opportunity to grow the business over time. It's about achieving economies of scale, eliminating duplicated costs and consolidating resources. We've certainly realized some or all of those benefits with the purchases we've made so far, and I fully expect the company to continue in that direction in the years to come.

Our own employees were not always thrilled when we announced to them that we were buying another PEO business. From their perspective, it meant a tremendous amount of work. It would have been better on the staff if we just purchased the stock of the selling company and allowed their management to continue the operation under new ownership without interruption. We chose not to do that, however, due to the unknown risks that are inherent in a business like ours. We did not want to assume responsibility for prior actions the selling company may have committed (or omitted), such as unknown tax liabilities, potential employee discrimination, lawsuits not yet filed, possible violation of fiduciary obligations on benefit plans, and more. The safer route is to purchase the assets and leave all those unknown problems behind.

In 2019, recognizing the company's need to diversify and expand its HR service offerings geographically, CEO Britt III made the decision to purchase hrQ, an established HR consulting firm based in Denver, Colorado. The company offers interim HR staffing, national HR executive search, and human capital consulting services. With over 35 professionals, six offices, and a nationwide clientele, including many Fortune 500 and Fortune 100 companies, this acquisition is by far the largest our company has made to date, which gives Landrum a physical presence in six additional cities including Denver, Atlanta, Austin, Houston, Dallas, and San Francisco. The acquisition, an asset purchase, offers great promise in that it positions our company to expand our footprint with a larger and more diversified customer base and suite of HR service offerings. With this acquisition, LandrumHR is now operating in 46 states across the country.

Diversification and Market Expansion

It has long been my feeling that HR consulting is an area of need that we are uniquely qualified to fill because of the expertise we have in-house and our reputation as an HR company. Over the years, our HR managers have been asked by one or two employment attorneys to investigate complaints of discrimination made by an employee of their client company. We have also assisted a few companies in writing job descriptions, producing employee handbooks, and performing other HR services, occasionally on monthly retainer for the company. One of our Senior HR managers, Holly McLeod, was especially interested in this area of our business and was asked to devote some of her time to developing it further. She met with some success in her efforts, but the arrangement didn't work very well as she had to divide her time between consulting and taking care of the HR needs of our growing base of PEO clients and worksite employees. Realistically, we didn't put much emphasis on consulting, and it understandably failed to take off as we had hoped it would.

When Ted Kirchharr came to work for the company in 2003, we decided to make a more deliberate attempt to build the consulting side of our business. My expectation at the time was that a formidable consulting practice would further solidify our reputation as the "go to" source for anything relating to employees and employment and would become a viable profit center for the company. My hope also was that these assignments could lead to the development of PEO prospects and clients. Our PEO and Staffing sales staff were incentivized to sell consulting as part of our value proposition, and we did pick up several consulting assignments, including some training and HR On-Call (as-needed HR assistance) business, but again, we were only marginally successful.

In mid-2016, Becki Haines, an experienced HR manager, was placed in charge of the consulting division. With renewed effort and greater focus, the HR team defined the scope of services to be offered, created a standard pricing structure, educated our sales representatives, and developed and implemented a marketing plan. As a result, consulting has become an integral part of our business.

Our current offering of consulting services focuses mostly on the compliance side of human resources and includes HR and risk management assessments, HR On-Call, workplace investigations, salary surveys, the creation of employee handbooks, and training and enrichment workshops. Becki reported to me that the workshops are in highest demand, and Supervisor Boot Camp is the most popular of our training offerings. A two-year leadership program is offered with training done on a quarterly basis. The coursework includes the basics of labor law and progresses to competencies in areas such as empowerment, accountability, and emotional intelligence. HR managers (now called HR partners) manage a book of business for the PEO and also execute consulting work as assigned.

The combination of services provided by the PEO HR team, which is focused primarily on compliance and supervisory training, and the organizational development, HR executive search and interim HR staffing services provided by the staff of our newly acquired hrQ division mentioned earlier, provides new marketing opportunities for the company. These services also expand our geographical reach. As a result, the consulting division of LandrumHR is now a significant contributor to the company's bottom line.

The European Connection

While attending the annual NAPEO convention in May 2012, some of our SLT members and I listened to a presentation by Mark de Vries, owner of a business development company, EuroDev, with offices in Almelo, the Netherlands, and in Paris, France. Mark was looking to establish cooperative relationships with a few PEOs in the U.S. He explained that his firm assists more than 150 U.S. companies in establishing a market presence in European countries.

The firm offers sales and HR outsourcing, digital marketing, and mergers and acquisitions (M&A) consulting. Mark and his team research and identify markets, register the business entity, provide office and warehouse space, recruit and hire staff, and pay the employees on behalf of their clients.

Mark explained that the laws in many European countries are very stringent regarding obligations to employees, and businesses not familiar with those laws can unknowingly obligate themselves to pay employees for a lot longer than they intend. The prospect of a market presence in Europe sounded intriguing to us. We had worked with at least two client companies that were foreign-owned, and we knew that our knowledge of U.S. laws and regulations was a great help to them, so it made sense that the reverse would hold true as well. We invited Mark and a member of his leadership team to Pensacola for a visit.

Mark's idea was to create a branch office for our company in his headquarters building in Almelo. Essentially, his plan called for us to have a separate telephone number that would be answered by his receptionist with the name of our company. We would have a sign on their office wall showing that we were indeed located there, and our website would advertise the location–all at no cost to us. All we had to do was refer business, and we would share the fees paid by our mutual client. The plan sounded interesting, and we decided to pursue it.

On September 9, 2012, Britt III, Ted Kirchharr and I, accompanied by my wife, Nell, and Britt's wife, Keena, flew to Amsterdam. We took the train to Almelo to meet with Mark and his staff to get a first-hand look at his operation. It was everything he had represented. His staff of about thirty people was professional and gracious to us. Every consultant spoke two or three languages and had a connection to the countries in which their clients needed representation. It was an impressive operation. While we were there, we met with one of Mark's clients whose office was temporarily in the EuroDev building. He had nothing but good things to say about the service he and his company had received from the firm.

Later that month, we held a press conference in downtown Pensacola, announcing the establishment of a strategic alliance with EuroDev and the office of Landrum Europe in the Netherlands. To those in attendance, I explained our connection with EuroDev and introduced Mark de Vries as the Senior Advisor for Business Development for Landrum Europe.

Mark made a few remarks of his own, after which Pensacola Mayor Ashton Hayward and Chamber President Sandy Sansing spoke briefly, saying good things about our company. It was a proud moment for us.

In the following months and years, we had fairly frequent contact with Mark and his staff. Our sales staff tried to drum up business by encouraging a few prospects to take advantage of our European connection but to no avail. Over the years, there may have been one or two companies that made contact with Mark to explore the possibilities, but to my knowledge we have never landed a single client.

In spite of the failure of this venture to produce new business for our company, there were some tangible benefits. We got a good bit of positive publicity. We met some very nice people, and we learned a lot about business in Europe. And, if we ever come across a manufacturer or service company that wants to expand to Europe, we still have the connection and friends across the ocean who can help.

CHAPTER 10

Powerful Influences

—◆◇◆—

Liberty Mutual

IN **THE LATE 80's,** I met Ed Bongart and Rick Ratner who were partners in an employee leasing company and an insurance agency. Ed worked with me initially to obtain workers' compensation coverage for AmStaff through an established self-insurance fund. After a few years of working together, Ed learned that Liberty Mutual Insurance was looking at writing coverage for a select few employee leasing companies, and he thought we might qualify. By that time, we had established a well-run safety program and were paying many of the smaller claims directly. We also incentivized some of our clients to do more to prevent accidents in order to keep their claims low. These efforts caused our mod factor to drop to near or below 1.0, making us more attractive to quality carriers.

Ed explained to me that Liberty Mutual had its own sales staff and did not work through or pay commissions to agents. At that point, he put me in touch with Ralph Barnes, a sales representative for Liberty, who subsequently agreed to write the coverage for AmStaff and Landrum Staffing. I was elated and gladly paid a fee to Ed's agency for his introduction.

My relationship with Ralph Barnes lasted until his retirement about twenty-five years later. He was instrumental in assisting us with negotiations each year as we renewed our policy. The policies written for us went from being fully to partially insured with as much as a one-million-dollar annual deductible. That meant that we had to pay the first one million dollars of all claims in each policy year.

Incurred claims refer to the estimated future cost before the claim is closed. Over the years, our accumulated incurred claims, i.e., "the tail," had to be booked as reserves. That obligation stays with the company until the claim is closed, and even then, it can be reopened under certain circumstances. We used the actuarial firm, Willis Towers Watson, to properly determine the estimated amount of reserves to book as a liability on our balance sheet.

While I was serving on the Florida Board of Employee Leasing Companies, I saw a number of instances where other PEOs that had large deductible plans like ours, didn't use an actuary and significantly understated their reserves. With larger PEOs, those obligations can amount to several million dollars, so it's important to be accurate. In some of those cases when the Florida Board of Employee Leasing Companies forced them to apply the correct reserve amount, it resulted in the company not having a positive net worth, which is a violation of the Employee Leasing licensure law.

Being a Liberty Mutual customer had a fun side for me personally. Because of our strong reputation in the PEO industry, our track record as an insured customer, and my long-standing relationship with Ralph Barnes, I was invited to attend annual golf weekends in San Juan, Puerto Rico with many other customers and some of the top sales executives with Liberty. Chi Chi Rodriquez, a famous pro-golfer at the time, was a spokesman for Liberty Mutual and put on a golf clinic for attendees each year. He and his wife also hosted a dinner party in their home, and we got to enjoy their hospitality.

Liberty also sponsored the Legends of Golf Tournament, a Senior PGA event held annually in Savannah, Georgia. This was a grand affair lasting four days, with fine dining and outstanding entertainers. Nell and I enjoyed ourselves immensely at these events. For about ten years, I was invited to play in the Pro-Am event that preceded the tournament each year.

The first time I played in the Pro-Am in 2003 was a bit nerve-racking. The pro who was assigned to play with our foursome was Graham Marsh, an extremely personable guy. Up until the 15th hole, I had played miserably and embarrassed myself with poor shots more often than not. On the 15th, however, I managed to hit the ball perfectly and make a hole-in-one. One of the spectators asked for my autograph, and I was recognized as a hero in the clubhouse! Arnold Palmer and Fuzzy Zoeller were there, and Arnold asked me how I did it. I was more than a little intimidated at being in the presence of two of golf's greatest players and said something like, "I really didn't see the ball go in the hole."

That was only half of the truth. The fact of the matter was that I was so embarrassed about the way I played that I kept my head down after the shot–exactly what you're supposed to do. I didn't know it went in the hole until the spectators and my partners began shouting. A few years later, I had the opportunity to play in a foursome with Ed Kelly, then the Chairman and CEO of Liberty Mutual. I wasn't so intimidated by then.

Through Ralph Barnes, I was also introduced and got to know several of the managers and officers of Liberty Mutual. Those relationships were especially important to our company in maintaining workers' compensation insurance coverage during "tight" market conditions. In 2002, I was invited to serve on the Florida Advisory Board for Liberty Mutual. This was an outstanding opportunity to gain further contacts with Liberty executives and solidify our relationship with the company. That relationship became even more important as the workers' compensation market began to harden, and carriers stopped writing coverage for PEOs. A very large insurance company announced that it was terminating coverage on all PEO policies. Many PEOs were impacted and scrambled to find coverage. Thankfully, we were spared that experience. I have to believe that my relationship with Liberty Mutual's management had a little to do with our ability to retain coverage uninterrupted.

Presentation to Britt Landrum, Jr. by George Townsend, VP of Liberty Mutual Insurance, recognizing LandrumHR for 25 years of customer loyalty - 2011

Baptist Health Care

In 1993, I was invited to join the board of directors of Baptist Health Ventures, a subsidiary of Baptist Health Care (BHC). BHC was in the process of buying physician practices, and the Ventures Board was tasked with oversight of that process. As one of the largest nonprofit hospitals in northwest Florida, the Baptist organization had roughly 5,000 employees. I was honored to be asked to serve on one of its boards.

In 1998, Al Stubblefield, who had become CEO of BHC following the retirement of Jim Vickery, asked me to serve on the board of directors of Lakeview Center, a community mental health organization that was also a subsidiary of BHC. Lakeview was about to lose its long-time CEO and founder, Dr. Morris Eaddy, who was retiring, and I was asked to assist in the selection and later with the transition of the new CEO, Gary Bembry. I served three years as vice chairman of the Lakeview board and eleven years as chairman before leaving that board in 2016. During that time, I became well acquainted with Allison Hill, then CFO of Lakeview. Allison became CEO after Gary's retirement in 2017. In 2019, she was appointed by Britt III to serve on the Landrum Advisory Board.

In 1999, I became a member of the Baptist Health Care board, the governing board of the organization, and served at various times as an officer through the level of vice chairman. I also served on various committees that gave me insight as to the strategies used by such larger organizations in managing the business and human capital side of their operation. I chaired the HR Committee for many years and listened to reports and discussions regarding the organization's efforts to control employee health care costs and workers' compensation claims and costs, and to provide competitive employee salaries and benefits.

I mention all of the above because what I learned at Baptist had a profound impact on the way I chose to run my company. Prior to my joining the Ventures board, the hospital system was struggling with low patient satisfaction levels and low morale amongst its employees. It was also losing market share to two other hospitals in the area. As COO and later CEO, Al Stubblefield became convinced that the problems the hospital was facing could be solved by a dramatic improvement in the quality of services being offered. He announced to the board and his leadership team a new commitment to quality and service excellence.

When I joined the board, Quint Studer, founder of the Studer Group, and now a successful business owner, management consultant, real estate developer and philanthropist, was president of Baptist Hospital. Al had hired Quint to implement the organization's plan and to make good on the commitment to improve quality and increase patient satisfaction. Quint's focus on employee satisfaction as a way to improve patient satisfaction really got my attention. The story is best told by Al Stubblefield in his book, *The Baptist Health Care Journey to Excellence: Creating a Culture that WOWs!*

During that time, Baptist was also designated by *Fortune Magazine* as one of America's 100 Best Places to Work. In addition, the entire Baptist organization was working through a process to qualify for the Malcolm Baldrige Quality Award, the nation's highest award for organizational excellence. I saw the commitment made by the senior leadership in setting goals and making sure the staff was fully aligned with those goals so the hospital could perform to the best of its potential. It was a proud day for the staff and the board members when the announcement was made that the organization had won the Baldrige Award.

All of those experiences, especially the insights gleaned when Baptist applied for and earned the Baldrige Award, made a powerful impression on me. I had a passion to make my company the very best in the area of human resource services and felt that we could benefit from going through a similar quality improvement program. It didn't happen right away, but a few years later, our company went through a period of self-examination and correction using guidelines provided by Florida's equivalent to the Baldrige program, the Florida Governor's Sterling Award for Organizational Excellence. Our company was the proud recipient of that award in 2007.

I was also impressed with the hospital's annual budgeting and planning processes, its management of investments, and the extensive financial reporting provided by Baptist's CFO, Andy Remke. Andy was the CFO when I first joined the Baptist board. He took early retirement from Baptist, and after a year or so, he came to work for my company and brought many of the ideas and strategies used at Baptist.

Baptist Health Care, like many other large health care organizations, regularly borrowed large sums of money, using complex financing methods to create liquidity or to purchase the expensive equipment that was needed for patient care. Interest rates on bank loans, bond issues, agency ratings, and such strategies as credit default swaps were part of our regular discussions at board meetings. At that point, my company had always paid cash for what it needed and had very little debt, so I had limited knowledge in that area of finance and welcomed the opportunity to learn more about those creative financing strategies. Such knowledge, I believe, helped me to become a more astute manager of our company's finances.

Employer Services Assurance Corporation

Another organization that had a significant impact on my business knowledge and played a role in my quest to make my company the best it could be was ESAC. In the mid-90's, NAPEO was seeking a way to provide a higher level of membership, one that differentiated members that operated in a more professional manner from others. As I recall, Rex Eley and Carlos Saladrigas were two of the leaders in NAPEO who led that movement.

NAPEO's efforts resulted in the creation of the Institute for Accreditation of Professional Employer Organizations (IAPEO), an independent body that formulated operational and accounting rules and standards to which members were required to adhere. Members then had to submit to more stringent auditing of their companies' financial records and attest to certain required behaviors. Because there were only a few members at first, the price of admission was relatively high, but because I wanted our company to be viewed as one of the best and I wanted our clients (and prospective clients) to be confident in our financial stability and ethical practices, I paid the price to join–around $30,000 as I recall, which was a considerable investment for my company at the time.

IAPEO changed its name to "Employer Services Assurance Corporation" when it began including bonding provisions in its membership offering. Clients of ESAC members were, and still are, guaranteed to be reimbursed for losses incurred in the event a member defaults on payment of taxes or benefits. There are limits to the guarantee. In the beginning, it was one million dollars. Later the limit increased to ten million. But the fact that we could offer our clients a guarantee differentiated us from our competition.

Shortly after ESAC was launched, I was elected to the board of directors and served from 1997 to 2006, along with several other industry members. The board also included former state and federal regulators, a vice president of NCCI, and a former assistant chief counsel for the IRS. Having outside members with those credentials increased the credibility of the entire organization and enhanced the value of being an accredited member of ESAC.

While a member of the ESAC board, I served on the Strategic Planning committee and met with Rex Eley, Carlos Saladrigas and others to come up with a new mission and vision for the organization. Rex had read a publication from the *Harvard Business Review* entitled, "Building Your Company's Vision." The article was excerpted from the book by Jim Collins and Jerry Porras, *Built to Last: Successful Habits of Visionary Companies*. Referencing the article, our committee focused on determining ESAC's Core Purpose, its Core Values, and on setting a big, hairy, audacious goal ("BHAG"). I don't remember what we came up with, but I do remember the process and deciding to bring that back to my own company's planning sessions.

Federal Reserve Branch Board

Earlier, I mentioned my service on the Federal Reserve board. In 2004, I received a call from Chris Oakley, vice president of the Jacksonville Branch of the Federal Reserve Bank of Atlanta, asking for an appointment with me. Quite honestly, I was very apprehensive about the reason for his visit. He didn't explain why he wanted to see me. I began thinking that it might be because of something that our company had done wrong. At that point in time, we were well into making direct deposits of employee payroll checks, which would have meant that the Jacksonville Branch Bank was clearing thousands of our checks each week. We were also electronically drafting the accounts of our clients in order to be paid our fees. I assumed we must have been doing something wrong with check processing.

When Chris showed up, I had Mike Perkins and Andy Remke in the office with me for the meeting. I reasoned that if there was a legal issue, Mike, as our corporate counsel, could come up with a good explanation. Andy was our CFO at the time, and if the problem was related to bank rules or regulations, I felt he could provide the best answer. Chris quickly set my mind at ease by saying that the reason for his visit was to find out if I might be interested in serving on the board of the bank. I was relieved and told him honestly that I didn't know a great deal about the economy, nor was I that familiar with the rules and regulations of banking. I offered to give him names of friends who I felt would do a much better job. At that point, I think either Andy or Mike gave me a kick under the table.

Chris assured me that the bank had plenty of economic and banking experts on staff, and what he wanted from me was input on what was happening in the business community–how businesses were impacted by changes in the economy. I was still a little stunned that he would ask me but told him I'd give it some thought and let him know. After some discussion with Mike and Andy, I decided to accept, and in January 2005, became a member of the board of directors of the Jacksonville Branch of the Federal Reserve Bank of Atlanta. I served two three-year terms on that board and was twice elected to serve as chairman.

Serving on the Federal Reserve Branch board was one of the most interesting experiences of my career. Early in 2005, I attended an orientation session at the Federal Reserve headquarters in Washington D. C. New branch directors from all over the country were there as well. Alan Greenspan was chairman of the Federal Reserve at the time, and I was privileged to meet him and several Board Governors, including

Ben Bernanke, who would later serve as chairman during the "Great Recession," one of the most turbulent times in our country's economic history. (The COVID-19 pandemic in 2020 may prove to be even worse). New branch board members were assigned to meet with board governors as part of their orientation. I was fortunate to meet with Governor Bernanke, who explained to our group how the Federal Open Market Committee (FOMC) operated and set economic policy for the nation.

When I joined the branch board in 2005, the economy was strong and interest rates were rising. Our board meetings in Jacksonville were held a few weeks in advance of each meeting of the FOMC. Prior to our meeting, each board member was given a series of questions about the economy, and we were asked to gather input from business leaders in our respective parts of the state.

I developed a list of about thirty business leaders in northwest Florida who were most willing to share information about their sales, costs, pricing, plans to hire or lay off workers, and other economic variables impacting their businesses. I was and am still most appreciative of their openness and willingness to share that private information with me. After receiving their responses, I wrote an extensive report and provided it to the Jacksonville Branch Bank.

Occasionally, something I wrote would wind up in the "Beige Book," a book used by the president of the Federal Reserve Bank of Atlanta to help him prepare for his upcoming FOMC meeting held in Washington D. C. When questioned about the value of the information provided by the branch directors, Chairman Greenspan explained that, by examining the data, their economists could help them see through the rearview mirror of the economy, and the anecdotal information provided by the branch directors could help them see through the windshield and learn what is happening on the street.

During the six years I served on the Jacksonville Branch Bank board, there were some significant changes in the economy as well as in banking. In January 2005, at the beginning of my first term, the Jacksonville

Branch Bank served as just one of a number of locations in the district that provided check clearing services for member banks. On my tour of the branch, I saw a large room with sophisticated equipment and many employees performing some portion of that operation. The bank had just consolidated processing items from another office, an effort designed to reflect changing use of check payments by consumers and to improve efficiency. Airplanes flew out of cities each evening to deliver checks to be cleared. Trucks arrived each night with the same cargo. The branch was processing millions of checks every day. When I left the bank in December 2010, those machines and many of the employees were gone, replaced by digital imaging and electronic banking. This happened all over the country, and the clearing function for physical checks was ultimately consolidated to just one bank.

The other significant change during my tenure was the state of the economy. When I joined the Jacksonville Branch Bank board, the economy was humming, and the FOMC was raising interest rates by a quarter of a percent (25 basis points) on a regular basis. From 2008 to 2010 that picture changed dramatically as we all remember too well. In fact, I was surprised when the president of the Federal Reserve Bank of Atlanta, Dennis Lockhart, signaled his intention to recommend a significant lowering of the interest rate. Thankfully, Dennis and others, especially then chairman Ben Bernanke, had the wisdom to try to stimulate spending through lowering rates and by taking other drastic measures to prevent a collapse of the economy. Not everyone agrees with all the steps that were taken during the "Great Recession," but I think they made the right decisions. Overall, I gained tremendous respect for the wisdom and dedication of the staff and leadership in the Federal Reserve System.

I also got to know and respect the other six members of the Jacksonville Branch board. One member, Jack Healan, joined the board and served two terms along with me. At the time, Jack was president of Amelia Island Plantation near Jacksonville. His organization had recently won the Florida Governor's Sterling Award, the state's equivalent of the national Baldrige Award recognizing organizational excellence. When our company won the Sterling Award in 2007, Jack flew down to Orlando to participate in presenting that award to us.

While I was on the Jacksonville Branch board and annually since my term ended, we have invited Atlanta and Jacksonville Bank officers to Pensacola to make presentations to business leaders at our "Breakfast with the Fed" program. In the middle of my term, Dennis Lockhart, then the new President of the Federal Reserve Bank of Atlanta, accepted my invitation to be the featured speaker at our "Breakfast with the Fed" meeting. I learned that he also liked to play golf, and with the help of the staff in Jacksonville, we arranged a round of golf the day before the presentation was to be made. Being the president of the Atlanta Fed, or any Federal Reserve Bank, is a prestigious honor and carries with it a great deal of responsibility. I wanted to make a good impression on Dennis and show him some real hospitality while he was with us.

Unfortunately, on the drive from my home that morning to pick up Dennis at the airport and take him to Pensacola Country Club, I suddenly felt a strange sensation in my right eye and began to lose a portion of my vision. I correctly assumed that the retina was tearing, and I needed to get to the hospital or to my eye doctor right away. I knew this because the same thing had happened to my father many years before. I was more than a little concerned as you can imagine.

Before I turned my car into the parking lot for Sacred Heart Hospital's emergency room, using my cell phone I telephoned Bill Cleary, then vice president of Client Services for our company, and arranged for him to go to the airport to meet Dennis and take him to the country club. Next, I called one of my golf partners, Ed Moore, and arranged for him to meet Dennis at the club, get him signed up, and play a round of golf with him. I then proceeded to explain my eye problem to the receptionist in the emergency room.

To make this long story shorter, I had laser surgery on my eye later that morning. After getting the assurance from the doctor that I didn't need to go home directly and lie on my back for a week, I drove to the golf course and joined Dennis and Ed for the remainder of the round. An interesting day and, thankfully, I still have good sight in my damaged eye!

Dr. David Altig, executive vice president and director of research for the Federal Reserve Bank of Atlanta, has been a frequent speaker at our "Breakfast with the Fed" meetings, as has Chris Oakley, vice president and lead regional executive for the Jacksonville Branch Bank. These events are well attended and enjoyed by our clients and other business leaders in the area. They have also been good for the Federal Reserve Bank in enhancing its Regional Economic Information Network (REIN) program, which was initiated during my service on the Branch Board.

Breakfast with the Fed (L to R) Chris Oakley, Britt Landrum, Jr., Dr. Dave Altig - 2011

Participants in REIN—typically business, community, academic, and nonprofit leaders, provide grassroots information that helps inform the Fed's policy decisions. The bank reaches out on a periodic basis to gather insights from "Main Street" on-demand, regarding the availability of capital, employment, costs, and other economic conditions. This grassroots information is combined with other economic data to provide real-world input to the bank's economists and president. I am proud that LandrumHR continues to be engaged with the Fed as a member of the REIN program.

During my term on the Jacksonville Branch board, Chris Oakley got to know several members of the staff at our company. He was especially interested in hearing from Denise McLeod, who, as head of our staffing division, was keenly aware of what was happening in the job market in our area. That association led to Denise's appointment to the Labor, Education and Health Advisory Council of the Federal Reserve Bank of Atlanta. She was appointed to that council in 2009 and served two three-year terms, which ended in 2014. She continued to consult with them up until her retirement from the company in 2018. Our close association with both the Atlanta District Bank and the Jacksonville Branch of the Federal Reserve Bank of Atlanta led to the recent appointment of Denise's replacement, Mandy Sacco, to the Human Capital Advisory board of the Atlanta Bank.

CHAPTER 11

Corporate Culture

———————————◆━◇━◆━———————————

Strategic Planning and Core Ideology

O VER THE COURSE OF THE LAST FORTY YEARS or so, our company has held a number of strategic planning sessions. In the beginning, I convened senior staff members, directed the meetings, and presented my vision and plans for the next year or two. They were effective, but after a few years, we recognized the need for more strategic thinking, and engaged a trained facilitator.

The first facilitated meeting, held in 1994, was led by Dr. T. Joe Willey. "T. Joe" was a medical school professor, who just happened to get interested in the employee leasing field. Not only did he start a leasing business, he created the human resources information and payroll system ("PayPlus") that was used by our company and more than eighty others across the country. T. Joe also wrote several books about the employee leasing business and trained others in both operations and sales.

T. Joe came to Pensacola to install updates to our new PayPlus system and stayed over a day or two to facilitate our planning session. I don't recall any specific plans that we made from that session, but having an outside facilitator for those meetings proved to be more productive than conducting them on our own. In 1997 and 1998, we engaged Evon Emerson, a local executive coach and training consultant, to facilitate those sessions for us.

Not long after my experience with the ESAC planning committee in 1998, I picked up a copy of *Built to Last: Successful Habits of Visionary Companies*. The book was written by Jim Collins and Jerry Porras, and studied the best of the best corporations in the country, looking at the common characteristics of those companies that had "made it." The authors essentially found that the best, most enduring corporations had a "Core Ideology," a belief system that those companies placed ahead of profit. The book truly inspired me, and I tried to absorb every concept presented as I read it.

A few weeks later, while waiting for my wife to do some shopping during a brief trip to Dahlonega, Georgia, I sat in the backseat of our car and wrote down what I thought was "our" Core Ideology: "our" Core Values, "our" Core Purpose, and "our" Big, Hairy, Audacious Goal. I use the word "our" in quotes, because what I wrote was actually my Core Ideology, not one that our team created together. I was passionate about what I wrote and was hopeful that I could get everyone to embrace my ideas when I presented them to my leadership team.

CORE VALUES (our guiding principles)

Respect for the dignity and worth of every person

Absolute fairness with employees and clients

Highest quality service

Reputation for excellence

Passion for progress and improvement

Responsible behavior

CORE PURPOSE (our most fundamental reason for existence)

Landrum Staffing Services – to be the most reliable source for people to find meaningful work and for companies to find the best employees.

AmStaff Human Resources – to contribute to our client companies' success by helping them manage human resources.

I gave considerable thought to each one of the statements or tenets in my Core Values section. I listed **respect for people** first because of its importance to me. It has always been repugnant to me when one person treats another as less important than himself or herself. I had heard too many stories from applicants who came to our company saying that they had been brushed off or treated indifferently by the staff of a competitor. I never wanted that to be said by anyone who called or came in to see us about a job or anything else. People dressed in work clothes were to be treated the same as someone in business attire, and they were made to feel as important. Over the years, we received many compliments from people about how well they were treated by our staff. That indeed made me very proud.

The statement about **absolute fairness** is again about the way we interact with people. That included people who came to us looking for a job, a business owner looking for an employee, or an employer/client depending on us for service or advice. I wanted to make it clear to the staff that they could always depend on our company to do the right thing, being fair to all parties, and that is what we expected of them as well.

Striving to provide the **highest quality service** to our clients, applicants, and employees is a mindset that I wanted our staff members to have. Achieving that level of service and earning a **reputation for excellence** was and still is extremely important to me and to our leadership as well.

In order to keep getting better as a company, whether improving processes, procedures, or delivery systems, folks who are driving the effort have to be passionate about doing everything they do a little better. I wanted that *passion* to be in the DNA of our leadership and staff members.

The last tenet in my list of Core Values was **responsible behavior**. The people who come to our company place a tremendous amount of trust that we will not only be fair and honest, but we will also be capable of delivering on all of our promises. Business owners entrust us with millions of dollars with which we are to pay their employees' salaries, taxes, benefit premiums, and retirement contributions. They trust us to give them expert advice on all matters relating to their employees and to fulfill all responsibilities on their behalf with local, state, and federal taxing authorities. We not only have to know what to do and how to do it, but we have to deliver because we run our company in a financially responsible manner. Not only did I want our clients to feel this level of confidence in our company, but I wanted this to be a guide for the behavior of our staff members as well.

Prior to our 1999 planning session, I wrote this memo to my executive team regarding strategic planning.

A NEW LOOK AT VISION AND MISSION FOR LANDRUM/AMSTAFF

A couple of weeks ago our company directors held a meeting with Evon Emerson (our facilitator) to discuss our next strategic planning session. We spent time revisiting our vision and mission statements and made some preliminary plans for the meeting. We have scheduled that meeting for Friday morning, January 9th, and most of the next day, Saturday, January 10th.

Prior to that meeting, I'd like for you to do a little homework. I have attached a copy of a publication from Harvard Business Review called, "Building Your Company's Vision." I would like for you to read this document very carefully before our planning session. I was introduced to the publication earlier this year when I participated in a strategic planning session with a few other board members of the Institute for the Accreditation of Professional Employer Organizations (IAPEO), now ESAC.

The method of looking at mission and vision is from a management book written by James C. Collins and Jerry I. Porras, both professors of management at major universities. They studied successful companies for six years, and found that their common thread was a clear and well-articulated vision that was understood and accepted by company employees. Their book is entitled, Built to Last: Successful Habits of Visionary Companies.

I've never quite been happy with the vision statement we developed a couple of years ago. My guess is that if we had a test to see how many employees could recite that vision statement, a very high percentage would fail. I want to change that. Not by making employees memorize something, but by making them feel something. And then act on it.

The process outlined in the publication will give us a framework within which to consider and restate our vision, and to set goals for the next few years. As plans for the meeting progress, you will be informed about meeting places and times. I hope the article will inspire you as it did me.

My executive team, consisting of Mike Perkins, Britt Landrum III, Andy Remke, and Denise McLeod, did accept and endorse the Core Ideology I had written. Over the next few months, this information was presented and discussed with the department heads and other leaders within the company and eventually to every employee.

I was also inspired by another book written by Jim Collins, one of the authors of *Built to Last. Good to Great: Why Some Companies Make the Leap...and Others Don't* compared a number of companies that were once great but had ceased to exist while their competitors had thrived. The points made in the book were meaningful to me, and I made them the subject of our planning session in 2003.

At that 2003 meeting, I presented another book that inspired me even more. *The Servant: A Simple Story About the True Essence of Leadership,* written by James C. Hunter, describes leadership styles and why leading with authority granted to the leader by those who are being led, is far more effective than leading with power. Essentially, the servant leader builds trust over time by taking a sincere interest in the employees and providing for their needs. Hunter referred to this as "agape" love. I guess the reason the book resonated with me is because it gives credence to my own style of leadership. I focused on my employees as much as I could, trying to show them respect and appreciation and allowing them a lot of latitude in decision-making. They knew that I trusted them, and as a consequence, they trusted me. I urged our leadership team to study and adopt the concept of leadership presented in the book.

In the early 2000's, our executive team developed and adopted Five Foundations for our future. It was no coincidence that our Five Foundations pretty much followed the Pillars of Excellence that were adopted by Baptist Health Care a few years before. I was impressed with the way Al Stubblefield, the CEO of Baptist Health Care at the time, led his organization utilizing their Pillars of Excellence. Departmental and management performance was measured against the achievement of goals within the Pillars.

We adopted as our Five Foundations: Best People, Best Service, Highest Quality, Strategic Growth, and Strong Financial Performance. We developed goals under each one and worked diligently to achieve them. In our 2003 planning session, I referred to these Foundations from which I had derived my own goals for the company. Essentially, I narrowed them down to three "Big, Hairy, Audacious Goals." I wanted our employees to feel that our company was the best one that they had ever worked for; I wanted our employees to provide the very best service they could for our clients; and I wanted to make a reasonable profit.

Several years ago, I drafted an "Ethical Statement" or business philosophy for our company, expanding on those goals and stating the principles that I believed were essential to our continued growth, success, and profitability.

ETHICAL STATEMENT / BUSINESS PHILOSOPHY - 2005

After thirty-five years in business, I have arrived at what I believe to be the key to success for most any service-oriented company. This "key" has formed the basis of my philosophy and has resulted in personal goals that guide me in my decision-making.

*The first goal is to **make our company the best place our employees have ever worked**. I want our employees to feel that they are treated fairly and with respect; are compensated adequately; have input into the direction and operation of the company; have opportunities to progress in their jobs; are appreciated for their contributions; and rewarded for their performance.*

I want our employees to have a pleasant, well-equipped, comfortable place to work. I want them to be proud of our company's reputation, and to enjoy and to respect the relationships they have with their fellow employees. It is important that they look forward to coming to work, and develop over time that sense of acceptance and belonging that is present (or should be) in a family. I want employees to feel a sense of ownership and responsibility for the performance of the company.

To make sure that we are achieving the desired level of employee job satisfaction, we will periodically take employee satisfaction surveys. Any areas of weakness or dissatisfaction will be aggressively addressed so that a measurable improvement can be attained.

Additionally, we will begin participating in the "Best Places to Work" program so that there will be an objective measurement of employee satisfaction by an outside entity.

Creating an atmosphere and a culture that enables employees to enjoy where, with whom, and for whom they work is important and sufficient reward for doing all those things necessary to achieve the goal. Certainly, it is the key to keeping employee morale at a high level. The result will be extremely low turnover, which in turn will translate into lower training costs, longer-term client relationships, and consistent levels of service delivery to clients. Being known as **the best place to work** also means that we will always be in the best position to recruit the best employees.

To put it briefly, happy employees are much more likely to make clients happy. The result will be better service to our clients and greater client loyalty. Maintaining this type of reputation will also assist us in making sales. Happy clients tell their friends and associates about their experiences. More client referrals are the result.

My second goal for our company is similar to and very dependent on the first. I want our company to **provide the best service of its kind in America**. That means that employees must have a thorough understanding of the services provided, their particular jobs, and the overall mission of the organization.

Employees should have a **passion for progress and improvement** as stated in our list of Core Values. There must be a constant effort to examine all of our processes and procedures, looking to make them more effective, error-free, and client-friendly. We must constantly be on the lookout for additional value that we can bring to our clients.

We must remain aware of and timely take advantage of all advancements in technology and systems that improve the efficiency and effectiveness of our service.

In order to be the best, we have to have employees who are the best in their fields. That means they have to be oriented, trained, and tested. Payroll specialists need to work toward becoming certified payroll professionals. Human resources managers need to work toward earning their Senior Professional or Professional in Human Resources designation. Benefit administrators should

work toward becoming Certified Employee Benefit Specialists; risk
managers should be certified in that field, and so on.

To achieve the level of quality necessary to be known as best
in class, we have chosen to adopt the criteria and work toward
achieving Florida's highest award for organizational excellence–the
Sterling Award. The criteria and award are patterned after the
Malcolm Baldrige Award, the nation's highest award for quality. It is
my goal for Landrum Human Resource Companies, Inc., to be the
first in our industry to achieve that award. This will take enormous
effort and determination, but the reward will be improvement in all
of our systems, procedures, and outcomes, which translates into
the highest level of service to our clients.

That leads me into the discussion of my final goal for our company:
earning a reasonable profit. If our clients enjoy their relationships
with our staff members and they receive consistent high-quality,
high-value service, they will tell their business friends and
associates. Some of them will become "raving fans" of ours and will
be happy to tell our prospects good things about us. That will make
it easier to sell the concept of outsourcing, and will make the job of
convincing prospects to choose our company over a competitor's
much easier.

The adopted Core Purpose of our company is to **help our clients
become more successful**. We do this by providing them with
expert care of their most important asset, their human capital. To
the extent we can accomplish that purpose, our own success will be
realized.

Pursuing Excellence

In 2003, on the recommendation of our COO and General Counsel,
Mike Perkins, we hired Ted Kirchharr, a man who had a great background
and strong interest in organizational development. Ted's initial title was
director of strategic initiatives. We weren't quite sure what that meant at

the time and gave him no written job description. However, we asked him to assist in taking our company to a higher level as an organization. He asked me about my goals for the company and I repeated what I considered key: (1) become the best place to work, (2) deliver world class service for our clients, and (3) earn a reasonable profit for the company. Over the next few years, his focus was in helping us achieve those goals in a meaningful way.

One of Ted's first actions in getting to know the staff better was to establish a book club. For quite a number of months, twenty or more staff members, including some department heads, voluntarily met during lunch to review several books. Some books were on management while others were on subjects of common interest to the group. Employees took turns reading and outlining the chapters in the book, so those who hadn't read the chapters being reviewed that day could still participate in the discussion. It was a great learning experience as well as an opportunity to get to know and interact with staff members from all departments in the company. It also was a morale-builder for those who attended.

Another initiative that proved to be popular was the establishment of a running club. Actually, it was for both walkers and runners. After work, we would gather in the parking lot outside the office and walk or run on the service road near our building. After several weeks, we participated in the first of several local 5k races. There were about twenty of us who donned our company shirts and ran or walked the first race together. This, too, was a great opportunity for employee interaction and a boost to morale.

Over the years, our company has taken the initiative to sponsor speakers who present subjects of interest to the employees. They cover the gamut from healthy eating, financial investment strategies, stress relief, to personal protection or defense, and more. During the "Great Recession" in 2008, we sponsored the Dave Ramsey "Financial Peace" program. It was well attended, and some employees mentioned to me a few years later that they had gotten out of debt as a result of what they had learned. The programs were all voluntary, and most were presented during working hours or over lunch.

On their own, employees have used the building after hours for yoga classes, exercise classes, and Weight Watchers meetings. This still goes on today. We provide the space, but the initiative to start and continue these programs comes from the employees themselves.

For a number of years our company has encouraged the employees to take good care of their health. We have done this primarily for their own good, but also because healthier employees are happier, can better focus on their work, see a doctor less often, and make fewer claims on our company health insurance plans.

For many years, we have arranged for nurses from Baptist Health Care to come to our office and administer free flu shots to our employees. We can't convince everyone to have the shot, but a large percentage take advantage of it each year. Our health-oriented plan extends to include classes on healthy living and screening for high blood pressure, high cholesterol, and other health assessments. Individual counseling for those with health concerns is also offered. All services are voluntary and paid for by the company.

The company has also paid for smoking cessation classes, sponsors Red Cross CPR training, and purchased automatic electronic defibrillators to be placed at strategic locations in the building. Again, this is done for the purpose of saving lives, but such measures also send a message to employees that we are genuinely concerned about their health and safety.

On their own initiative, a few of our employees started a Toastmasters Club in the company. When I asked her about this, Lois Johnson, one of the founders, wrote the following:

> *Lorena Peterson (a long-term employee at Landrum) had been going to Toastmasters Cordova at Trinity Presbyterian Church. That made her late to work on Friday mornings, so she and I got into a discussion about starting a chapter here at Landrum. The*

idea was presented, and you were kind enough to see the value in this program and agreed to let us start Landrum Companies Toastmasters in April 2004.

We opened our club to all Landrum employees and had several clients participate as well.

Landrum Toastmasters had participation in all levels of speaking competitions in both Humorous Speaking and Table Topics.

Landrum Toastmasters was proud to sponsor several new clubs in the area including Toastmasters at Navy Federal and Navarre Toastmasters. We were coaches for several clubs in the area as well—Monday Night Toastmasters, Ellyson Park Toastmasters, and Spirited Speakers.

Dawn Danforth, Kevin Holcombe and I all served as club presidents, area governors and division governors, moving up the Toastmaster corporate ladder, which was quite a coup for our club. Landrum Companies Toastmasters was a very well-known and well-respected club at the District level.

Due to the time constraints and the level of everyone's workload, Landrum Toastmasters disbanded in October 2016.

We had a great run. Thanks so much for allowing us to do this.

During one or more of my presentations at general staff meetings, I called out the Toastmasters members, suggesting they made me a little nervous as I knew they were counting my use of "um's" and "ah's." In truth, I am extremely proud of their accomplishments and the desire of the participating staff members who chose to better themselves in this way.

Employee Satisfaction and Engagement

Earlier I mentioned that one of my main goals throughout these fifty years in business has been to make sure our employees enjoy working for our company. Actually, I have always wanted them to feel that our company is the best one they have ever worked for. Our first attempts at measuring employee satisfaction are described in this excerpt from our 2006 Sterling Award application.

EXCERPT FROM 2006 STERLING AWARD APPLICATION

To help measure their degree of satisfaction, our company began surveying employees in the year 2000. We were pleased with many of the results of that survey, and took seriously the areas our employees identified that needed improvement. A series of small group meetings with the employees was held to make sure we understood the issues. We then set about to develop a plan for both immediate and long-term improvements in the areas of most interest to our employees.

We focused on the areas of communication, working conditions, and professional development/advancement. We immediately instituted a paid time-off program that improved and replaced our vacation/sick leave plan. We pledged to improve our response time to correct technical issues faced by the employees, and added a staff member in IT to support that pledge. To give employees an opportunity to advance to higher level positions within the company, we began posting internal job opportunities on our Intranet. We also increased reimbursement amounts for company travel. We received very positive feedback on these immediate action steps.

Committees of employees were formed to assist us in developing our longer-term plans. As a result, we developed an employee recognition program we called, "Kudo's," to give employees an opportunity to recognize their fellow staff members. When clients complimented one or more of our employees, we began highlighting their remarks on our Intranet, and we began a formal Employee of the Month recognition program.

We also looked closely at our professional development program and focused on four major areas. First, each employee needed to develop his or her computer skills. Our company offers training in personal productivity products such as Excel, Word and PowerPoint, in addition to training on the software specific to our industry. Employees may also choose self-study on a technology issue important to them. Our second area of emphasis is personal development. We offer training that addresses such issues as stress management and personal finance as well as health and wellness programs.

Serving our customers is a strong part of our company's values, and our employees added training opportunities in the field of "customer service excellence" as the third element of our professional development program. Courses in dealing with difficult people and service recovery are examples of courses in this field of study. Finally, a business-related component was identified to assist our employees in learning to be better communicators, better managers of time, and to develop other related skills to assist them in their work.

Our employee suggestion program was redesigned to encourage employees to share their ideas for improvement with us–we called this our "Bright Ideas" program. We began sharing employee birthdays and anniversaries with the company through the Intranet as well as encouraging department celebrations on important occasions. We revamped our employee appraisal process to place greater emphasis on employee development and to provide more meaningful feedback to employees regarding their performance.

A second Employee Satisfaction Survey was taken in 2002, which showed a significant percentage improvement (from the high 80's to the high 90's) in employee responses about their pride in the company, their willingness to recommend our company to others as a good place to work, and about their decision to work for our company.

In 2004, we learned about a new "Great Place to Work" initiative. Previously, this program had targeted much larger companies with thousands of employees, notably those among *Fortune* magazine's Fortune 100. The new program, sponsored by the Society for Human Resource Management (SHRM), was designed to honor small and medium-sized businesses that could qualify. We recognized that participation in this national survey could offer benchmarking and might help us better assess employee satisfaction levels and identify priorities for improving the work environment, so we enrolled in the program. The employees were excited about participating in the survey, and later that year, a very high percentage of them took the time to answer the questions.

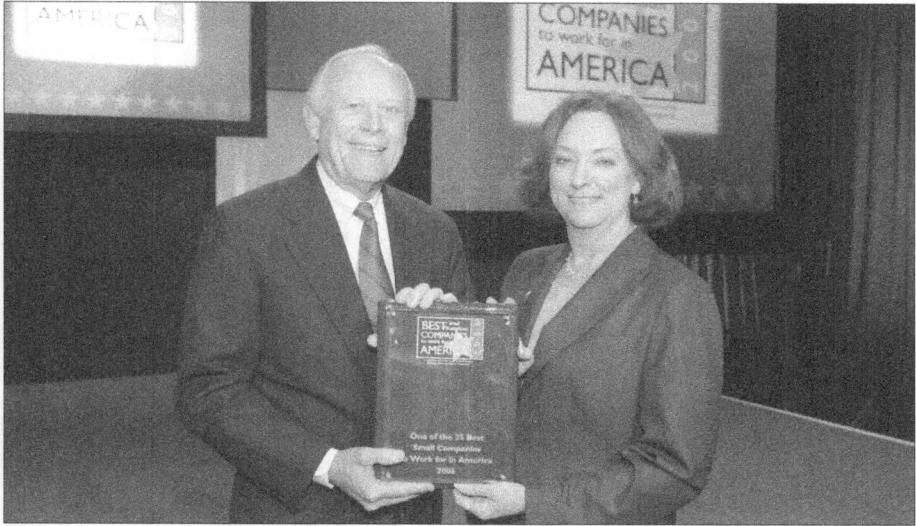

Presentation of award accepted by Britt Landrum, Jr. on behalf of his company as one of the '25 Best Small Companies to Work for in America' - 2006

In 2005, to our surprise and delight, our company received notification that we had been chosen as one of the Top 25 Best Small Companies to Work for in America! We were invited to attend SHRM's national conference in San Diego, California, where the winners and their rankings would be announced. I was on stage with the other winners, looking out at more than two thousand attendees, including several of our employees who made the trip when SHRM announced that we were ranked tenth out of the group of twenty-five! It was a proud day for all of us.

LandrumHR staff members attending the
'Great Places to Work Award' ceremony - 2008

We continued to survey our employees and participate in the Best Places to Work program for the next four years, winning the award each year by ranking in the top twenty-five. We also continued to make improvements in areas that our employees ranked lower than the benchmarks, or lower than the averages of the other participants in the program. The SHRM organization eventually ceased to sponsor the Best Places to Work program, and we decided to take a break from the surveys as well.

About that same time, experts were pointing out that employee satisfaction was only part of the ingredient for achieving success. Employee "engagement" was of equal if not greater importance. The book, *Hundred Percenters* by Mark Murphy, caught the attention of Denise McLeod, head of our staffing division. The book references the author's company, Leadership IQ, and how *Hundred Percenters* aspire to achieve the extraordinary, and they give 100% in striving to achieve greatness. Denise convinced our leadership team to invite Mark Murphy to our office to consult with and train our department heads. He did an outstanding job, and our department managers learned a great deal from him. He conducted an Employee Engagement Survey of our employees and was taken by the result, which showed that a very high percentage of our employees were fully engaged in their work and in our company.

A Culture of Compassion

One of the best indicators of the kind of culture present in the workplace is how employees treat each other and how they care for each other in times of need. Signs of personal compassion and caring have been expressed in many ways throughout our history.

I have always been impressed when our staff members, without hesitation, prepare and deliver meals to fellow employees who are sick or grieving over the loss of a loved one. Often, they take up a collection among themselves in order to provide for someone in an emergency situation. To make this easier, we created a company relief fund. Employees are offered the opportunity to contribute a little from each paycheck through payroll deduction, which is placed in the fund. A committee of employees makes the decision as to how the money is distributed when the needs arise.

As mentioned earlier, in the late 90's I became involved with the 90 & 9 Boys Ranch in Cantonment (local folks know this is a small community just north of Pensacola). The Ranch housed about twenty boys who had been abandoned by their parents or removed from their homes for one reason or another. I learned very quickly that those boys were in tremendous need of shoes, clothing, school supplies, and more. When I shared this news with our staff members, they were quick to offer their help. Many of them joined me in sharing a meal with the boys at the Ranch and providing presents at Christmas. Several of our staff members also participated in shopping sprees at Gayfer's Department Store (now Dillard's) in Pensacola, buying the boys clothing and shoes for school. Mike Perkins, who later became vice president and COO of our company, was on the Ranch board even before I joined and served with me for the duration of my term. He opened his home to some of the boys on occasion to share a meal with his family and provide them a positive influence away from the Ranch.

In prior years, our staff held Christmas parties and shared gifts with each other. When we became involved with the 90 & 9 Boys Ranch, we stopped giving gifts to each other and started giving gifts to the boys or to other needy children instead. That practice has continued and been expanded over the years as we have annually provided gifts to foster children through the Families First Network Angel Tree project at Christmas.

Around 2000, I served on the United Way of Escambia County board of directors as campaign chairman and ultimately as chairman of the board. During those years, our company became a strong supporter of United Way. Joni Humphreys served as our community relations coordinator and annually organized United Way luncheons that resulted in record levels of giving from our staff. Our company has been recognized on several occasions as being one of the strongest supporters of United Way in our community.

In 2006, we created the Landrum Employees Charitable Foundation. One of the first gifts made from our new foundation was a $20,000 endowed scholarship in honor of Dan McLeod, the deceased husband of Denise, our long-time employee and vice president of the staffing division at the time. Since 2006, additional gifts have been made to the University of West Florida Foundation and numerous charitable organizations in the community.

Landrum Employee Foundation check presented by Britt Landrum, Jr. and Britt Landrum III to President John Cavanaugh (center) of the University of West Florida to fund the Dan McLeod Scholarship - 2006

Funding for the Foundation comes primarily from payroll-deducted contributions made by employees. Some who participate in the funding serve on the board of directors and determine how the funds are distributed.

For years, a committee of employees (our "Fun Committee") has planned and conducted luncheons and raffles to raise funds for charity. Employees get a chance to show off their cooking skills, basket-making skills, and other creative talents, all for the sake of helping those less fortunate folks in our community. These events have raised many thousands of dollars annually in support of many nonprofit organizations.

Presentation of check from the Landrum Employee Foundation
by Joni Humphreys (left) to Susan Byram, past president
and co-founder of Autism Pensacola - 2008

Taking Care of Our Employees

It has long been my belief, and is borne out by many studies, that employees are motivated more by how they are treated by their supervisors and peers than by their compensation. They want to be treated fairly, appreciated, recognized for their accomplishments, kept informed, involved in decision-making, and offered opportunities for growth. Over the years, we tried to do all those things, and when we fell short, as revealed in our Best Places to Work survey results, we listened, took note, and tried to do better. When we learned that employees wanted to be better informed, we increased the level of communication and gathered them for a meeting at least once each month to share financial and other company information.

When we learned that the employees wanted to be given the opportunity to apply for jobs within the company, we made sure to advertise all openings internally and interview those who were interested. More positions were filled from within as a result. We also created a mentoring program where an employee wishing to advance or learn more was paired with a more experienced staff member or a department supervisor who became a mentor or advisor.

The fact that we won the award for being one of the 25 Best Small Businesses to Work for in America for five years in a row is evidence that our employees truly appreciated the way they were treated. The real proof, however, is in the low turnover rate of our staff. Since the company was founded in 1970 with some 700 employed as staff at LandrumHR, there have been 99 employees who worked for the company ten years or more. At the end of 2017, when I retired from the company, over 40 of our 170 or so employees then working had been with the company ten years or more.

Treatment of employees aside, making sure that they are compensated fairly and sufficiently is the goal of most employers, and it certainly was mine as well. As much as possible, I wanted our employees to be paid at a level that was at least as much and preferably more than the market average in our area. Because we had access to the salary information of thousands of employees, we were able to stay in touch with what other employers were paying. Just as important, our staffing coordinators were regularly recruiting to fill job orders for local companies and were keenly aware of what those employers were having to pay to attract, employ, and retain quality workers.

In addition to paying an adequate salary, the SLT and I tried to come up with plans that would compensate all employees based on their performance and the performance of the company. We created quarterly and annual bonuses based on the gross margin achieved by the company–up to as much as $1,000 for every employee if our annual goal was achieved and $500 more for a total of $1,500 for each employee if our "Super Goal" was achieved. Our staff members seemed to enjoy and were motivated by this plan, and we achieved our goals almost every year.

On the staffing services side of the business, a significant portion of the pay of each staff member was based on the gross margin achieved by that division of the company each month. Each person also received an annual bonus based on whether or not certain gross margin goals were met. This proved to be a strong motivator for them, encouraging each person to work a little harder at finding job orders, screening applicants, and placing employees with our clients. Denise McLeod deserves the credit for installing the incentive system for her staff, and I believe that system, along with the caliber of the outstanding members of her team, enabled our staffing company to achieve a much higher level of performance than most similar companies our size.

On the PEO side of the house, trying to find just the right formula for measuring performance was a little more difficult. We also wanted to motivate each employee to the fullest extent possible and reward each one directly for good performance. For quite some time, we chose to set goals each month for an increase in the number of worksite employees added to the payroll, paying a bonus to all staff members who worked for the PEO when the goal was met. I'm not sure this plan provided the motivation we intended. It was pretty hard for staff members on the operations side of the business to connect their performance output to a change in the number of worksite employees. Rather, they were motivated by the knowledge that providing good customer service to our clients would help retain them and the worksite employees we already had enrolled, and that keeping those clients would in turn help us reach our financial targets each month.

Taking care of our employees through the benefits program was always a high priority. As we became more successful financially, we tried to pay for those benefits out of company funds rather than have the money come out of our employees' paychecks. Some benefits were for immediate needs, like health insurance, but others were intended to take care of unexpected emergencies, such as disability and life insurance.

In the long term, we want our staff members to have a good retirement plan, funded in part by the company, but also with their own tax-deferred contributions, which we match. We settled on setting up a 401K plan with the company matching up to 6% of the employee's salary, 100% of the first 3% and 50% of the next 3% of their deferred annual contribution. In addition, we set up a 3% company contribution for all employees whether they contribute into the plan or not. The latter is discretionary, meaning that the company isn't required to make the contribution in lean years, but we have made a contribution each year since the plan was established.

It was particularly rewarding for me to have some of our recently retired staff members praise the company for making that bonus benefit available to them as it gave them the assurance that they could live comfortably in retirement.

Achieving Sustainable Operational Excellence

Our journey to the Sterling Award actually began in 2003. Harry Booros, our special projects manager, strongly encouraged me to attend the Sterling Showcase presentation sponsored by Boeing Aerospace Support, a company that had just won the award. Saying that I'm glad I went is an understatement. Harry had been our director of safety and risk management. After his retirement from that job, we weren't ready for him to leave and placed him in charge of special projects. His interest had always been in quality improvement, as evidenced in 1994 when he helped us become designated as an ISO 9000 contractor. This was especially important to our client, Monsanto, where we had several hundred production workers assigned at the time.

After Ted Kirchharr started with the company as our director of strategic initiatives in 2003, our SLT began to talk seriously about pursuing the Sterling Award. We learned that most companies hired an outside consultant to guide them through the process. Ted had some experience with Sterling at his previous job and a strong interest in helping our company pursue the award, so I decided to assign that task to him.

Initially, we decided to apply for the Sterling Challenge (a precursor to the actual Award application), which enabled us to go through the process as a learning experience to see just where we were and how much more we had to accomplish in order to meet the Sterling requirements. We began using the Sterling framework to assess our performance capabilities and to systematically improve our processes and results. A requirement for going through that process was a site visit by a team of Sterling examiners. The feedback report we received from the examiners after that visit proved to be extremely helpful and an excellent source for identifying improvement opportunities.

Over the next three years, teams of staff members examined current practices in every area of our company with the view in mind of making them better and more efficient. "Current Best Standards" were written to document each process as a best practice. Ted implemented a "One Page Plan" that was used by departments and by the SLT in planning and reporting progress throughout the company. The process also caused us to look carefully at the capacity of our staff members and identify additional training that was needed to insure full coverage of company requirements.

Writing and editing the Sterling application was a monumental task. Several staff members took on that responsibility including Leslie Gordon, Yvonne Nellums, Susan Hunsucker, Jim Guttman, Melissa Miller, Tom Knox, and Gayle Meacham, with Leslie pulling all of the information together and putting it in final form. Also, during this time, Leslie qualified for and served as a Sterling examiner for other applicants in various stages of the process, fulfilling our obligation to the Sterling organization.

After three years of working to bring about these improvements in our company, we formally submitted our application in November 2006. A final site visit by the Sterling examiners occurred in early 2007, after which time we were notified that we had won the award!

Presentation of Sterling Award (L to R) Britt Landrum, Jr., Lt. Governor Jeff Kottcamp, and Ted Kirchharr - 2007

I consider that three-year period to be one of the most important times in our company's history. There is no question that it was expensive and time-consuming, and there were occasions when the pressures of the day-to-day operation caused us to question our decision. However, the benefits we received from the experience were invaluable.

To: Am Staff Human Resources – Congratulations! Jeb Bush

Awards Ceremony commendation from Florida Governor Jeb Bush (L to R) Sterling Council President John Pieno, Britt Landrum, Jr., Ted Kirchharr - 2007

In May 2007, a large number of us traveled to Orlando to attend the annual Sterling Convention where we were to receive the award. We tried to include as many employees as we could on the trip, inviting one or more staff members from each department in the company, in addition to the SLT and other staff members who had contributed to the application process. In appreciation for his introducing me to Sterling and encouraging me to have our company participate in the process, I also invited Harry Booros, who by that time had retired from the company.

The formal presentation of the award itself was to be made by Florida's Governor, Charlie Crist. Because he was not available, Lt. Governor Jeff Kottcamp made the presentation. What was even more meaningful for me, however, was to have my friend, Jack Healan, participate in the presentation. I was surprised and honored to have him speak on our behalf. Jack was a fellow Federal Reserve Branch board member, and, as CEO of the Amelia Island Plantation, a former winner of the Sterling award himself.

Landrum staff members, officials and guests at the Sterling Convention - 2007

Winning the award brought our company a great deal of publicity. Newspaper articles, requests for interviews, and lots of congratulations were received from business associates, fellow NAPEO members, and friends. Our staff came together with a great sense of pride in our company and all that we had done to achieve the recognition.

In October 2007, after winning the Florida Governor's Sterling Award for organizational excellence, our company sponsored two showcase presentations, the first in Pensacola and the second in Jacksonville.

Those events were attended by several business leaders and heads of government organizations who were curious about the nature of the award. Winners of the award traditionally sponsored such presentations each year in order to explain the process and encourage new applicants. It was a proud moment for our team, and we were happy to participate as a sponsor.

My opening remarks at one of the Showcase events in 2007 told the story.

> It was about this time four years ago when I was invited to attend just such a meeting as this. That meeting was held in Fort Walton Beach and was hosted by Boeing Aerospace Support, a division of The Boeing Company. This company had just won the Governor's Sterling Award and was there to tell us what winning the award had meant to their company.
>
> What those speakers talked about that day was not about winning an award, as great as that might seem. Rather, it was all about making your company the best it can be. It was all about achieving excellence as an organization—and that's what really appealed to me.
>
> Since my introduction to Sterling on that day in Fort Walton Beach, I have also learned a lot about the Baldrige Award, the nation's highest award for quality. The Baldrige Award is similar to the Sterling. The criteria for the two are basically identical.
>
> I happen to serve on the board of Baptist Health Care and, as some of you may know, in 2003 Baptist won the Baldrige Award. During that time as a board member, I got to see first-hand the tangible improvements in the overall performance of the hospital that resulted as its entire staff got involved in that process. Since that time, as you may know, Baptist has won a number of national awards for quality and has achieved some of the highest rankings in our part of the state with regard to employee and patient satisfaction.

These two experiences, with Sterling and with Baldrige, helped drive home for me a simple truth. That truth is that the high quality that we strive for and the high quality that gives any company the competitive advantage it seeks is a product of organizational excellence. And in order for any company or any organization to consistently deliver that high quality to its customers and to its stakeholders, it has to attain a state of excellence in its overall operations.

How a company goes about doing that is what we're going to talk about here today.

All too often we, as leaders of our companies, spend almost all of our time working IN the business–taking care of today, tending to operational issues and staff issues that are important, but time spent that way doesn't do much for tomorrow. We don't spend nearly enough time working ON the business, which can help us prevent some of the issues that are causing us problems and eating up our time today.

The discipline of Sterling forced our staff to look at the big picture, to focus on aspects of our organization that could, and in fact have, resulted in a dramatic overall improvement in the way we operate and in the bottom line for our company.

This improvement has been especially evident in our Risk Management department. In case some of you don't know, our company assumes the risk for workplace injuries on more than 11,000 employees. We partner with Liberty Mutual Insurance in managing that risk, but claims up to one million dollars are our responsibility. So, as you can well imagine, preventing injuries and managing claims are extremely important to us.

Sterling caused us to take a close look at all of our risk management processes and procedures. We benchmarked our performance against companies that we thought were doing it right and also with Liberty Mutual's other clients, and we changed our approach.

I'm proud to say that those changes have resulted in dramatically reduced claims and lower costs.

The man in our company who deserves the credit for bringing about those changes in risk management and for guiding us through the entire Sterling process is our vice president and COO, Ted Kirchharr. Ted is an organizational development expert, and we are fortunate to have him on the Senior Leadership Team of our company. Ted will be sharing a lot of information about our experience a little later in the program.

One final point before I close. Sustainability. It's one thing for an organization to be at the top of its game today, but it's equally important for it to be able to sustain that kind of performance year after year as changes occur. Key staff members move on; market conditions change; sometimes the regulatory environment changes. I can tell you, that's the kind of thing that has kept me awake more than a few nights in my thirty-seven years in business.

But I can honestly say that Sterling has changed that for me. It has done that by helping our company develop and document processes and procedures that I am convinced will sustain us over the long haul. It's important to get to a state of excellence, but it's even more important to be able to keep that level of excellence in the years to come. I believe Sterling can help.

CHAPTER 12

Looking Forward

Refusing to Sell Our Family Business

SINCE I OPENED THE BUSINESS IN 1970, the Landrum companies have been owned 100% by me and members of my family. For several years, all of the stock in the company was in my name. However, as the years passed, for estate planning purposes and a number of other reasons, much of the ownership was transferred to my wife and two sons.

I have turned down several opportunities over the years to sell all or a portion of the business. Part of my reason for declining all offers was personal. I got into business so I could make my own decisions and determine my own destiny. I didn't want other people to take that away. My attorney, Bob Hart, and my wife before him, advised against taking on a partner. Bob shared with me that he had seen too many companies suffer and even fail because of the failure of one of the partners to live up to promises and expectations.

I confess that I did consider the idea a few times. In 1997, the economy was strong, the stock market was hot, and a few PEOs were considering an Initial Public Offering (IPO). My good friend, Carlos

Saladrigas, principal owner of Vincam, a PEO based in Coral Gables, Florida, was making plans to take his company public. In preparation, he wanted to get commitments from other PEOs to join with him and "roll up" into a new public company. He came to Pensacola and did his best to convince me to join him along with the one or two others that had already committed. I told him, "No." If I had said, "Yes," our company as we know it today would be owned by ADP, the largest payroll processing company in the U.S. That company merged with Vincam a year or so after it successfully became publicly traded. I'm still glad I declined.

One year before Carlos Saladrigas came to visit me, I had a brief visit with a representative from Paychex, the second largest payroll processor in the country. That visit didn't go well. Frankly, I forgot that I had accepted an appointment with anyone that morning and decided at the last minute to take the morning off. When I got a call from my assistant to let me know that I had someone waiting in the lobby to see me, I was embarrassed. I spoke by telephone with the gentleman for a few minutes. He explained that he didn't have much time and couldn't wait for me to come to the office. He was cordial and didn't appear upset about my mistake, but I certainly couldn't blame him for being put off. It didn't register with me until later that he had flown to Pensacola especially for our visit. A short time after his visit to the office, I learned that Paychex had agreed to purchase a St. Petersburg PEO, National Business Solutions, reportedly for a very large amount of money. It occurred to me then that the gentleman I didn't see was most likely on a scouting visit, looking for PEOs to purchase. I wasn't upset when I realized his purpose. I wouldn't have agreed to sell anyway.

In the year 2000, not long after Andy Remke joined our company as CFO, I took a serious look at selling the company. My objective was to make sure that the company continued to thrive and provide income for my family after I was gone.

Raymond James and Company, a Florida firm that had a specialty in PEOs, prepared an analysis of our company and came up with what they felt would be a fair selling price. It was far less than I had imagined, which quite honestly didn't upset me. Deep down, I knew I wasn't ready to sell anyway. I was testing the waters in case I should ever seriously consider it.

Over the years, several of my friends have sold their companies and become financially well off. The trouble with that, in my opinion, is they lost their sense of purpose, and no longer had the enjoyment of working with others, striving to achieve a goal. One of my peers became seriously depressed. Another took a part-time job working for a friend. Still others started new PEOs. One former PEO owner came to see me and wanted to open a staffing company, offering me 10% of the new business. I turned down the offer, but I took him and his partner to see Denise McLeod, who told them what they needed to know and provided copies of all our material. Their experiences just confirmed to me that my decision not to sell was the right one. Now, I know that isn't the case for every business owner. Some use the money to do greater things, but more than one of those who sold told me that they regretted their decision.

Another important reason I didn't want to sell my company to a larger one was the impact I knew it would have on the lives and futures of some of our employees. They were the ones who had worked hard to create the success that made us attractive to buyers in the first place. Personal relationships that were important to me, would be viewed only from an impersonal business perspective by a new owner looking for a positive return on the investment made. I learned that lesson in 1970 when the *Pensacola News Journal* sold to Gannet Company. The word on the street at the time was that there would be no changes made in the operation, and employees should not fear losing their jobs. That turned out not to be true. Since my office was located right across the parking lot from the newspaper building, several of the long-term employees came to me looking for jobs after receiving their notices of termination.

This line of thinking may have resulted in slower growth and less value overall for our company, but it has suited me just fine. My real enjoyment has been in the journey with my employees, building a reputation for excellence, and the knowledge that we are doing something important for people. That isn't to say that I haven't enjoyed the financial wealth that success has brought. It's just that the success without the journey wouldn't be very fulfilling.

This may sound strange to some, but I learned that about myself a number of years ago when my small company was making much more money than I had dreamed possible. To my surprise, it didn't make me happy. What did make me happy was making a little progress each day toward whatever goal we had set, and after reaching that one, making another. I call that the journey, and, for me, that's what success is all about.

Succession Planning

Making sure our business survives over time has long been an objective of mine. Many thoughts have crossed my mind on that subject in recent years, such as these:

Concern for the employees who were critical to our success.

My own health and the possibility that I might die suddenly or have a debilitating illness.

If that happened, who would run the company?

Who would make that decision, and how would it be made?

Around the year 2000, I started giving such matters serious consideration. At that time, Britt III had not been with the company very long, and his primary focus was on improving our technology. Neither he nor I had any way of knowing how his career would progress. So, I began to think about the possibility that my successor could be a non-family member.

Also, I needed to prepare the company for the possibility of my sudden departure, either through death or severe disability. Mike Perkins, then vice president and COO of the company, and I had discussed the prospect and agreed that should it play out, he would step into the role of president. I made Britt III aware of our agreement.

At that point, with the help and advice of my estate attorney, Bob Hart, senior partner with Clark, Partington, Hart, shares of ownership in the company were transferred to Nell, Britt III, and my younger son, Brian, a small business owner in Asheville, North Carolina. If I were not in the picture, they would have the authority to decide who should run the company and would need help in making the best choice.

My research on succession planning led me to the Family Business Consulting Group in Atlanta. That firm published newsletters and books targeting family-owned businesses, which I signed up to receive. The newsletters contained articles written by consultants in the field, covering such topics as creating and working with boards of directors, exit strategies for CEOs, and more. One of the books I read contained stories and testimonials from business owners regarding the benefits of having an outside board of directors.

The idea of having a board of directors intrigued me. It made sense that the board could provide much needed help to my family in the event of my death or incapacity, either to help sell the company or select new leadership. I was not sold on the idea of having a governing board, but I did like the idea of an advisory board. As it turns out, the latter relieves board members of liability for company actions and makes them more willing to serve.

My initial thought was to name at least three directors to our new Advisory board, but, after thinking about it for a few weeks, I could only come up with two people who I felt would be a good fit and offer great advice and counsel to me, to the senior leadership of the company, and to my family. Those two people were Eric Nickelsen and Mort O'Sullivan. Eric was a friend and had been my bank officer during my first few years in business. Mort, also a friend for many years, headed up O'Sullivan Creel (now Warren Averett), one of the largest CPA firms in the area. Both had years of experience in business, banking, and finance, and were well known and respected in northwest Florida, and likely throughout the state. Both were quite willing to serve on my new board and agreed to step in to assist my family if I was suddenly taken out of the picture.

Eric Nickelsen – about 2001

Mort O'Sullivan – 2017

Before convening our first advisory board meeting, I contacted the Family Business Consulting Group to request a visit by one of their consultants. This led me to a conversation with Dr. Jennifer Pendergast, a management consultant specializing in family businesses. Jennifer came to Pensacola in August 2004 and did a survey of our business. Before her arrival, I had given her a written description of every Landrum corporate entity, its history, operation, ownership, and leadership. During her visit, she interviewed the key leaders in the company plus all family shareholders and their spouses.

Dr. Pendergast's summary report included recommendations to implement the advisory board and to create a family board. She listed a number of other suggestions as well, including the creation of written policies and procedures on hiring and compensating family members and business governance. I found her recommendations to be very helpful and tried to implement some of them over time.

Our advisory board held its first meeting in late 2004 and has been meeting regularly with the senior staff of our company since that time. The board has proven to be a tremendous asset, with the members providing advice on financial trends, business opportunities, acquisitions, and other matters of vital importance to the company.

In 2015, when Britt III became president of the company, we decided to increase the size of the board. At that time, we added Andy Remke, our former CFO, and, in 2016, we added Sergio Fernandez, former CFO of ADP TotalSource. Andy served from 2015 to 2018, and Sergio remained on the board only a few months, opting to resign and devote his time to other business interests.

Britt III became CEO of our company in 2017, and the following year, the board was reorganized. Mort O'Sullivan and Eric Nickelsen continue to serve, along with new member, Allison Hill, CEO of Lakeview Center, a subsidiary of Baptist Health Care. Jeff Phillips, CEO of Accountingfly, a Pensacola-based company that recruits and places accounting professionals, was appointed to the Advisory Board in 2017 and served until his departure in 2019.

Preparing for the Transition in Leadership

Another important step in making sure that the business would survive after my departure was our decision in 2007 to hire Sperduto & Associates, Inc., a group of corporate psychologists headquartered in Atlanta. I became aware of the firm and the work it did through my long association with Baptist Health Care and Lakeview Center. Baptist had used the firm to conduct executive coaching and to assist in evaluating candidates for hiring and staff members who were being considered for promotion to higher-level positions. Andy Remke, our CFO at that time, and, as mentioned earlier, the former CFO of Baptist Health Care, was personally aware of the good work done by Sperduto. He highly recommended that we begin working with the firm.

I have to confess that I was shocked when I was told how much this was going to cost our company each month, but, as it turned out, retaining Sperduto & Associates was a prudent decision. Over a period of months, Gary Sperduto and his associates got to know each of the members of our executive team very well. We each submitted to a psychological evaluation and an extensive interview regarding our positions with the company. We also carried out exercises designed to help each member of the team get to know each other better. The monthly sessions conducted by the psychologists, aimed at establishing open and honest communication among us, produced real value to our team.

In addition to the group sessions, each member of our executive team, including Britt III and me, had a monthly coaching session with one of the psychologists. Over a period of about ten years, Gary Sperduto met with us separately and with Britt III and me together, helping us understand our strengths and weaknesses, and work through differences of opinion. The purpose of that exercise, of course, was to help both of us prepare for the transition of leadership that we knew would one day occur. Looking back, I have to say that bringing in the Sperduto organization to assist was indeed well worth the sizeable investment.

The psychological evaluation done on me by Gary Sperduto pointed to some characteristics of mine that definitely had an impact on my management style. For one thing, Gary said that the results of my survey indicated that I had a tendency to avoid confrontation. That wasn't news to me, but he reminded me that this wasn't a positive trait for the CEO of a company, who has to hold staff members accountable and point out their mistakes as well as dealing with other challenges. I agreed that being more assertive might have made me a better manager, but I told myself that I had built a pretty successful company in spite of that shortcoming.

Without question, I have always found that directly confronting others about behavior which I don't like, or mistakes they may have made, or some other unpleasant situation, is one of my least favorite things to do. I know I'm not alone in that regard. Several of our PEO clients often turn for help from their assigned HR manager to take care of counseling one or more of their employees (our co-employees) and even terminating an employee when that needs to be done.

Having said that, I didn't completely shirk my responsibility with regard to holding employees accountable. It just took me a little longer to decide that it was warranted or necessary. Every manager has to take care of the unpleasant task of counseling with or terminating an employee from time to time, and I had my share of doing that over the years. When I did personally handle employee terminations, I almost always gave the person as soft a landing as I could, maybe adding a few more weeks to their severance pay or something like that. It didn't hurt the company financially and made a big difference to someone being forced to begin looking for a new job.

My tendency to avoid confrontation also impacted the way I handled employee performance evaluations for the managers who reported to me. I never liked doing them or filling out those forms. I know I didn't set a very good example, but my department heads believed in doing them. They developed some fine performance evaluation forms and held regular meetings with their direct reports to give them feedback on their performance. Our HR managers for the PEO regularly provided such forms for our clients and recommended that they use them in evaluating their employees.

Filling out the evaluation forms requires one to make judgments about people and give opinions. I just didn't want to do that. I kept an open door and much preferred to have regular conversations with those who reported to me so we could discuss what was happening in their department, any concerns they had, what they were hoping to accomplish, and what help they might need from me.

In addition to not wanting to confront people, I have never liked for someone to tell me what to do and how to do it–unless I asked them, of course. I assumed others felt the same way, so my way of managing was to give people fairly wide latitude in doing their jobs. I think the majority of staff members who reported to me rather enjoyed my non-directive approach and the freedom to be creative in coming up with their own ideas as to what needed to be done in their particular areas. I didn't tell Denise McLeod how to develop the staffing service or Susan Hunsucker how to develop the benefits department or Yvonne Nellums how to develop the HR department. Neither did I tell Leslie Gordon, Andy Remke, and Johnathan Taylor how to develop and operate the finance department, or Britt III how to develop his IT department. The same goes for safety, payroll, and most other areas in the company.

I also didn't tell my team how to manage their departments. I respected those leaders and trusted them, and they knew it. When they wanted to hire an additional staff member, they came to me to ask permission and to help me understand the need. The fact that each department grew to become a very successful part of the operation, and we had happy, long-tenured employees is evidence in support of doing it my way. At the very least, it points out that there is more than one way to effectively manage people. Sperduto uncovered leadership qualities in each member of the SLT and better prepared the company for my imminent departure.

Letting Go

I've entitled this last section, "Letting Go," as that is exactly what I did with regard to control over our company. I credit my wife, Nell, with helping me make that decision. For a couple of years, we had discussed when I should retire and what that might feel like for me.

The time came when there was no question in my mind that my son, Britt III, was ready to take over the job as CEO. Over the years since he joined the company in 1993, I had seen his passion for learning and for developing his skills in each area of responsibility given to him—first in sales, then in IT, and later in management. He had over ten years of experience as vice president over several departments within the company and had served as a valuable member of the SLT. He was appointed president in 2015, during which time he was the architect of some important management changes that proved to be very beneficial to the organization. We had worked for quite a few years with Gary Sperduto, our executive coach and counselor. Gary had assured me that Britt was very capable and ready to assume the role of CEO. Still, giving up "my" company, the one I created and built, was a hard decision to make.

Intellectually, I understood and accepted that there were good reasons for me to let go. I had read articles about company founders who just refused to give up, often with a detrimental effect on their companies and on leaders who were ready to take over. I knew that it was far better for me to leave while my health was good, and my exit would give Britt III the opportunity to step fully into the leadership role without me looking over his shoulder. I knew also that I could be available to serve as an advisor to him when needed.

Still, the comfort of being in the familiar surroundings of the company, being involved in the dynamics of the day-to-day business activity, and interacting with the people I had grown so fond of over the years made the timing of my decision more difficult.

To make the separation a little easier and because I can't find room in my house for all my "stuff," I have chosen to maintain an office in the company and drop by there on occasion. When long-term employees retire, I am called on to tell a story or two about them and the memorable times that we shared. I enjoy that.

I also serve on the company's advisory board and attend those meetings. These are stimulating and keep me informed on the strategic aspects of the business. I have a new title, "Founder and Chairman." Actually, I'm the chairman of our "family board," which meets officially once each year. The four of us, Nell, Britt III, Brian, and I still own all the stock in the company and serve as directors of Landrum Human Resource Companies, Inc. At those meetings, we review the status of the company and approve actions taken or planned to be taken the same as any other corporate board. Johnathan Taylor, our trusted CFO, prepares all the documents for us and schedules and attends the meetings.

Landrum family board members (L to R)
Brian, Britt Jr., Nell, Britt III - 2018

I need to give credit to Bob Hart, our long-time tax and estate attorney, who was a trusted advisor for many years. Bob prepared many of the legal documents we now use for our various corporations, and through the years, he gave us excellent legal advice. He and members of his firm guided us through the legal quagmire when negotiating and purchasing other businesses. He also served as an advisor to me and to my family in the preparation of wills, trusts, and other estate planning documents that enable us now to have all of our affairs in order. His advice and genuine concern for us has been invaluable.

It has been almost three years since we called the staff together and announced Britt III's promotion to CEO and my retirement. I can say without reservation that it was the right decision to leave when I did. I truly enjoy the freedom that has come from clearing my calendar of meetings and freeing my mind of the problems and more difficult aspects of running a business. It gives me a great sense of relief and pride knowing that the company now rests in the capable hands of Britt III and his entire team.

Writing this book has taken several months of my time, and, if my advisors are correct, will undoubtedly take several more before it is published. Then, I'm hopeful I'll be able to get back to my original plan, which is to continue perfecting my skills in photography and brushing up on Photoshop and Lightroom so that I can create great pictures.

Thanks for taking time to read my memoir and the history of our company. If you've been a part of my story, that means that I've been privileged to be a part of yours. I hope I haven't disappointed you by what I said or what I didn't say.

If you've read this book to gain some insight as to what it takes to be successful in business, I hope there has been something in it for you that will inspire, encourage, enlighten, or confirm what you might have known all along. Trust and believe in yourself. Find good people to help you as I did. Show them love and encouragement. Help them to be all they can be. It sure worked for me.

AFTERWARD

A PARTING MESSAGE FROM MR. LANDRUM

Adapted from an article written by Mr. Landrum for the
August 2011 issue of *PEO Insider,* a publication of the
National Association of Professional Employer Organizations

Working a Better Way – It's All About Relationships

In 2020, LandrumHR celebrates fifty years in the human resources business. Opening in August 1970 at the tail end of a recession, we have survived as many as six others since that time, providing some evidence of our success. Our history of growth and profitability support that claim as well. Relationships have been the key.

I have written this memoir and history not to impress you, because others have surely done better, but to impress upon you that the establishment of solid, trusting relationships is essential if you want to position your company for growth through referrals from those with whom you conduct business. In our case, those relationships have been both personal and professional and have extended from our company to the people and communities we serve. And, whether it's you personally or your company, you want those relationships to be based on trust.

When you establish relationships, you're establishing your reputation, which later becomes your brand. As you know, most businesses (including ours) spend lots of money trying to build and protect their brand because it tells the public not only who we are, but what the public can expect when they do business with us, lend us money, issue us an insurance policy, or decide to come to work for us. Whether you're establishing relationships with employees, clients, vendors, or bankers, it's vitally important for them to know that they can trust you and that you are going to treat them fairly. The Golden Rule applies.

Fifty years ago, I didn't have any idea how important such relationships were going to be to my business. But it is my strong belief that they have made a measurable difference in the success of our company.

Relationships with Peers – Over the years, through membership and participation in the National Association of Professional Employer Organizations (NAPEO), I have been able to meet many friends who were willing to share information with me when I needed it. Those trusting relationships helped me in the early years to grow and learn while avoiding some of the mistakes that others might have made. We visited their offices, and they visited ours, openly sharing so that we both could learn. The lesson here is that successful companies aren't afraid to share their secrets and help others along the way.

Relationships with Employees – Most employers are well aware that they have to treat employees fairly if they're going to develop trusting relationships and a loyal, effective work force. Our goal is to hire the best employees and strive to make them feel that our company is one of the best they have ever worked for. Higher production, more loyalty, and lower turnover are just some of the results. We've also found that happier employees are much more likely to provide the exceptional service that we expect. They are strong advocates for us in the community and enable us to attract the best candidates when openings occur.

Relationships with Clients – Giving our clients even better service than they expect is our primary goal, but reducing client turnover and getting referrals from them are two other goals. Every member of our staff works hard to establish those trusting relationships. Years ago, we decided to be very deliberate about nurturing those relationships and hired a "chief relationship officer." His title was actually director of client relations, and his job was to get to know our clients and to make sure they were happy with us.

Relationships with Vendors, Bankers, and Insurers – The people who run those businesses and others have to learn from experience that we can be trusted, we're not going to take unfair advantage of them, and they are going to be paid on time every time. Developing that reputation makes establishing the right kind of relationships much easier. Over the years, we've had many referrals from these companies.

Never forget that the people who run the businesses you touch serve on boards of directors of many of the important organizations in your market. If you don't treat them well, that reputation can do you great harm. On the contrary, if you earn their trust, they will spread that word for you and be your advocate when you need them. Paying attention to that detail has helped us sign up many nonprofit organizations, churches, chambers of commerce, the United Way, Better Business Bureau, several banks, credit unions, and others.

Relationships with Auditors and Government Regulators – As PEO owners, we place ourselves in a position of great responsibility. Our companies have control over millions of dollars and thousands of employee records. We have the obligation to accurately collect and timely pay insurance premiums and taxes, to keep accurate, legally compliant records, and to serve as fiduciaries for multimillion-dollar retirement plans. Such responsibilities are enough to keep you up at night.

To be trusted with all this responsibility, it is imperative that we demonstrate the highest level of integrity and reliability in every aspect of our business. We want to cooperate with state and federal regulators. We want to hire the best auditors and have them do a thorough job of examining our records. In addition, we want that third party verification that we are in full compliance with every requirement. That is why we chose years ago to undergo the scrutiny required to become accredited by the Employer Services Assurance Corporation (ESAC). It's the reason we have become SAS 70 compliant and worked to earn the Governor's Sterling Award for organizational excellence. We even have an internal auditor whose job is to make sure we're doing everything that is expected and required of us.

Our external accountants and auditors have become our advocates. They have many clients and serve on many boards of directors. Their circle of influence is quite large. And they speak with the highest degree of credibility. Over the years, we've added a number of new clients on the books because of them. A trusting relationship with them is priceless as they say.

I could go on trying to impress upon you the importance of establishing and taking care of relationships, but I'm sure by now you get the idea. It's my own belief, after living for more than 80 years and being a business owner for 50 of those years, that success in life and success in business are due in large measure to the establishment of healthy, trusting relationships along the way.

Best wishes for your success in both.

POSTSCRIPT

A s this book is nearing publication, the world is going through one of the most trying periods of our lifetime, brought about by the rapid spread of the novel coronavirus known as COVID-19, which causes severe respiratory problems for many who become infected. Our community, our state, and our country have been virtually shut down now for several weeks, which may extend longer as we wait for the virus to run its course. People are strongly encouraged to stay inside their homes, wear masks if they have to go out, and keep away from others—even family members who live apart.

Non-essential businesses have been ordered closed. Many have been forced to reduce staff in order to survive. Unemployment rates have reached double digits for the first time since the 80's.

LandrumHR is feeling the impact of all of this. Before it was required, our staff members were encouraged to work from home, and our offices were essentially closed to the public. The leadership has discovered new ways to provide staff with the means to support clients, interview applicants, and fill jobs—all from their homes via the Internet. I have just listened in as CEO Britt Landrum III held a virtual meeting with key staff members across the country, giving an update on what the company has done and will be doing to survive the crisis and take care of our clients.

As I listened to Britt III inform, thank, and encourage the staff members who were listening over their telephones or attending via Zoom, I could not help but feel pride and confidence in the leadership of our company. Britt III has assembled a strong team of leaders who have demonstrated their ability and their commitment to the company and its mission to enhance the lives of our clients and employees. One example is how the staff came together quickly and worked around the clock to prepare information for all PEO clients so they could apply for loans under the Coronavirus Aid, Relief and Economic Security ("CARES") Act as soon as it became law. Because the funds were limited, the need to be among the first to apply was imperative.

There is no question that our company will continue to feel the stress of this crisis for a while longer. In spite of that, I know we are well positioned to survive and thrive going forward. Not only do we have strong, capable leadership in place, we also have a strong balance sheet to withstand the setback.

Our fiftieth year in business has provided some not so pleasant surprises, but I am convinced that it will also present some opportunities, and we'll be there to take advantage of them for the benefit of the people we employ and the clients we serve.

REFLECTIONS OF NINE LEADERS

Following are reflections shared by the nine people who were interviewed for this book. All are leaders. All played a pivotal role in helping to create the success that LandrumHR currently enjoys as perhaps one of the longest running mid-tier players in the HR services industry. Each grasped the meaning of *working a better way.*

PEGGY FORTUNATO
Retired Corporate Director
of Human Resources

I knew right away when I started (in 1976) that it was a different atmosphere. Mr. Landrum treated the employees like family and with respect. That was the comment I heard throughout my whole career–the respect for Mr. Landrum and the culture. It was not like other places where people had worked. Mr. Landrum's patience and forgiveness to employees set the example. He always took an interest in us.

What's unique about LandrumHR goes back to culture. The culture started at the top with Mr. Landrum and then trickled down to managers and supervisors, in the way you treat people, with respect.

The commitment of staff to being their best and doing the right thing sets LandrumHR apart. It's the devotion to the clients that stands out, and from the internal side, it's the values-driven culture inspired by Mr. Landrum and instilled in each of us.

DENISE MCLEOD

*Retired VP and COO for Landrum Staffing
and VP of HR for the PEO Division*

I realize how lucky I have been to work for someone like Mr. Landrum–someone who we could have complete trust in, who valued us, included us in everything, who was very generous, and who had and still has such a leadership style that being committed to him is a no-brainer. Mr. Landrum's method of managing is to treat people the way he would want to be treated. He brings out the best in people.

Throughout my forty-two years at Landrum, the philosophy was always the same. Take care of the client. Do the right thing. We're not here to be the biggest–we're here to be the best.

Looking back, I believe that the values that set our company apart were integrity, love, and a culture of family. Mr. Landrum can be proud of the company he built. He built it out of truly wanting to help people. That attitude and those values withstand the test of time. To me, that is what this book is all about.

YVONNE NELLUMS

*Retired Director of HR
for the PEO Division*

I recognize how blessed I've been to be able to do what I've been doing for 35 years. I've had a good employer, and I've been surrounded by good, honest people. As employees of LandrumHR, we have had great lives. We've been able to support our families and make a good living while doing something we love!

Mr. Landrum was a great leader, and I never wanted to disappoint him. He taught us about dignity and respect, and how to treat each other. We had the opportunity to grow. We weren't micro-managed, so we could spread our wings. Everyone worked so well together. We were like a family. Everybody trusted each other. Everyone loved each other.

I loved what I did every day. I loved the company that I worked for. I believe that we were very good at what we did. We put our customers first and were sincere in wanting to help them. Our company's mission was *working together to enrich lives*. I think that's what we did every day.

SUSAN HUNSUCKER

*Retired Director of Employee Benefits
for the PEO Division*

Mr. Landrum was definitely an innovator, and very involved in the early years of employee leasing–now "PEO." Our company benefitted from his involvement in all of that. When we went to a PEO conference and others saw on our name badge that we're with Landrum, they would say, 'You must be awesome because you work there!' It gave us credibility. The company itself has always had an excellent reputation and is well known in the industry.

Mr. Landrum's reputation in the community made clients feel secure knowing it was a reputable company and helped us to get and maintain clients. He also created a very close-knit caring culture, one that allowed you to grow and fail occasionally without being made to feel badly about that, being able to learn from your mistakes, and being supported and encouraged. It was wonderful.

Mr. Landrum instilled the values that the employees had toward the clients and towards each other. One of our values was the respect and dignity of all individuals, treating everybody with respect and dignity.

As I look back, what strikes me is that it wasn't just my journey–it's my whole family, really. My kids grew up there and remember boat rides with Mr. Landrum at the company picnic. I wouldn't be where I am now, as far as being able to retire and financially set, without the benefits that were available to me, and that were provided to all of us. Of course, all of that impacts my whole family. Also, our values aligned. That's part of why it was such a good fit for me, and why I was there so long. It was very much the same ethics and values that I was brought up with myself– hard-working, honest, trustworthy, diligent, persistent. All those things.

MIKE PERKINS

*Former VP, Corporate Legal Counsel
and COO for the PEO Division*

Mr. Landrum was one of the pioneers of PEO licensing. He brought a lot of credibility to us, first of all for doing things right–he was on the State licensing and oversight board and couldn't afford for us not to do everything right, but it brought a lot of credibility for us, and sometimes put him in the uncomfortable position of monitoring some other PEOs out there that weren't doing things right.

Mr. Landrum is responsible–whether he admits it or not, for raising the image, raising the reputation, raising the bar of the whole PEO industry, particularly in Florida. And Florida is a leading state in the industry, so the impact was national.

There is a whole level of devotion and reverence from the people who worked with him. Mr. Landrum set his own brand, a high standard. There's a level of devotion to this guy that I have never seen before in business. Long-term employees who are very dedicated would knock down walls for him. And he would have done the same for them.

There were times when we had to have a lot of mercy for people who were going through tough times. That was one of the beauties of a company like that, with a leader like that–if things were tough, you weren't going to be cut loose to fend for yourself. It's not always that way in a big company. The company even the size of LandrumHR had a heart. Mr. Landrum set the tone and still does.

ANDY REMKE

*Retired VP and Chief Financial Officer
of LandrumHR*

I can't say I've worked for a better person than Mr. Landrum. I mean, he is non-selfish–all parts of everything he does. I saw that all the way back when he was on the Baptist board in the late 1990s. Though he was reluctant to fire anyone, he scores a 99% on everything else. He has put together a tremendous company, and has been very good at picking who, when, and why when building his team.

TED KIRCHHARR

*Former VP and COO
for the PEO Division*

We applied for and won the 'Great Places to Work Award' for five years in a row, starting around 2004. The 'Great Places to Work Award' in turn helped us with the 'Sterling Award.' That was another form of validation of what we had been doing well.

I recall asking Mr. Landrum on our return from a business trip, 'How would you sum up your business philosophy?' His response ...

I want my customers to have world-class customer service.

I want my employees to think 'this is the best place I've ever worked.'

I want to make a reasonable profit.

That's it. And I thought, WOW...that's pretty cool. We lived that. That became part of what we used in strategic planning, and when we eventually went to a one-page strategic plan, we captured it in several versions, because that was Mr. Landrum's philosophy, and the sales guys could talk about that philosophy, 'This is what we're trying to do.' It was about strategic growth, not growth for growth's sake. It was about getting a little bigger every year and growing a little bit every year. It was about managed growth. That's what we did.

I think Mr. Landrum's three-point philosophy on the business is very profound. To me it's your emphasis on all the right things–employees, clients, and profits. The employees were always aware that Mr. Landrum took the approach of always putting money back into the business. He wasn't flamboyant with the way he spent money.

I consider Mr. Landrum my mentor. The biggest lesson I took from him is the power of relationships. I watched him make decisions where "relationships" became the overriding factor. That was a huge piece of his decision-making process. It was about the relationships that were involved.

Mr. Landrum's is a story of how you can apply strong personal beliefs in a business setting. That is what he brought to the table. He would agonize over people decisions–what to do with someone. It was the depth of the anguish he reflected sometimes, because relationships were so important to him. Also, in the final analysis, even if it cost him money–Mr. Landrum's money, he's still going to opt for making the right decision when he is ready to make that right decision.

Character is a big piece of it, too. Many of us are really good at teaching tactics and techniques and helping people with visioning and helping people with employee engagement and all of that. But in my opinion, with many companies there is a big hole in the 'character of leader' piece. What does the 'character of a good leader' look like? What does that mean? How does one make decisions based on a personal set of values? That's a piece where Mr. Landrum has something to say.

Mr. Landrum is someone whose life is about service to others. It's about love. It's about relationships. That's what his life has been about. That's the message people need to hear. Everybody needs to hear it. Businesspeople need to hear it, in particular.

BRITT LANDRUM III

LandrumHR President and CEO

Dad's legacy has much to do with what sets us apart. What I most respect about his legacy as pertains to the business—is the family atmosphere we have as a company. Most people say to me in orientations, even to this day, "I just feel appreciated here, and valued."

"Mr. L," as I referred to Dad as my boss, would never take credit for something someone else did. I've seen that happen many times. You just can't replace that. Also, Dad's wisdom—it is something I will always aspire to have. Whether it be a spreadsheet, or a law, or a sales situation, he could figure it out and find a solution. Often times I sat in amazement like, "How did you know that?" A lot of that comes with experience, I know, but you've got to be pretty smart and creative to work through the difficult situations you face along the way.

Preparing to take the reins from Dad as President then CEO came from lots of individual experiences with him and with other people. It came from the interactions and practical advice on how to deal with issues and opportunities. I would strongly encourage anyone transitioning to lead a family-owned business to seek out mentors. The turning point for me was when I stopped trying to be like Dad and instead tried to be the best version of me I could be. I had to focus on what I'm good at. Sperduto helped me with that.

Although Dad was thrifty, he was willing to spend money where it made sense. He made a significant investment in bringing in third party expertise to help with leadership development and with succession planning when we needed an independent point of view. Because of "Mr. L's" willingness to invest in the company, it has now afforded us a lot more opportunities to grow and diversify.

ERIC NICKELSEN

LandrumHR Advisory Board Member

Good stories have a beginning, middle, and end. Britt's covers the 50 years since founding his company. When he first came to me looking for a banker as he was getting under way, there was confidence. There was integrity. There was a vision, and a reality–a reality meaning, "I don't think I'm going to do this overnight and make a million dollars tomorrow." He had vision that was doable.

You get to the middle of that–I wasn't involved, but he was in a quandary then. Do I sell this company? Do I go forward and take more risk? Am I able to do this? Am I able to hire people who are good enough? He hired a psychologist to help him out with those type of things, to grow the company and have the right people on board.

You get to the end–the end is that he's got a CEO who he tutored, he educated, he believes in, he trusts, and he knows that after he's gone from here, the company is in good hands.

THROUGH THE YEARS

LandrumHR staff - 1986

(Front L to R) Joni Humphreys, Michele Stinson, Peggy Fortunato, Harry Booros, Susan Hunsucker; (Back L to R) John McBride (partially hidden), Harry Rasmussen, Billy Price – 1987

Landrum staff - early 1990's

YMCA Corporate Cup Games – 2001

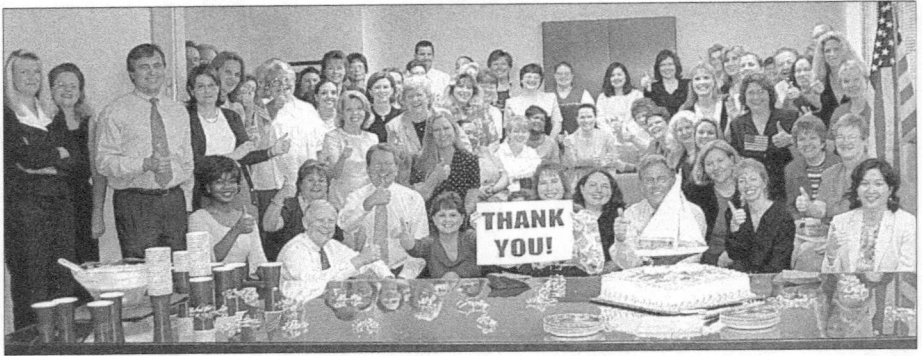

Staff celebration – early 2000's

Landrum Staffing - early 2000's

Britt Landrum, Jr.'s 65th birthday celebration – 2002

*Landrum Staffing recognized by the Greater Pensacola Chamber as
'Small Business of the Month' – about 2003*

Junior Achievement Mardi Gras Bowl - early 2000's

Fiesta Run – 2007

Team Landrum - about 2014

IMAGE CREDITS

All photographs displayed in Working a Better Way came from the archives of LandrumHR.

LANDRUMHR'S
LONGEST SERVING EMPLOYEES

40 Years or More

Margaret A. (Peggy) Fortunato   1976 - 2018

Denise T. McLeod   1976 - 2018

30 Years or More

Valerie C. Cole   1988 - Present

Joni K. Humphreys   1986 - 2018

Susan Hunsucker   1980 - 1982; 1984 - 2018

Darlene S. McClendon   1990 - Present

Yvonne C. Nellums   1984 - 2019

20 Years or More

Cynthia L. Bigalow   1996 - Present

Dawn D. Danforth   1999 - Present

Carol J. Eggart   1999 - Present

Rhonda E. Freeman   1989 -2018

Sheila Golden   2000 - 2019

Leslie T. Gordon   1993 - 2014

Margaret E. (Meg) Harris   1999 - 2019

Eileen M. Hess   1992 - Present

Andrea K. Johnson   1998 - 2020

Kimberly L. (Kim) Johnson   1998 - 2018

Lois A. Johnson   1994 - 2020

David D. Keleher   1993 - 2018

H. Britt Landrum III   1993 - Present

Alice L. Malloy   1997 - 2018

Diana Gayle Meacham   1995 - 2017

Lisa N. Nagem   1996 - 2018

Jennifer C. Osburn   1997 - 2018

Lorena B. Peterson   1997 - Present

Johanna J. Pohlmann   1998 - Present

Melanie R. Rhodes   2000 - Present

Angela Thornton Jones   1999 - Present

Grace A. Whalen   1993 - 2014

10 Years or More

Jo-Anne Audette-Arruda   2005 - Present

Frazer Banks   1971 - 1987

Jessica H. Beal   2009 - Present

Kathryn E. (Kathy) Black   2008 - Present

Harry L. Booros   1987 - 2005

Elizabeth A. (Liz) Carpenter   2000 - 2017

Deborah Sue Carroll   2007 - 2018

William A. N. (Bill) Cleary   2006 - 2018

Jamie Lynn Constantakos   2010 - Present

Carole Cox   1995 -2004; 2016 - 2020

Julie H. Creedon   2002 - Present

Carolyn R. Davis   1975 - 1986

Brenda D. Dean   2002 - 2020

Dinna B. Dizon   2006 - Present

Julie Kristy Dolihite   2001 - Present

Martha M. Dolihite   2004 - 2016

Thomas L. Downey   1988 - 2006

Rachel A. Dubose   2005 - Present

Susan D. B. Edmonston   2002 - 2016

Susan D. Fleming   2007 - 2017

Christopher M. Fortunato   2006 - 2017

Michael M. Fortunato   1994 - 2007

Cassandra R. (Casey) Gardner   2000 - 2010

Katherine M. Gebler   2000 - 2017

James M. Guttmann   2001 - 2018

Jerold D. Hall   2002 - 2019

Tisonia T. Hallford   2006 - Present

Jana D. Hand   2007 - Present

Sandra R. Hardy   1999 - 2015

W. Jason Heuer   2003 - Present

Sarah M. Hockman   2006 - 2016

Edward M. (Ted) Holz   2000 - 2018

Deborah A. Horak   1997 - 2014

Ingrid R. Horil   1991 - 2001

Robert C. Horne   1989 - 2000

Wanda Y. Jones   1997 - 2012

10 Years or More (continued)

Matilde A. Keith   2007 - 2017

Ted A. Kirchharr   2003 - 2016

Thomas R. Knox   2001 - 2014

Sue A. Lane   2007 - Present

Amanda D. Lloyd   1998 - 2009

Mark Lundquist   2005 - Present

Sharon M. Mathews   2000 - 2013

Karena G. McCafferty   2005 - Present

Holly E. McLeod   1998 - 2015

Brenda Miller   2005 - Present

Melissa K. Miller   2004 - Present

Lisa K. Millikin   2003 - 2013

Emile Dianne Milling   1987 - 2000

Don Nelson   1971 - 1983

Michael A. Perkins   1997 - 2007

Luz V. Pitre   1989 - 2008

William G. (Billy) Price   1981 - 1995

Leann Pugh   2007 - Present

Amie A. Remington   2005 - Present

Adrian P. (Andy) Remke   2000 - 2014

Rochelle Richards   2005 - Present

Deborah (Debbie) Russo   2008 - Present

Mandy R. Sacco   2007 - Present

Sandra Kay Smith   1997 - 2016

Marsha Jane Spann   2004 - 2017

Charles J. (Chuck) Studeny   1997 - 2007

Jill S. Swilley   2002 - Present

Johnathan M. Taylor   2005 - Present

Susan L. Varner   2002 - 2017

Kelli Watson   2005 - Present

Angela T. White   2007 - Present

Sharon D. Williams   2006 - Present

Jean M. Wojnarowski   2005 - 2016

Betty R. Wright   1990 - 2003

BIBLIOGRAPHY

Collins, Jim and Porras, Jerri I. *Built to Last: Successful Habits of Visionary Companies.* HarperCollins Publishers, Inc., 1994.

Collins, Jim. *Good to Great: Why Some Companies Make the Leap...and Others Don't.* Williams Collins, 2001.

Gorman, Leon. L.L. Bean: *The Making of an American Icon.* Harvard Business School Press, 2006.

Hunter, James C. *The Servant: A Simple Story About the True Essence of Leadership.* The Crown Publishing Group, 1998.

Lencioni, Patrick. *The Five Dysfunctions of a Team.* Jossey-Bass, 2002.

Murphy, Mark. *Hundred Percenters: Challenge Your Employees to Give It Their All, and They'll Give You Even More.* McGraw-Hill Education, 2009.

Stubblefield, Al. *The Baptist Health Care Journey to Excellence: Creating a Culture that WOWs.* John Wiley & Sons, 2004.

APPENDICES

Appendix A: Acronyms

Appendix B: Business Evolution of LandrumHR

Appendix C: Companies and Ownership Interests Since 1970

Appendix D: Pensacola-based Office Locations Since 1970

Appendix E: People Referenced in *Working a Better Way*

Appendix F: Associations Referenced in *Working a Better Way*

APPENDIX A
ACRONYMS

AMFI	American Fidelity Life Insurance
AmStaff	American Staff Leasing Corporation, later known as LandrumHR
ASA	American Staffing Association
BHAG	Big, Hairy, Audacious Goal [Built to Last: Successful Habits of Visionary Companies, by Jim Collins and Jerry Porras]
C&P	Citizens & Peoples National Bank
CARES	Coronavirus Aid, Relief, and Economic Security Act
CEO	Chief Executive Officer
CFO	Chief Financial Officer
COBRA	Consolidated Omnibus Budget Reconciliation Act
CPA	Certified Public Accountant
CRM	Customer Relationship Management
CTO	Chief Technology Officer
CU	Credit Union
CRT	Cathode-ray tube (computer display)
DBA	'Doing business as'
DEC	Digital Equipment Corporation
DOAH	(Florida) Division of Administrative Hearings
EAP	Employee Assistance Program
EASI	Employer Administrative Services, Inc.
EBITA	Earnings before interest, taxes, and amortization
EEOC	Equal Employment Opportunity Commission
EPLI	Employment Practices Liability Insurance
ESAC	Employer Services Assurance Corporation
FBI	Federal Bureau of Investigation
FEA	Florida Employment Association, later known as Florida Association of Personnel Consultants
FEMA	Federal Emergency Management Agency
FICA	Federal Insurance Contributions Act (tax employees and employers pay on portion of employee income)
FMLA	Family Medical Leave Act
FOMC	Federal Open Market Committee
FSU	Florida State University
FUTA	Federal Unemployment Tax Act

GE	General Electric
HBL	H. Britt Landrum, Jr.
HR	Human Resources
HRCI	Human Resources Certification Institute
IAPEO	Institute for the Accreditation of Professional Employer Organizations (now ESAC)
IRS	Internal Revenue Service
ISO	International Standards Organization
ISP	Internet Service Provider
IT	Information Technology
ITSA	Independent Temporary Services Association (now TempNet)
LHR	LandrumHR (name for PEO, Consulting, and Workforce Solutions divisions)
LHRC	Landrum Human Resource Companies, Inc. (LHR's parent corporation)
LINK	Landrum Information "NetworK"
LPA	Landrum Personnel Associates
M&A	Mergers and Acquisitions
MRO	Medical Review Officer
NAPEO	National Association of Professional Employer Organizations
NAS	Naval Air Station
NATS	National Association of Temporary Services
NCCI	National Council for Compensation Insurance
NEA	National Employment Association
NLRB	National Labor Relations Board
NPA	National Personnel Associates
NSLA	National Staff Leasing Association, now National Association of Professional Employer Organization (NAPEO)
OSHA	Occupational Safety and Health Administration
PC	Personal computer
PEO	Professional Employer Organization
PTO	Paid time off
SLT	LHR's Senior Leadership Team
SSA	Social Security Administration
SSAE	Statement on Standards for Attestation Engagements
SUTA	State Unemployment Tax Act
TEFRA	Tax Equity and Fiscal Responsibility Act
Y2K	Year 2000

APPENDIX B
BUSINESS EVOLUTION OF LANDRUMHR

1970   Launched Landrum Personnel Associates (later known as Landrum Personnel Resources), as a private employment agency to recruit and place personnel

1970   Rented office space at 21 South Tarragona Street in downtown Pensacola, Florida

1973   Incorporated and launched Britt Landrum Temporaries, Inc. dba Landrum Temporary Services, later known as Landrum Staffing Services, now LandrumHR

1974   H. Britt Landrum, Jr. commenced a decade-long, part-time run as a Vocational expert, testifying in court as an expert witness on employment matters

1975   Purchased office space at 1207 West Garden Street near downtown Pensacola; relocated to the remodeled space in 1976

1976   Launched resume preparation service

1977   Bought and remodeled an old house at 238 East Intendencia Street in the historic downtown district to provide office space for Landrum Temporary Services

1977   Established a medical transcription service called Medicom

1983   Incorporated and launched American Staff Leasing Corporation dba AmStaff, an employee leasing company (later known as a professional employer organization (PEO))

1985   Opened Landrum Temporary Services branch office in Fort Walton Beach, Florida

1985   Purchased and opened Landrum Temporary Services branch office in Panama City, Florida

1986   Closed Panama City office

1986   Completed construction and consolidated offices into company-owned building in Plantation Road Office Park at 6708 Plantation Road

1988   Sold Fort Walton Beach branch location

1993   Completed construction and moved to new building at 6723 Plantation Road

1999   Purchased the assets of Evergreen Systems (staffing service)

2001   Launched CU Personnel Solutions, an entity within AmStaff focused on credit union personnel

2001   Launched Medical Personnel Solutions, an entity within AmStaff focused on medical personnel

2001   Purchased a partial interest in PayPlus along with nine users of the human resource information and payroll system as a collaborative venture

2003   Created Landrum Consulting to provide human resources consulting services to employers

2003   Listed all operating entities as subsidiaries of Landrum Human Resources Companies, Inc.

2004   Applied for and won the Great Places to Work Award (won the award during the next four years for a total of five consecutive years)

2004   Established captive workers compensation entity, Accredited Insurance, Ltd, domiciled in Bermuda, providing the first layer of insurance on all workers' compensation claims incurred by Landrum entities

2004   Formed an Advisory Board comprised of Eric Nickelsen and Mort O'Sullivan

2004   Formed the Landrum family board of Landrum Human Resource Companies, Inc.

2006   Created Landrum Employees Charitable Foundation, pooling employee-directed funds to benefit charitable initiatives in the community

2006   Rebranded AmStaff as Landrum Professional Employer Services

2007   Won the Florida Governor's Sterling Award for operational excellence in first year the application was submitted

2010   Formed a licensed self-insurance company providing workers' compensation coverage for Florida clients, which is augmented by insurance through Liberty Mutual Insurance Company

2012   Established a strategic alliance with EuroDev and the office of Landrum Europe in the Netherlands

2012   Purchased the assets of Employer Administrative Services (EASI), a PEO in Asheville, North Carolina

2012   Purchased the assets of Synergetic, a PEO in Columbia, South Carolina

2012   Purchased the assets of Tangent Insurance, an insurance agency affiliated with Synergetic in Columbia, South Carolina

2013   Incorporated Garden Street Insurance in South Carolina

2013   Purchased the assets of Staff Payroll, a PEO in Pensacola

2015   Began rebranding all operating entities as "LandrumHR"

2015   H. Britt Landrum III became president of the company

2017   H. Britt Landrum, Jr. retired, and H. Britt Landrum III became President and CEO of the company

2017   Purchased the assets of The Employee Management Team, a PEO in Sarasota, Florida

2019   Made largest acquisition in the company's history with the purchase of a nationwide consulting firm, hrQ, with offices in Atlanta, Austin, Dallas, Denver, Houston and San Francisco

2019   Rebranded Landrum Staffing as "Workforce Solutions," acknowledging the services LHR provides in hiring and managing a portion of the workforce for a company

APPENDIX C
COMPANIES AND OWNERSHIP INTERESTS SINCE 1970

Accredited Insurance, Ltd. (captive insurance company in Bermuda, later Vermont)

American Staff Leasing Corporation dba AmStaff

AmStaff (later Landrum Professional and then LandrumHR)

Britt Landrum Temporaries, Inc. dba Landrum Temporary Services (later Landrum Staffing now Workforce Solutions, a division of LHR)

CU (Credit Unions) Personnel Solutions

Employer Administrative Services (EASI) in Asheville, North Carolina (LHR acquisition)

Evergreen Systems (LHR acquisition)

Garden Street Insurance

hrQ (LHR acquisition)

Landrum Consulting (now LandrumHR Consulting)

Landrum Employees Charitable Foundation

Landrum Europe

Landrum Family Partnership, Ltd. (owner of Accredited Insurance and all properties)

Landrum Human Resource Companies, Inc.

Landrum Personnel Associates (later changed to Landrum Personnel Resources)

Landrum Personnel Resources (formerly Landrum Personnel Associates)

Landrum Professional (formerly AmStaff)

Landrum Staffing

Landrum Temporary Services

Medicom

PayPlus (partial ownership interest)

Staff Payroll (LHR acquisition)

Synergetic in Columbia, South Carolina (LHR acquisition)

The Employee Management Team, Sarasota, Florida (LHR acquisition)

Workforce Solutions (a division of LandrumHR)

APPENDIX D
PENSACOLA-BASED OFFICE LOCATIONS S NCE 1970

1970   Rented office space at 21 South Tarragona Street in downtown Pensacola, Florida

1975   Purchased office space at 1207 West Garden Street near downtown Pensacola

1977   Bought and remodeled an old house for office use at 238 East Intendencia Street in the historic district in downtown Pensacola

1986   Completed construction and consolidated offices into company-owned building in Plantation Road Office Park at 6708 Plantation Road

1993   Completed construction and moved to company-owned building across the street at 6723 Plantation Road

1995   Completed phase II remodeling and expansion of 6723 Plantation Road building to accommodate growth of staff

1997   Completed phase III remodeling and expansion of 6723 Plantation Road building to accommodate growth of staff

2003   Purchased office building and five vacant lots with associated parking at 7100 Plantation Road, adjacent to and north of 6723 building

2004   Purchased additional office building at 7100 Plantation Road for possible expansion and to obtain more parking privileges

2006   Remodeled and moved Payroll and later Benefits operations into previously purchased office building located at 6715 Plantation Road, adjacent to 6723 building

2015   Purchased 3.5 acres of vacant property across the street from 6723 building for future expansion

APPENDIX E
PEOPLE REFERENCED IN
WORKING A BETTER WAY

Beside each name are the corresponding roles assumed currently, or at one time or another during LHR's 50-year history.

Mike Adkins	Saltmarsh, Cleaveland and Gund audit manager
David Altig	Executive Vice President and Director of Research for the Federal Reserve Bank of Atlanta
Clyde Anderson	Owner of Associated Insurance
Christy Arnold	LHR Benefits Compliance Attorney
Jo-Anne Audette-Arruda	LHR Safety Manager
Henry Baggett	Vice President of Finance for American Fidelity Life Insurance (AMFI)
Irene Baldi	Owner of Pensacola-based Staff Payroll
Joe Baldi	Owner of Pensacola-based Staff Payroll
Frazer Banks	Landrum Personnel Associates job placement counselor
Ralph Barnes	Liberty Mutual sales representative
Dempsey Barron	Florida State Senator
Larry Barrow	Architect on LHR buildings at 6708 and 6723 Plantation Road
Jessica Beal	CPA tax specialist and former LHR internal auditor
Lorita Bee	Member of the AmStaff team in the division's earliest years
Gary Bembry	Lakeview Center CEO
Bob Bennett	Retired Air Force officer and owner of Snelling and Snelling franchise in Pensacola
Ben Bernanke	Chairman of the Federal Reserve
Cindi Bigalow	LHR Claims Adjuster
Ed Bongart	Co-owner with Rick Ratner of Modern Employers, Inc.

Harry Booros	LHR Safety and Risk Manager, and later Special Projects Manager
Barclay Bourdeau	PayPlus programmer
Betty Bowles	Mr. Landrum's second secretary
Kevin Bowyer	CPA with O'Sullivan Creel
Wilbur Boyd	Florida State Senator
Bert Brown	CPA with Brown, Kirkland and Campbell
Jim Brown	Personnel Manager for Baptist Hospital
Earl Caldwell	Co-owner of a temporary help service in Atlanta
Steve Caldwell	Owner of Caldwell Systems and co-owner of a temporary help service in Atlanta
John Calhoun	Mr. Landrum's former Sigma Chi fraternity brother at FSU, and owner of a private employment agency in Tallahassee, Florida
W.D. Childers	Florida State Senator
Bill Clark	Attorney with Clark, Partington, Hart
Bill Cleary	Vice President of LHR, Director of Client Services, Director of Sales and Risk Management, Senior Leadership Team (SLT) member
Valerie Cole	Senior HR Specialist for LHR Workforce Solutions division
Jim Collins	Co-author of *Built to Last: Successful Habits of Visionary Companies* with Jerry Porras, and author of *Good to Great: Why Some Companies Make the Leap...and Others Don't*
Larry Cowan	Former client and business broker
Carole Cox	LHR Human Resources Manager for PEO division
Charlie Crist	Florida Governor
Richard Cruitt	Independent Temporary Services Association (ITSA) member from Birmingham, Alabama
Bob Crumpton	Army Reserve and Jaycee friend of Mr. Landrum

Sarah Damson	Co-owner of Mobile, Alabama-based Long's Human Resource Services with her husband, Tom Damson
Tom Damson	President and co-owner of Mobile, Alabama-based Long's Human Resource Services with his wife, Sarah Damson
Dawn Danforth	LHR staffing services employee, formerly with Evergreen Systems
Carolyn Davis	Manager of Landrum Temporary Services
Mark de Vries	Owner of business development company, EuroDev and Senior Advisor for Business Development for Landrum Europe
David Denham	Owner of D & B Builders
Joe Dorsett	Job placement counselor with Landrum Personnel Associates
Tom Downey	AmStaff sales representative
Steve Durko	Son-in-law of Joe and Irene Baldi, and minority owner of Pensacola-based Staff Payroll, then LHR customer service representative
Morris Eaddy	Founder and CEO of Lakeview Center
Rennee Edwards	LHR Administrative Coordinator
Rex Eley	Past President of the National Association of Professional Employer Organizations (NAPEO) and Employer Services Assurance Corporation (ESAC)
Evon Emerson	Executive coach and training consultant
Sarah Entrekin	Family friend and County Court Judge in Jones County, Mississippi
Wayne Etheridge	Personnel Manager for the City of Pensacola
Sergio Fernandez	Chief Financial Officer of ADP TotalSource and LHR Advisory Board member
Tom Fife	Insurance and investment executive

Mary Flynn	LHR accounts receivable staff member
Chris Fortunato	LHR (PEO) payroll delivery driver
Mike Fortunato	LHR (PEO) payroll delivery driver
Peggy Fortunato	LHR Corporate HR Director and staff payroll administrator
Chris Fountain	LHR Workforce Solutions team member and General Electric (GE) Site Manager
Rhonda Freeman	PayPlus expert for LHR
George Gersema	President of Employers Resource of Boise, Idaho, and Chairman of PayPlus management committee
Leslie Gordon, CPA	LHR's first Controller, later Director of Finance
Alan Greenspan	Chairman of the Federal Reserve
Mary Griewisch	LHR Director of Payroll for PEO division
Dick Grimes	Early AmStaff sales representative
Pat Groner	First president of Baptist Health Care
Jim Guttman	HR Manager for LHR PEO division
Jim Haggerty	Owner of Sarasota-based Employers Management, Inc.
Becki Haines	HR Manager and head of LHR's Consulting division
Jerold Hall	LHR Director of Business Development
Meg Harris	Executive Assistant to Mr. Landrum, then Director of Client Reporting, and later HR Assistant
Bob Hart	Senior law partner with Clark, Partington, Hart, and long-time tax and estate attorney to LHR
Ashton Hayward	Pensacola Mayor
Jack Healan	Board member of the Jacksonville Branch of the Federal Reserve Bank of Atlanta, and President of Amelia Island Plantation

John Heaton	Owner of Pay Plus Benefits of Kennewick, Washington (different from PayPlus Software), and Vice Chairman of PayPlus Software management committee
Jason Heuer	LHR systems engineer, and later Technical Director
Allison Hill	Lakeview Center CEO and LHR Advisory Board member
Lou Hipp	Independent Temporary Services Association (ITSA) member from Stamford, Connecticut
Kevin Holcombe	LHR marketing associate
Bill Holt	Employee leasing company owner
Ted Holz	LHR Sales representative for PEO division
Ray Howell	Owner of Adcom advertising agency in Pensacola
Joni Humphreys	LHR Director of Marketing and Communications, and Community Relationship Coordinator
Susan Hunsucker	LHR Director of Benefits
James Hunter	Author of The Servant: A Simple Story About the True Essence of Leadership
Martha Hunter	Co-owner of Pensacola-based American Life Assurance, a subsidiary of First National Life Insurance Company
Skip Hunter	Co-owner of Pensacola-based American Life Assurance, a subsidiary of First National Life Insurance Company
Lois Johnson	LHR Risk Management assistant, then licensed Claims Adjuster, and co-founder of Landrum Toastmasters
Wayne Josephson	Executive Director of Independent Temporary Services Association (ITSA)
Brianna Keen	Mr. Landrum's great niece and Britt III's cousin (provided inspiration for 'thought for the day' on Harmony)
Dave Keleher	LHR sales representative
Ed Kelly	Liberty Mutual Insurance Company Chairman and CEO
Kay Kendrick	One of first two AmStaff hires

Gene Killinger	Owner of Killinger Marine
Ted Kirchharr	LHR Vice President, Chief Operating Officer and SLT member
Jerry Kirkland	CPA with Brown, Kirkland and Campbell
Jeff Kottcamp	Florida Lieutenant Governor
Britton Stamps Landrum	Mr. Landrum's grandfather
Brian Landrum	Mr. Landrum and Nell's younger son, shareholder and director of Landrum Human Resource Companies, Inc. (LHRC), LHR's parent corporation
Henry Britton Landrum	Mr. Landrum's father
L. G. Landrum, MD	Mr. Landrum's uncle
Nell Landrum	Mr. Landrum's wife, shareholder and director of LHRC
H. Britt Landrum, Jr.	LHR founder ('Mr. Landrum'), shareho der and Chairman of LHRC's family board
H. Britt Landrum, III	Mr. Landrum and Nell's older son, now LHR President and CEO, and shareholder and director of LHRC
Cecil Lanier	Former Vocational Rehabilitation Counselor and family friend
George Lehor	Employee leasing company owner
Patrick Lencioni	Author of The Five Dysfunctions of a Team
Larry Lewis	Former Cox Cable Manager and fundraiser for Florida Senator W.D. Childers
Bob Liken	Independent Temporary Services Association (ITSA) member from Pittsburgh, Pennsylvania
Dennis Lockhart	President of the Federal Reserve Bank of Atlanta
Myrtle Long	Owner of Long's Personnel in Mobile, Alabama
Tom Long	Founder and owner of Long's Personnel in Mobile, Alabama
Mark Lundquist	LHR safety and loss prevention staff member

Dick MacNeil	Mr. Landrum's Jaycee friend, architect and co-landlord at 21 South Tarragona Street
Alice Malloy	LHR payroll manager for PEO division
Chuck Marks	National Personnel Associates (NPA) Executive Director
Graham Marsh	Professional golfer
Bob Martinez	Florida Governor
John McBride	Early AmStaff sales representative
Karena McCafferty	LHR Director of Payroll for PEO division
Darlene McClendon	LHR Technical Support Specialist, early PEO payroll specialist
Ann McIntyre	CPA and LHR accounting specialist on captive insurance
Dan McLeod	Husband of Denise McLeod and subject of endowed UWF scholarship award
Denise McLeod	LHR Vice President and General Manager of Staffing (Workforce Solutions) division, and (SLT) Team member
Holly McLeod	LHR Senior HR Manager
Gayle Meacham	LHR Unemployment Claims Administrator and former Florida Unemployment Claims Adjudicator
M. J. Menge	Law partner with Shell, Fleming, Davis and Menge
Melissa Miller	LHR IT staff member
Mike Miller	Tampa-based labor attorney, long-time PEO advocate
Guy Milner	Franchiser with Southeastern Personnel Associates in Atlanta
Gonzalez ('Gon') Montiel	Controller with Long's Personnel, Mobile, Alabama
Dan Mooney, MD	LHR Medical Review Officer (MRO)
Ed Moore	Attorney and personal friend of Mr. Landrum
Bill Morland	Contract Staffing of America owner
Bill Mullis	Co-founder of Staff Leasing and former sales manager with Sarasota-based Employers Management, Inc.

Mark Murphy	Author of Hundred Percenters
Lisa Nagem	Payroll and collections supervisor for LHR Staffing Services division
Yvonne Nellums	LHR Director of HR for PEO division and one of first two AmStaff employees
Don Nelson	Landrum Personnel Associates job placement counselor
Eric Nickelsen	LHR Advisory Board member, banker and real estate developer, C&P loan officer, and later President
Margie Oakes	LHR contract accountant
Chris Oakley	Vice President and Lead Regional Executive of the Jacksonville Branch of the Federal Reserve Bank of Atlanta
Eileen O'Brien	Landrum Personnel Associates job placement counselor
Mort O'Sullivan	CPA and LHR Advisory Board member, founder and managing partner of O'Sullivan Creel (now Warren Averett)
Arnold Palmer	Professional golfer
Jennifer Pendergast, PhD	Management consultant with the Family Business Consulting Group in Atlanta
Mike Perkins	LHR Vice President, COO and General Counsel, SLT member; formerly with Clark, Partington, Hart law firm
Joan Perryman	First job placement counselor for Landrum Personnel Associates
Lorena Peterson	HR Assistant and co-founder of Landrum Toastmasters
Jeff Phillips	Accountingfly CEO and former LHR Advisory Board member
Luz Pitre	LHR receptionist and telephone operator
Johanna Pohlmann	LHR Client Relations Manager, Workforce Solutions division
Jerry Porras	Co-author of Built to Last: Successful Habits of Visionary Companies with Jim Collins

Billy Price	Job placement counselor and Vice President of Landrum Personnel Resources
Tim Quinn	Actuary with Towers Perrin
Dave Ramsey	Founder of the Financial Peace program
Paul Randall	LHR staff member who wrote and installed 'Employee on Board' proprietary software
Rick Ratner	Owner of The Employee Management Team in Sarasota, Florida; co-owner with Ed Bongart of Modern Employers, Inc. and an insurance agency
Melissa Redmon	LHR Client Services Specialist in Sarasota, formerly with The Employee Management Team
Jim Reeves	Attorney, Mr. Landrum's Jaycee friend and co-landlord at 21 South Tarragona Street
Howard Rein	Mayor Pro Tempore for the City of Pensacola
Amie Remington	LHR General Counsel and employment attorney
Andy Remke	LHR CFO, SLT member and Advisory Board member, and CFO for Baptist Health Care
Melanie Rhodes	LHR Managing Director of Operations
Robert ('Bob') Riegel, Jr.	Labor attorney with Jacksonville-based Coffman, Coleman, Andrews and Grogan
Buzz Ritchie	Florida House of Representatives member
Chi Chi Rodriquez	Pro-golfer and spokesman for Liberty Mutual Insurance Company
Hon. Casey Rogers	District Judge of the United States District Court of the Northern District of Florida
Mandy Sacco	President of LHR Workforce Solutions, and member of the Human Capital Advisory Board of the Federal Reserve Bank of Atlanta
Carlos Saladrigas	Principal owner of Vincam, a PEO based in Coral Gables, Florida

Sandy Sansing	Co-owner of Pensacola-based Digital Systems, with Wally Yost; now owner of multiple car dealerships
Joe Scarborough	Florida Congressman
John Schill	Mr. Landrum's Jaycee friend and co-landlord at 21 South Tarragona Street
Rev. Michael Schulenberg	Episcopal priest and former Rector of Holy Cross Episcopal Church in Pensacola
Ron Sedlacek	Independent insurance agent and adviser to LHR
John Shattuck	AmStaff sales representative, then sales manager
Wanda Silva	PEO business broker engaged by LHR to facilitate acquisitions
John Slavic	Owner of Slavic401K, and administrator of LHR's 401K plans
John Slavich	Manager of LHR's Columbia, South Carolina office following the Synergetic acquisition
Sandra Smith	Sandra Smith, LHR staffing service sales representative / Sales Manager
Andrew Sowell	LHR senior business consultant, PEO division
Nobie Sparks	First employee of Landrum Personnel Associates and former co-worker (secretary) at the Florida Division of Vocational Rehabilitation
Gary Sperduto, PhD	Sperduto and Associates owner
Michele Stinson	LHR administrative assistant
Murray Stinson	Owner of Spartin Systems, and co-owner with Steve Caldwell of Caldwell-Spartin, Inc.
Al Stubblefield	Baptist Health Care CEO and author of The Baptist Health Care Journey to Excellence: Creating a Culture that WOWs!
Quint Studer	Baptist Hospital Administrator and founder of the Studer Group

Johnathan Taylor	LHR Chief Financial Officer and SLT member
Angela Thornton Jones	LHR staffing services employee, formerly with Evergreen Systems
Neil Thorsen	LHR Safety and Risk Manager
Todd Torgerson	Florida Blue Vice President, then Combined Insurance founder (now dba Torgerson Causey)
Elaine Tracey	LHR (AmStaff) Site Safety Manager at the Monsanto plant
Jim Vickery	Predecessor to Al Stubblefield as CEO of Baptist Health Care
Suzanne Walker	Part of the AmStaff team in the division's earliest years
Bill Watson	AmSouth Bank President in Pensacola
Grace Whalen	Registered Nurse and LHR's first Drug-Free Workplace Coordinator
Peter Willets	Head of Liberty Mutual Bermuda
Grace Williams	Landrum Personnel Associates (LHR) job placement counselor
T. Joe Willy, PhD	Expert in employee leasing industry and originator of PayPlus software system
Charles P. Woodbury	Founder and principal owner of American Fidelity Life Insurance (AMFI)
Cooper Yates	LHR advertising consultant
Wally Yost	Co-owner of Pensacola-based Digital Systems, with Sandy Sansing
Frank "Fuzzy" Zoeller	Professional golfer

APPENDIX F
ASSOCIATIONS REFERENCED IN
WORKING A BETTER WAY

90 & 9 Boys Ranch

Accountingfly

Accredited Insurance, Ltd., captive insurance company domiciled in Bermuda, later Vermont

AdaptSuite

Adcom, advertising agency adjacent to LHR's office in downtown Pensacola

ADP (Payroll Services)

ADP TotalSource (PEO)

Affordable Care Act

Allstate Insurance

Amelia Island Plantation

American Fidelity Life Insurance (AMFI), LHR client

American Life Assurance Corporation, a subsidiary of First National Life Insurance Company

American Red Cross

American Staff Leasing Corporation, dba AmStaff, later known as LandrumHR

American Staffing Association (ASA), formerly known as National Association of Temporary Services (NATS)

AmSouth Bank, now Regions Bank

AmStaff (American Staff Leasing Corporation), now known as LandrumHR

Ascend, formerly Solutia and before, Monsanto

Assigned Risk Pool

Associated General Contractors Self Insurance Fund

Associated Industries of Florida Self-Insurance Fund

Associated Insurance

Baptist Health Care

Baptist Hospital

Bermuda Monetary Authority

Better Business Bureau of Northwest Florida

Big Oak Ranch

Blue Cross of Florida, now Florida Blue

Board of Employee Leasing Companies

Boeing Aerospace Support

Bond International Software

Britt Landrum Temporaries, Inc., dba Landrum Temporary Services

Brown, Kirkand and Campbell

Caldwell Systems

Caldwell-Spartin, Inc., a merger of Caldwell Systems and Spartin Systems

Central Credit Union of Florida

Champion Paper

Citizens & Peoples National Bank (C&P Bank)

City of Pensacola, Florida

Clark, Partington, Hart, Pensacola law firm

Coffman, Coleman, Andrews and Grogan, Jacksonville-based law firm

Combined Insurance Services, Inc.

Consolidated Omnibus Budget Reconciliation Act (COBRA)

Contract Staffing of America, California-based employee leasing company

Coronavirus Aid, Relief, and Economic Security (CARES) Act

CU Personnel Solutions, an entity within AmStaff later known as Landrum Professional

D & B Builders

Digital Equipment Corporation (DEC)

Digital Systems

Dillard's Department Store, formerly Gayfers

Dodson, Craddock and Born Advertising Agency

Ellyson Park Toastmasters

Employee Assistance Program (EAP)

Employer Administrative Services (EASI), a PEO acquired by LHR

Employer Services Assurance Corporation (ESAC), fka Institute for Accreditation of Professional Employer Organizations (IAPEO)

Employers Management, Inc., Sarasota, Florida

Employers Resource, Boise, Idaho

Employment Practices Liability Insurance (EPLI)

Equal Employment Opportunity Commission (EEOC)

EuroDev, Almelo, The Netherlands

Evergreen Systems

Families First Network

Family Business Consulting Group, Atlanta, Georgia

Federal Bureau of Investigation (FBI)

Federal Emergency Management Agency (FEMA)

Federal Open Market Committee (FOMC)

Federal Reserve Board

Fiduciary Partners Retirement Group

First National Life Insurance Company, parent of American Life Assurance

Fisher Brown Insurance Company

Flexential Corporation

Florida Association of Employee Leasing Companies

Florida Association of Personnel Consultants (formerly Florida Employment Association)

Florida Blue, formerly Blue Cross of Florida

Florida Board of Employee Leasing Companies

Florida Commission on Human Relations

Florida Division of Administrative Hearings (DOAH)

Florida Division of Vocational Rehabilitation

Florida Employee Leasing Association, now Florida Association of Professional Employer Organizations

Florida Employment Association, later Florida Association of Personnel Consultants

Florida Governor's Sterling Award for Organizational Excellence

Florida League of Credit Unions

Florida Self-Insurers Guaranty Association, Inc., LHR licensed self-insurance company

Florida State University

Florida Trend Magazine

Fortune Magazine

Gannet Company

Gayfers Department Store, now Dillard's

General Electric (GE)

Harvard Business Review

Highland Associates

Holy Cross Episcopal Church

hrQ, an HR consulting firm acquired by LHR

Human Resources Certification Institute (HRCI)

Inc. Magazine

Independent Temporary Services of America (ITSA), now known as TempNet

Institute for Accreditation of Professional Employer Organizations (IAPEO), now known as Employer Services Assurance Corporation (ESAC)

International Standards Organization (ISO)

Jacksonville Branch of the Federal Reserve Bank of Atlanta

Judges of Compensation Claims

Kelly Services

Kentucky Unemployment Compensation Commission

Killinger Marine

Lakeview Center

Landrum Consulting, now part of LandrumHR

Landrum Europe (LHR)

Landrum Personnel Associates (LHR)

Landrum Staffing, formerly known as Landrum Temporary Services, now Workforce Solutions division of LandrumHR

Landrum Temporary Services, later Landrum Staffing, now Workforce Solutions, a division of LandrumHR

Landrum Toastmasters

LandrumHR (LHR)

Lanier Business Products

Leadership IQ

Legends of Golf Tournament

Liberty Life Assurance, a venture of Liberty Mutual Insurance Company

Liberty Mutual Bermuda

Liberty Mutual Insurance Company

Long's Personnel

Long's Human Resource Services, Mobile, Alabama

Malcolm Baldrige National Quality Award

Manpower

Masters, Mates and Pilots Union

Medical Personnel Associates, an entity within AmStaff later known as Landrum Professional

Medicom, a former LHR company

Microsoft Corporation

Modern Employers, Inc.

Monday Night Toastmasters

Monsanto, then Solutia, then Ascend

National Association of Personnel Consultants (formerly National Employment Association)

National Association of Professional Employer Organizations (NAPEO) (formerly National Staff Leasing Association)

National Association of Temporary Services (NATS), now American Staffing Association (ASA)

National Baldrige Award

National Business Solutions (PEO)

National Council for Compensation Insurance (NCCI)

National Employment Association (NEA), later National Association of Personnel Consultants, then the National Association of Personnel Services

National Labor Relations Board (NLRB)

National Personnel Associates (NPA)

National Staff Leasing Association, now known as the National Association of Professional Employer Organizations (NAPEO)

Naval Air Station Pensacola (NAS)

Navarre Toastmasters

NetWise Technology (ClientSpace CRM software)

Occupational Safety and Health Administration (OSHA)

Oglethorpe University, Atlanta, Georgia

Olsten Staffing Services

O'Sullivan Creel, now Warren Averett

PaperWise

Pay Plus Benefits, Kennewick, Washington

Paychex

PayPlus Software

PayStaff

Pensacola Jaycees

Pensacola Junior College, later Pensacola State College

Pensacola News Journal

Pensacola State College, formerly Pensacola Junior College

Peoplenet

Port of Pensacola

Prism Software

Raymond James and Company

Regional Economic Information Network (REIN) of the Federal Reserve Bank

Regions Banks, acquired AmSouth Bank

Rehabilitation Institute of Northwest Florida

Saltmarsh, Cleaveland and Gund, CPAs

Sedlacek Insurance Service

Shell, Fleming, Davis and Menge

Slavic401K

Snelling and Snelling

Society for Human Resource Management (SHRM)

Solutia, formerly Monsanto, now Ascend

Southeastern Personnel Associates

Spartin Systems

Sperduto & Associates

Staff Leasing

Staff Payroll

Statement of Auditing Standards 70 (SAS 70), now Statement on Standards for Attestation Engagements (SSAE 16)

Statement on Standards for Attestation Engagements (SSAE 16), formerly SAS 70

Sterling Challenge

Stonegate Office Park

Studer Group

SubWest Rotary Club

Synergetic, a PEO acquired by LHR

Tangent Insurance, an insurance agency acquired by LHR

Tax Equity and Fiscal Responsibility Act (TEFRA)

TempNet, formerly known as Independent Temporary Services Association (ITSA)

The Employee Management Team, a PEO acquired by LHR

Toastmasters at Navy Federal

Toastmasters Cordova

Top 25 Best Small Businesses to Work for in America

Torgersen Causey, formerly known as Combined Insurance Services

Towers Perrin, now known as Willis Towers Watson

Trinity Presbyterian Church

United States District Court of the Northern District of Florida

United Way of Escambia County

University of West Florida Foundation

Vincam (PEO)

Warren Averett, formerly O'Sullivan Creel

WCOA AM station

Wharton School of Business of the University of Pennsylvania

Willis Towers Watson, formerly Towers Perrin

Workforce Solutions, division of LandrumHR, formerly Landrum Staffing Services

Zurich Insurance Company

ABOUT THE AUTHOR

H. Britt Landrum, Jr.

H. Britt Landrum, Jr. is the founder of LandrumHR and current chairman of the board for the parent corporation, Landrum Human Resource Companies, Inc. After founding the company in 1970, he served as its chief executive officer until turning the reins over to his son, H. Britt Landrum III, and retired from the company in 2017.

Mr. Landrum has been active in several industry-related organizations, serving as a board member and officer of the National Association of Professional Employer Organizations (NAPEO) and Employer Services Assurance Corporation (ESAC). He has served as president of the Florida

Employment Association (FEA), National Personnel Associates (NPA), and TempNet, formerly Independent Temporary Services Association (ITSA). He was appointed by the Governor of Florida to serve as a member of the first Board of Employee Leasing Companies and served a term as chairman.

Active in civic affairs, Landrum is a past member and chairman of the board of the Jacksonville Branch of the Federal Reserve Bank of Atlanta. He served on the advisory board of AmSouth Bank and on the Florida advisory board of Liberty Mutual Insurance. He is past chairman of the board of Lakeview Center, and past vice chairman of the board of Baptist Health Care. He is past chairman of the board of trustees for the University of West Florida (UWF) Foundation, past chairman of the Better Business Bureau of Northwest Florida, past vice president of the Pensacola Area Chamber of Commerce, past chairman of the 90 & 9 Boys Ranch, and past chairman of the United Way of Escambia County.

In 1998, Mr. Landrum was named Business Leader of the Year by the Pensacola Area Chamber of Commerce. In 2003, he was named Trustee of the Year by the Florida Coalition for Children. In 2005, he received the Ethics in Business Award, granted by the University of West Florida College of Business and Combined Rotary Clubs of Pensacola, and in 2008, he was named a Foundation Fellow by the UWF Foundation Board of Trustees. Also in 2008, he was chosen by Baptist Health Care Foundation to receive the Hollinger Award as Volunteer of the Year. In 2016, NAPEO presented him with the Michaeline Doyle Award, its highest award for service to the industry.

Mr. Landrum earned a Master of Science degree in 1969 and a Bachelor of Science degree in 1959 from Florida State University in Tallahassee, Florida. He and his wife, Nell, have been married for fifty-six years, have two sons, two daughters-in-law and five grandsons, and reside in Pensacola, Florida.

www.ingramcontent.com/pod-product-compliance
Lightning Source LLC
Chambersburg PA
CBHW031841200326
41597CB00012B/219